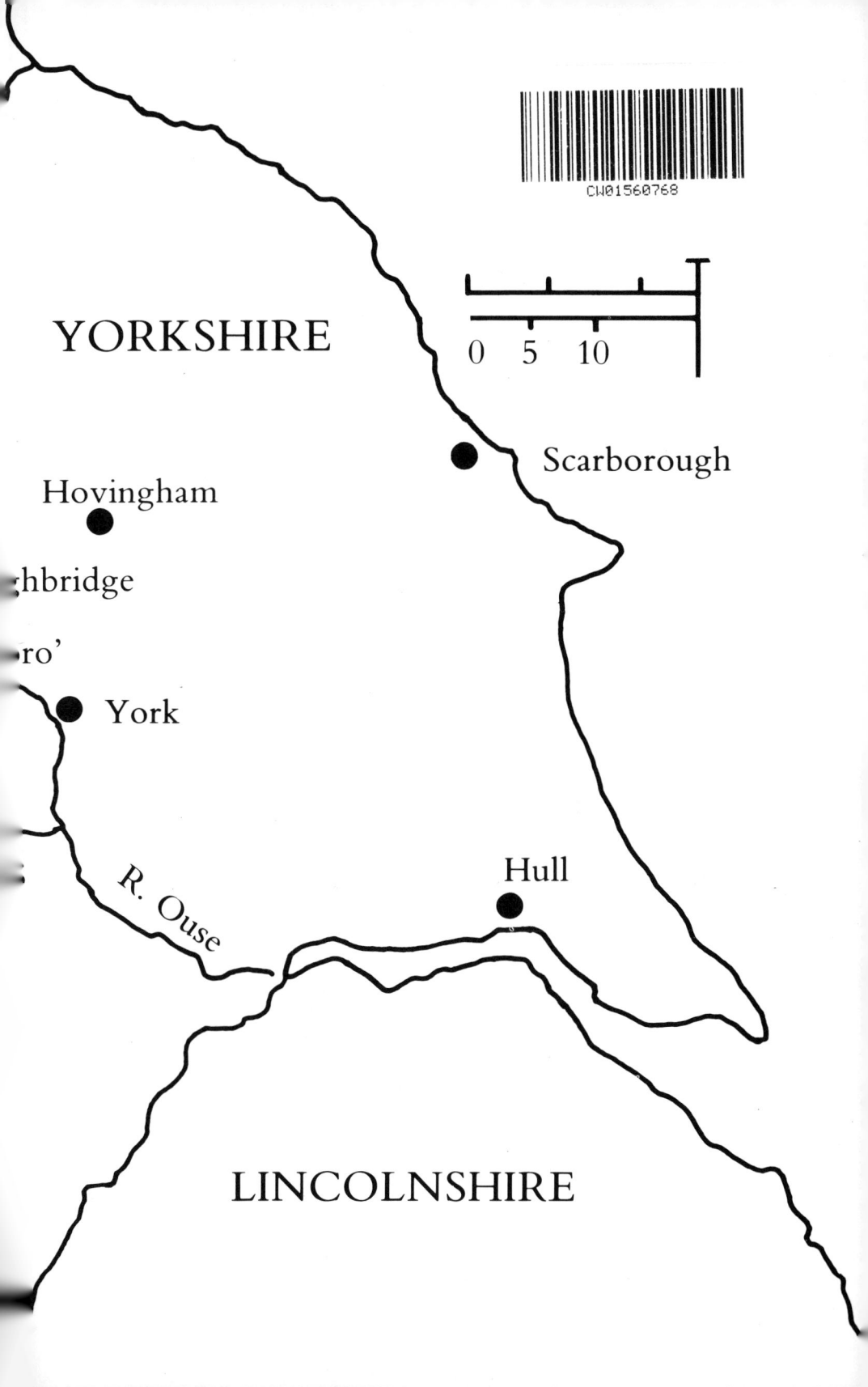

Margaret and Tony

With very best wishes

for Christmas and the New Year

Anne

1988

YORKE COUNTRY

To my nephews
John and Charles Yorke

'And here's to the line that we follow,'

YORKE COUNTRY
BY ANNE ASHLEY COOPER

Published by Mrs. Ashley Cooper
Hexton Manor, Hexton, Nr. Hitchin, Hertfordshire

November 1988

© Anne Ashley Cooper 1988

British Library Cataloguing in Publication Data

Ashley Cooper, Anne
Yorke country.
1. Yorkshire. Families. Genealogical Aspects
i. Title
929' 2' 094281

ISBN 0 9511112 21

All rights reserved. No part of this publication may be reproduced, stored in a retrieval system, or transmitted in any form or by any means, electronic, mechanical, photocopying, recording or otherwise, without the written permission of the publisher.

Produced and Printed for the Publisher by
White Crescent Press Ltd., Luton, Bedfordshire

CONTENTS

		Page
List of Illustrations...............................		vii
Acknowledgements.............................		ix
Prologue		xi
Chapter I	Early History	1
Chapter II	Sir Richard Yorke of York 1430?–1498 married 1. Jane Mauleverer 2. Joan Whitfield	11
Chapter III	John Yorke of Gouthwaite 1460?–? married Katherine Patterdale	39
Chapter IV	Sir John Yorke of London 1490?–1568 married Anne Smyth..................	41
Chapter V	Peter Yorke of Gouthwaite 1525?–1589 married Elizabeth Ingilby	58
Chapter VI	Sir John Yorke of Gouthwaite 1566?–1634 married Juliana Hansby................	80
Chapter VII	John Yorke of Gouthwaite 1592?–1638 married 1. Florence Sharpe 2. Katharine Ingilby Daniel........................	94
Chapter VIII	Sir John Yorke of Gouthwaite and Richmond 1633–1663 married Mary Norton..................	98
Chapter IX	Thomas Yorke of Richmond, Gouthwaite and Bewerley 1658–1716 married Katherine Lister................	111
Chapter X	John Yorke of Richmond, Gouthwaite and Bewerley 1685–1757 married Hon. Anne Darcy	134

Chapter XI	Thomas Yorke of Halton West and Gouthwaite 1688–1768 married Abigail Andrews	150
Chapter XII	John Yorke of Richmond and Bewerley 1733–1813 married 1. Sophia Glynne 2. Elizabeth Woodstock Campbell	164
Chapter XIII	Thomas Yorke of Halton Place 1738–1811 married Jane Reay	178
Chapter XIV	John Yorke of Bewerley and Halton Place 1776–1857 married Mary Wright	193
Chapter XV	John Yorke of Bewerley 1827–1883 married Alice Simpson	218
Chapter XVI	Thomas Edward Yorke of Bewerley and Halton Place 1832–1923 married 1. Augusta Baillie 2. Fanny Walsham	222
Chapter XVII	John Cecil Yorke of Bewerley and Halton Place 1818–1915 married Marion Elizabeth Stansfeld	248
Chapter XVIII	John Edward Evelyn Yorke of Halton Place 1904 married Eleanor Assheton	261

Envoi ... 278

Records of the Yorke family ... 279

Chapter notes ... 280

Bibliography ... 292

Glossary ... 294

Family trees { Watson / Yorke } ... 295

Index ... 297

LIST OF ILLUSTRATIONS

		Page
1.	Sir Richard Yorke and his sons	x
2.	The Yorke Achievement	9
3.	South East Prospect of York 1745	22
4.	Seal of the Mercers and Merchant Adventurers	25
5.	The Yorke memorial window	38
6.	The Man with the rose	42
7.	Edward VI coin	50
8.	Parcevall Hall	66
9.	'Notification by Symon the dean'	68
10.	Sir Edward Yorke	77
11.	Gouthwaite Hall 1837	82
12.	Middlesmoor Church	92
13.	Halton Bridge	96
14.	Maulger Norton of Richmond	99
15.	South West Prospect of Richmond 1749	104
16.	Abbot Huby's Chapel, Bewerley	113
17.	Dame Mary Yorke	116
18.	Mary, wife of Sir Edward Blackett	117
19.	Thomas Yorke	119
20.	Katherine, wife of Thomas Yorke	120
21.	The Bewerley estate	124
22.	Thomas Yorke when older	131
23.	Anne, wife of John Yorke M.P.	137
24.	John Yorke M.P.	140
25.	Miners underground	147
26.	Abigail, wife of Thomas Yorke M.P.	151
27.	Thomas Yorke M.P.	153

28.	Sophia, first wife of John Yorke	165
29.	Colonel Coore with John Yorke	166
30.	Field Book of Halton Place	179
31.	Halton Place	182
32.	Interior section of Halton Place	189
33.	Miniature of John Yorke 1802	196
34.	Bewerley Hall 1815	198
35.	Bewerley Hall 1821	201
36.	Silhouette of Jane, wife of Thomas Yorke	206
37.	Mary, wife of John Yorke	210
38.	Bewerley School	211
39.	St. Cuthbert's, Pateley Bridge	217
40.	Bewerley, August 1858	219
41.	Augusta, wife of Thomas Edward Yorke	229
42.	Family group at Halton 1883	232
43.	Thomas Edward Yorke	235
44.	Miners at Harris Shaft 1890	239
45.	Jacobean oak overmantel	245
46.	John Cecil Yorke	250
47.	May, wife of John Cecil Yorke	251
48.	Map of Halton West estate	253
49.	Edwardian tea party	256
50.	St. Mary's, Long Preston	260
51.	Mr. and Mrs. Moon's Golden Wedding 1909	262
52.	The stableyard at Halton Place	264
53.	The hall at Halton Place	267
54.	David, Eleanor and Anne Yorke 1936	269
55.	Halton West tenants 1958	272
56.	John Edward Evelyn Yorke	273
57.	Halton West tenants 1964	275
58.	Stump Cross Caverns	276
59.	Charles, Sophia, Susan, David and John Yorke	277

ACKNOWLEDGEMENTS

During my researches I have been greatly helped by a large number of people. I cannot hope to name them all, but there are some to whom I must express my gratitude. The inspiration for the book came first from my mother, whose efforts in preserving the family archives are detailed elsewhere. My father, my brother and my husband have all made notable contributions to the preparation of material.

Professor Bernard Jennings M.A. of Hull University was kind enough to read drafts and comment on them, and has encouraged me greatly. Mrs. R. J. Freedman, City Archivist of York, Mr. Michael Ashcroft, County Archivist at the Northallerton County Record Office, and Mr. Mark Dorrington, Archivist of York Minster Library, have all assisted me personally in my preparation. Mr. W. R. McKay, Clerk of the Journals at the House of Commons, allowed me to use vital material from the House of Commons library, and my brother in law, Sir Paul Bryan, has contributed much information on Parliamentary procedure.

Miss Muriel Swires and Mrs. Barbara Gill were kind enough to lend me photographs. Without them, and the expertise of Juliet Muskett who made the fine photographic reproductions of the family portraits and all the other illustrations, the book would be poor indeed. Without the counsel and patience of Helena Pickup in drafting, or the typing and collating done by Heather Massie, publication would have been greatly delayed.

The personal advice and experience of Mr. Dean Iszatt and the staff of White Crescent Press Ltd., and Mr. Christopher Springford of MFK Typesetting Ltd., have been invaluable in the final production.

1. Detail of the Yorke window

PROLOGUE

IN THE NORTH TRANSEPT OF YORK MINSTER, in St John's Chapel, (the regimental chapel of the King's Own Yorkshire Light Infantry), the sun shines through two of the rare and beautiful lights of ancient glass on the west wall, and reveals, across the centre panels, a delightful family scene. A father is kneeling with his six sons behind him, and his four daughters facing him, also on their knees, all wearing simple robes of a rich blue.

The father is wearing armour, which is covered with a tabard, or surcoat, charged with his armorial bearings, a silver saltire on a blue

By courtesy of the Dean and Chapter of York

ground. His round basin shaped helmet lies beside him and his armoured shoes have huge spurs attached. An open book lies on the gold fringed altar cloth before him and his hands are raised in prayer.

Both he and his sons have their hair quite long, over their ears, and the boys, who are similar in size, each have a lively and different expression.

Under them in Latin is the inscription: 'Pray for the soul of Richard York knight, twice mayor of the city of York and former mayor of the Staple at Calais, and for the souls of Jane and Joan his wives, and also for all his children and benefactors; who died on the . . . day of April anno domini 1498'.

Above him are eight angels supporting shields which carry coats of arms, and below them four panels depicting the Trinity, St Christopher, a Corpus Christi procession and St George. Other citizens of York are shown also.[1]

My family is directly descended from this man, Richard. We are fortunate to have this memorial, and even more so to have some twenty five portraits of his descendants. These have come down the five centuries and fifteen generations since his day. As far back as I can remember the faces of these men and women have been part of my familiar surroundings. We were on Christian name terms – we even gave some nicknames. Some of them gaze pensively into the distance. Some are dark and rather sinister looking. One or two are handsome, in fine clothes, and some are very plain indeed. The last six generations have a definite family look, but earlier than that it is hard to trace.

All have been born and bred in Yorkshire, owning farmland, lead mines, moorland and woods in various areas at different periods, but each has played a part in the wider world too.

Richard, in addition to his civic offices and mercantile career, served as a member of Parliament for York over a period of nearly twenty years, under four successive kings. His grandson John, Sheriff of London, and Master of the Mint at one time, was thrown into the Tower in 1553 for supporting Lady Jane Grey.

One of John's sons, Edward, sailed on voyages of discovery with Sir Martin Frobisher, his first cousin.

Another John, Richard's great-great-grandson, came up before the Court of the Star Chamber for allowing a play to be acted in his house which derided Protestant beliefs. He was imprisoned in the Fleet, and heavily fined.

The great nephew of that John stood as Member of Parliament for Richmond in Yorkshire, where he then lived, and both his son and grandson also held the seat – the three members covering a period from 1660–1760. The sixth John Yorke travelled to Russia in 1802, as attaché to the Ambassador, Sir John Borlase Warren. He left a diary describing the strange and exotic life in St Petersburgh at that time.

The next four generations held office as High Sheriff or Justices of the Peace, and were all concerned with very many aspects of local life.

From the extensive records of the lives, wills, business and land transactions of the family it has been possible to bring each one alive in his generation. At one time or another they owned land around York, Darlington, Kingston on Hull, Richmond and Halifax, as well as from Sleningford across to the Lancashire border, so the story of the Yorkes is very much part of the story of their shire of York.

Chapter I

EARLY HISTORY

In the earliest days the North of England shared with the South the successive invasions of men from other lands who were searching for hunting grounds, pasture, minerals and farmland on this island. Their pre-history appears similar, but from the time history was written down, differences begin to appear. Even today these differences are still discernible. In the north there is a rugged disregard for frills and fancy ways, and the sense of straight forward, no nonsense attitudes. A warm welcome is given to visitors by the country people, but they can sum up a character in a very short time. Sparing with words, they will give any practical help willingly and not wait for thanks. What ever needs to be done is tackled head on, and shirkers are despised.

As David Hey says, Yorkshire people have acquired a belief that they are a breed set apart from the rest. Those living beyond the boundary acknowledge this separateness, but not always in the most flattering manner.[1]

Their characteristics must stem from the mixture of differing races in their past. The strong strain of warrior Scandinavian blood was coupled with the native hardiness necessary to survive the harsh climate and wild terrain.

After the Roman invasion it took some considerable time before the southern counties were subdued. The rough mountainous land on both sides of the Pennines enabled the fierce native Brigantes tribe to resist the invaders even longer, using what we would now call guerilla tactics, and harrying the disciplined legions from locally known vantage points. Nevertheless Yorkshire too was eventually conquered, and gradually the people settled down.

In 122 Hadrian came to Britain, and over the next five years the military barrier between the Tyne and the Solway, which bore his name, was built. Five thousand troops patrolled its length, with a cohort garrisoning each fort. A supporting legion was based in York which by then was established as the military centre, while London was the centre of Roman government. The area enclosed by the walls of York is still more or less that of the Roman fortress, together with its residential part. The Roman villa system spread across the country but none have been found north of Yorkshire.

The Romans had considerable skill in mining and a fund of technical knowledge drawn from a flourishing industry in Spain. The evidence for

Roman mining in Yorkshire lies in some pigs of smelted lead bearing Latin inscriptions from which dates can be deduced. Two of these were found alongside an old trackway leading from Greenhow Hill to a ford over the River Nidd, near Heyshaw Bank. These can be dated to A.D. 81. A third pig was found about four miles west at Nussey Knot. All three appeared to have been hidden away, perhaps by one of the captive Brigantes working for the Romans, who was unable to return for his treasure.

Roman organisation was excellent and the actual mining work was mostly done by prisoners or slaves, sometimes even working in fetters. The extensive water works entailing hundreds of yards of piping for baths and heating created a great demand for lead, which was also used for coffins by the Romans.[2]

Up to the year 293, Hadrian's Wall barred out the more northerly hordes. Then the Picts pierced it. Again and again Roman-trained British troops drove back the barbarians, but by the beginning of the fifth century Britain was drained of troops and commanders, who were needed to aid the Empire elsewhere.

This gave the Saxon invaders their chance and more and more gained footholds around the coast, moving gradually further inland. As their numbers increased, despite fierce opposition, the Britains were once again forced back to the upland areas of Wales and the North, or else overcome and enslaved. This Christian island, once part of the great Roman Empire, orderly and civilised, then descended into barbarism again. The art of writing was largely lost, pagan worship reigned and it is hard to trace the unrecorded struggles for survival that took place.

By 547, Ida had founded the huge kingdom of Northumbria, which stretched from Hadrian's Wall to the southern boundary of Yorkshire. Later Edwin, who had established himself in York as overlord of Northumbria and all the other kingdoms except Kent, was baptised in York on Easter Day 627, in a wooden church dedicated to St Peter. A larger stone church was built later on the site of the present Minster. (The roof of this church 'was protected from injury by storms with sheets of lead,' an indication that lead mining was flourishing.)[3]

The conversion of Northumbria antagonised the heathen king Penda of Mercia, who, joining forces with the Welsh king Cadwallon, laid waste all the land of the Northumbrians and overthrew Edwin. Over the next hundred years the rivalries of the various succeeding rulers of the seven or eight Anglo-Saxon kingdoms occupied the scene. Northumbria was beset on all sides – the Picts from the north, the Mercians from the south, the Welsh from the west. Mercia's power increased and, under the long reigns of Ethelbald and Offa, Christianity and culture grew and flourished. Then came the Danish threat. The Anglo-Saxon Chronicle gives brief but compelling glimpses of the turbulent history of the north.

737   King Aethelbald ravaged Northumbria.
741   York was burnt to the ground.
789   'There came for the first time three ships of Northmen, the first ships of Danish men which came to the land of the English.'
793   A great famine in Northumbria, then the ravages of the heathen men miserably destroyed God's church on Lindisfarne with fire and slaughter. (The shock of this atrocity was felt all over Europe.)
794   The heathen ravaged Northumbria.
851   For the first time heathen men stayed through the winter.
867   Heathen men ravaged Northumbria and broke into York and made immense slaughter and killed the king.

In the south, Alfred, at twenty-four years old, had given the English new confidence and shown such determination that the Danes made a truce, and retreated to the north. There they began to settle and till the land. They differed from the earlier Saxon invaders in that they worked alongside the local people instead of exterminating them. The two languages were not dissimilar, and their methods of cultivation much the same.

The Chronicle continues:

876   Healfdene shared out the land of the Northumbrians and they (the Danes) began to plough and support themselves.

It seems that this division of land became, during the next hundred years, the shire which was named after the military centre of Eoforwic, which the Danes pronounced Jorvik, and we call York. The city was described in 980 as densely populated with rich Danish merchants but poor buildings.

Yorkshire stretched from the Tees in the north to the Humber in the south, and from the east coast to the peaks of the Pennines. In the tenth century it was even larger and included parts of Lancashire (north of the Ribble), and of Westmorland, Cumbria and Nottinghamshire.

The Viking word 'thrithing', meaning a third part, gave the three ridings their names, and the whole shire lay in the heart of Danelaw, the boundary agreed by King Alfred in 886. The profound Scandinavian influence on the development of the law, language and agricultural customs is still visible today.

Viking York was ruled by a Christian king from 882–895, but monastic life had been all but wiped out by the invaders, and only a few churches survived. During the late ninth and early tenth centuries many of the Danes were converted to Christianity, married local wives and settled down. The patterns of land ownership by the thegns that was laid down then carried on, in many cases, to medieval times and some of the boundaries of the manors and parishes can be traced far back. The ancient and extensive lordships were complex, with multiple estates and outlying properties, (called berewicks or sokelands). They often combined rough moorland and woodland with good arable ground in their calculations, to make a satisfactory whole.

Specific customary services had to be performed for the lord in due season, such as washing and shearing the sheep, or repairing the mill and a few set days a year for ploughing, but the north countrymen were not obliged to do weekly work, as were those on the southern manors, so were relatively free. Master and man lived more closely together, and 'there was always a breath of freedom blowing off the moors'.[4]

The Anglo Saxon Chronicle continues,

994 · The Danish king Sweyn Forkbeard attacked London with ninety four ships and harried all the coast. King Ethelred was forced to give them £16,000 and provision them all winter

997–1001   The Danes burnt and ravaged almost everywhere. They went about as they pleased and nothing withstood them . . . on sea . . . nor land. It was in every way grievous for they never ceased from their evil doing.

1005   A great famine – the cruellest ever remembered.

1006   A great fleet returned and ravaged and burnt and slew everywhere.

1013   All England submitted to Sweyn, except Ethelred with a small band of followers.

1014   Sweyn died and his son Cnut became king.

After Cnut's death, Edward the Confessor became king. The last great Viking of York, Earl Siward, ruled Yorkshire for twenty two years, but on his death, the King made Earl Tostig, third son of Earl Godwin, his new Northern earl.

The new King Harold, (Godwin's eldest son), was obliged to march north and defend his throne. He defeated the united forces of Tostig and Hardrada of Norway at Stamford Bridge on September 25th 1066. This was the last major battle that the Vikings fought on English soil.

Immediately afterwards, King Harold had to make a forced march south to face the Norman invasion. On October 14th he lay dead on the battlefield at Hastings. William I was crowned king on Christmas Day.

Just before the Norman Conquest, the major landholders in Yorkshire were the Archbishop of York and the Earls Morcar, Harold and Edwin.

The two remaining northern earls were still powerful and they rebelled fiercely against the Conqueror's heavy taxation. William marched north against them and left a garrison of five hundred men at York, under his sheriff, William Malet. A fresh rebellion broke out, and a large scale revolt seemed likely. William sacked York and killed hundreds of rebels. He strengthened his defences with a second castle added to the one he had built in the earlier emergency.

At their next uprising the northern rebels were supported by the Danes. From September 1069 they held their ground and harrassed the Norman troops, but William reached York finally and spent Christmas in the devastated city. He came to an agreement with the Danes who sailed away home, but he could not subdue the proud northerners. He then embarked upon a ruthless campaign during which, as the Anglo Saxon chronicle says 'he laid waste all the shire'.

Orderic Vitalis describes how 'he punished the innocent with the guilty – the whole region north of the Humber was stripped of all means of sustenance – and so terrible a famine fell on this defenceless population that more than 100,000 Christian folk of both sexes, young and old, perished'.[5]

Symeon of Durham wrote 'Between York and Durham no village was inhabited', and states that the countryside lay desolate for nine years. Seventeen years later the Domesday book records that 44·5% of all the Yorkshire manors were 'waste'. Even if the term 'waste' did not in every case mean that the manor was totally deserted or valueless it is still a vast proportion, and gives us some indication of the terrible effect William's policy had had on the people of the county.[6]

Huge castles were erected for defence against invasion from Scotland, or by the Vikings, or local revolts. The castles were built by forced labour, roofed and guttered with local lead, and held all the strategic positions on the routes north, east and west. Richmond, Knaresborough, Pontefract and later Skipton, were some of the many massive Norman constructions.

The shire was divided between just twenty eight great tenants-in-chief, upon whom the King could rely. He chose strong ambitious men to establish and maintain Norman control. Each in their turn parcelled out land to lesser knights who had supported them in battle. Every land-owner needed local men to work their land and farm it profitably, so gradually small farmers moved back into the wasted areas from around. (There was not however a peasant society, as in Europe or Asia, for individual ownership of property, and considerable mobility of labour was established.)

The old boundaries and place names remained the same. Some of the horror slowly began to fade.

The Norman lords loved hunting as well as war, and every castle had its chase or forest nearby. Inside these thinly wooded 'forests', however, many small patches could be grazed or cultivated by villeins and their families.

Another factor which brought new life to the wasted manors was the great encouragement given by the Normans to religious houses. The first generation or two of the Norman barons often granted some of their English estates to monastic orders. Selby, Whitby, Jarrow and York were some of the earliest Benedictine abbeys to be founded or restored, but it was the Cistercian monks who made the greatest contribution to Yorkshire.

These 'white monks' were founded on the principles of the early Benedictines. They wanted to live simply, far from other settlements on wild uncultivated acres near moorland or marsh. Their lay brothers were the farmers and herdsmen who far outnumbered the monks themselves. (By 1150 Rievaulx Abbey had 140 monks and over 500 lay brothers.) One of the eight Cistercian abbeys in Yorkshire, Fountains, lay in empty undeveloped Nidderdale, and another, Byland near Helmsley, had land there also.

In 1150 the Norman, Roger de Moubrai, granted 'to God and the monks of St Mary of Byland two stags and two hinds caught annually in his Forest of Nidderdale for the use of the sick of the monastery'. He also granted pasture for 80 mares and foals, and thirty sows and five boars. His grandson Roger, however, when he came to hunt in Nidderdale, 'had the lay-brothers and servants beaten and by his wishes cattle were taken violently to his kitchin'. He vexed the monks until he 'had the satisfaction of £10 of silver from them and a horse worth 100 shillings' then he renewed the grant.

By 1251 the Abbot had obtained an undertaking that Roger would not enter his boundaries except for 'a chase in the season of grease' if their quarry entered the boundaries, and the convent would not have to entertain or house Roger.[7]

Despite these shifts of fortune, the Cistercians acquired extensive pasture rights for their flocks of sheep, as well as mineral rights, over great tracts of moorland across the Dales. They developed the grange system for farming their outlying land. A small group of lay brothers and labourers lived around the grange or barn at first, but later these developed into small settlements, with arable land around them. With the profits, chiefly from the wool but also from the mutton and cheeses, the monks built their beautiful abbeys. They also developed Yorkshire's economy and turned unprofitable rough land into arable. They engaged in lead and iron mining for use on the roofs and gutters of their abbeys and churches. (In 1365, 48 fothers of lead, or over ten tons, from Nidderdale were transported by ox wagon to Boroughbridge then by water to York and London to be used on the roof of Windsor Castle.) The monks continued to use many of the same methods of mining employed by the Romans, such as 'hushing' and 'fire setting'.[8]

Medieval farmers grew far more corn on the Pennines than was grown later, as they were obliged to be self sufficient. Nearly every settlement had its own corn mill. Much toil was needed to produce even small yields with the poor undrained soils, shallow ploughing and lack of manure. Livestock too only brought in very low returns by todays standards. Thanks to the improving economy the population growth in the 12th and 13th centuries in Yorkshire appears to have been faster than in any other county. This was in spite of the seven terrible years of harvest failure between 1315–22, which in turn brought famine and cattle murrain. During these same years, Scottish armies ravaged Yorkshire as far south as Pontefract and added fresh miseries to the lives of the already weakened people. The 1341 tax returns show that much tax relief had to be allowed to compensate for these various disasters.

Scarcely was there some recovery amongst the farming community when the Black Death struck in 1349. Death rates of between 40–45% are estimated around Knaresboro' and in Nidderdale, and 'great mortality' occurred throughout the shire.[9] Few villages were completely wiped out but if only a handful of people were left, the landlord sometimes enclosed the land around, and the remaining people moved elsewhere.[10]

As in the south, however, after the Black Death, and the subsequent smaller outbreaks of plague, there was more land available, and fewer people requiring to be fed. The families who survived were better off than they had been, and labourers could ask for higher wages. With less demand for corn the wool market increased. R.E. Glasscock has estimated there may have been as many as eight million sheep in the county at that period.

By 1396 when York received the status of a county borough with its own sheriff and a powerful city council, York merchants were on the ruling body of the wool staple at Calais. 1,600 of the 2,700 sacks of wool exported from Hull came from York, and this wool reached York from the great sheep runs across the shire. The Ouse was a major thoroughfare whose navigable tributaries reached into many parts of Yorkshire.

The woollen and cloth cottage industries were carried on all over the countryside, spinning, weaving, dyeing and fulling and the products were sold at fairs or sent into town.

By 1430 the turbulent stream of the history of the North had flowed into calmer waters. Its wars, invasions, devastations, plagues and famines had passed. Life was still hard and uncertain and death a common sight, but a pattern had been established. Justice was administered by the county court and manor courts dealt with petty law and order, dues, boundaries and tenures. In the town the Mayor and city council regulated civic order, and the Guilds dealt each with their own sphere of trade. From the lowest cottager to the Lord Mayor, the system provided for every eventuality on a reasonably fair basis. The church touched life at all points and lent discipline and teaching to a medieval man, and also cared for the sick and needy. Trade flourished.

EARLY HISTORY

2. The Achievement of the Yorke family

The family name was spelt York or Yorke for many years, but I have kept to Yorke throughout except when quoting directly from a text.

YORKE COUNTRY

CHAPTER II

SIR RICHARD YORKE 1435? – 1498
OF
YORK

THE NAME OF WILLIAM YORKE DE BERWYKE is mentioned in Richard Rupell's will of December 1st 1435, when William and his wife, (the daughter of one John Barker), were left a bequest by Rupell, a merchant of York.[1] People had begun to be identified by where they lived, and surnames generally became hereditary during the fourteenth century.

If William and his wife had left Berwick on Tweed and settled in York, as seems likely from the evidence we have,[2] their young son Richard grew up in a busy centre of commerce and in an exciting period. York was at the height of its prestige as a leading provincial city. A new spirit had dawned over plague-ravaged, war-racked Europe by the 15th century. New concepts of freedom were glimpsed. It seemed to many that reason and knowledge would liberate the minds of men, and that the boundless secrets of the universe could be discovered. 1450 was the height of this age of discovery.

William Caxton, with his printing press, was an immediate contemporary of Richard Yorke's, and later a fellow merchant. The arrival of the printed word enabled knowledge and argument to flow through society in medieval Europe, and revolutionised communications. Wider paths of study were opened up by the new universities. The first questionings and debates began in the second half of this century which led to the movement known as the Reformation.

Amongst other famous contemporaries were Leonardo da Vinci, with his amazing combination of skills as artist, scientist, architect and sculptor; the painters Botticelli, Piero della Francesca, Jan van Eyck, and Rogier van der Weyden. Lorenzo de Medici was living his life of magnificence in Florence.

While the forces of the Renaissance and Reformation were gathering strength in Europe, the world beyond was yielding its secrets to traders and explorers like Diaz, Columbus, Cabot and Magellan.

Henry V's victory at Agincourt had been a glittering one but the miseries brought about by the campaigns that followed had overshadowed Europe. Although Joan of Arc was burnt at the stake in 1431, her spirit had re-inspired the French. That same year ten year old Henry VI, who had succeeded to the throne when only a baby, was crowned.

A strong king was desperately needed to control the noble factions in England, but Henry VI was feeble in mind and body, although gentle and devout. He married a remarkable wife, Margaret of Anjou, niece of the King of France, but despite her support he allowed England to drift into a state of indiscipline and near anarchy. By 1451 of all his father's conquests in France only Calais remained.

The great landowners kept bands of armed retainers and the many experienced ex-soldiers from the French wars were glad to join such retinues on their return home. They were rewarded with land, or money, and often livery too, and some almost private armies were formed.

As the rivalries grew between the legitimate house of Lancaster in the shape of Henry VI, and his cousin, the Duke of York, so the country became divided. The Lancastrian party was strongest in the war-like north, with York as a centre and most of the nobility on their side. The Yorkists were based in the south and in the midlands. The names of the two factions must not be confused with the counties of those names. The great mass of the people were surprisingly little affected by the struggles, and, by and large, local government carried on as normal.

As a boy, Richard Yorke grew up in a busy urban society which had not lost the tang of country air. The gates of the walled city were locked at sunset, but each morning country people streamed in. Women brought their baskets of vegetables and fruit, fishermen carried buckets of tench, roach and carp caught in the local rivers and ponds, and peasants drove in cattle and sheep for slaughter. This produce was all sold in open booths.

The shopkeepers in the city sold the goods they had made themselves, in open fronted shops. Their wares lay on a bench outside and they sat plying their trade within. An apprentice slept in the shop at night. The work of the tailor, cobbler, candlemaker, saddler, barber and weaver was there for all to see. The baker drew his hot loaves out of his great oven and cooled them in the open air, and the fullers washed their cloths in the river. The butcher killed his cattle in the street, throwing the entrails into the central gutter. The trades tended to stick together so streets were named Coppergate, Fishergate, Swinegate, Peasegate and so on, and the sign of a fish or a boot or a barrel hanging outside showed those who could not read where to go.

Through the narrow cobbled alleys roamed pigs and chickens picking at the rubbish. The wooden houses were crowded together and an unwary passer-by could be soused if a bucket of water were thrown out from a top window. Ragged beggars, hardworking tradesmen and sober-gowned merchants jostled together, occasionally being pushed against the wall as a richly dressed nobleman rode by with his retinue. Thieves and lazy apprentices were birched down Whip-ma-whop-ma-gate, horses and cattle were watered at the great stone troughs, and carts and barrows trundled back and forth. From time to time the town crier stood at the street corner and shouted out the news of the day – 'A merchant's ship is lost at sea! A felon is to be burnt in the square! The Mayor's procession is approaching! A man has been fined for allowing his pigs to stray!'

The great Minster, almost completed in its present day form, towered over the city – a wonder for all to behold.

Richard watched the heavy wagons rattling over the cobbles, bringing the woollen fleeces into York market from the villages with outlying sheep pastures. The English wool was some of the finest and most expensive in the world. It was brought in sacks after the clip, or, in the autumn, as wool fells – the wool left on the skins – after the Martinmas slaughter. As Richard grew older, he probably rode out with his father to visit the farmers who had wool to sell. He had two sisters, Joan and Elizabeth, but may himself have been the only son. His father would have been keen therefore to interest him in the business at a young age.

The huge bales of cloth, fodders of lead and other commodities being loaded on to the ships in the port of Kingston on Hull were a common sight for him too. He was no stranger to the bustle of the quayside where wooden handworked cranes hoisted aboard the hampers, nets and barrels containing the varied goods. A toll had to be paid to use the great weigh beam with its 50lb iron weights. Very heavy loads were dragged on sledges by horses across the cobbles. Whole tree trunks lay waiting to be planed into masts. Onlookers mingled with rope-makers, and sail menders, ship builders and crews, as they made preparations or bade their farewells. In the broad dialect of the day he heard prices discussed and tales of fortunes lost and made. Blunt phrases and earthy adjectives were in everyday use. We can read the Mystery Plays which were performed in the streets of York and which Richard certainly watched every year, to catch the flavour of their speech and the views and attitudes prevailing.[3] So many of the words are still in use today that it telescopes the centuries between us and him, and even between him and his Norse ancestors. Many local place names ended in the Norse thwaite, by, scale, thorpe or toft. Becks (brooks) and laithes (barns), gills (small valleys) and dales were part of his world, as they are part of ours still.

'Stop laikin' about! Shape thi'sel and mek yon rope fast,' or 'Bray yon stoup an' lug yon bale ower 'ere or it'll be marred in't wet,' were orders he would have heard and acted upon, very often.

From what we know of his achievements, he must have received a good education. Much store was laid on learning in his day and he probably attended a Guild School, where he learnt Latin, or was taught by a chantry priest. His reading was from books of devotions, grammars, translations of Latin authors such as Dante, Virgil, Bocaccio, Petrarch, and of course, Chaucer's Canterbury Tales. He heard the descriptions of distant lands found by the new explorers. He met his father's merchant friends who travelled regularly to the Continent, and experienced many adventures on their journeys across Flanders to the markets of Bruges, or Antwerp or to Italy or Spain. Well schooled and disciplined in the church, the weekly mass and great festivals were an integral part of his family life. The Mystery Plays were acted each year on movable stages around the city, and these helped to give him a vivid knowledge of the Bible. Outbreaks of plague and pestilence could strike at any time, and death was never far away. Every man was greatly concerned for the good of his soul, and gave alms and did penances regularly.

His letters and business notes were dated by Saints Days, as was the general practice, and often ended, 'Sweet Jesu have you in his keeping', or some such valediction, and 'May God and the Holy Virgin and all the Saints in Paradise send you sound health and a good profit'.

Family morality was stern, children were harshly brought up and Richard may well have been bound apprentice at twelve for seven years to one of his father's fellow merchants. Even if he were related to the master, an apprentice had to learn the trade from start to finish. He slept with the other apprentices in the attic and served at table.

Each boy learnt to pick and card the wool, then spin it till his thread was strong and even. Next he filled and refilled the shuttles for the weavers until he, too, was allowed to try to weave. His slightest mistake was met by a box on the ears, so he learnt fast. He hated the hot and steamy dye house where he had to stoke the fires and lift the heavy wet cloths from the vats. Then he had to carry the dripping cloths from the fulling mill where it had been pounded, shrunk and thickened, to the tentering grounds. Here, as he helped to peg out the cloths on the racks (or tenters), to stretch them back to the original length, he was at least out of doors. He and his mates could have a game on their way back, or a joke with a passer by. As he grew older he was taken to fairs to learn the marketing side of the business, and to handle the raw wool to feel the quality. His master taught him accounting and bookkeeping, and oversaw his every step in the business.

It was a hard training indeed, but the best way to get on and to become a factor and then later a member of a Guild.

Marriage was regarded as a business arrangement. A daughter had little say as to the match made for her, and cruel pressure, amounting in some cases to beatings and starvation, was used to persuade her. Once married, however, she often played an important part in her husband's business affairs, as Margaret Paston did.[4]

Nicholas Mauleverer, whose family had come over with William the Conqueror, and had been granted land at Allerton Mauleverer, (nine miles from York), arranged a match for his daughter Jane, with Richard. (Her coat of arms bore three greyhounds, so possibly the name arose in the first place from keeping the King's coursing hounds. Her family held 13 carucates of land (about 1,560 acres) at Hellifield in 1303, 'from the lady of the castle of Skipton and paid homage'.)[5] Various members of her family held important offices in the county and in the city. This marriage was clearly a good match for a young merchant and probably brought some land with it.

Jane evidently shared an interest in Richard's business as well as being a fruitful wife. He and she both became members of the Merchant Guild[6] and she bore him six sons and four daughters.

Any portrait of a wife in those days has to be reconstructed from details of the life her husband lived. Apart from wills, or marriage settlements, there is virtually no written record, unless by lucky chance letters have been preserved, as in the case of the Paston family, or the Datinis in Italy. Richard led an extremely full and busy life, and must constantly have been absent from home for long periods, both on journeys to the Continent, and later on long sojourns at Westminster. Jane therefore had to deal with a multiplicity of affairs, as well as the daily oversight of a medieval household. She brought up at least ten children, and almost certainly bore others who miscarried or died in infancy.

From their early married days, every item that came into the house had to be checked, noted down and carefully preserved. If Richard was the hard headed business man he appears to have been, he must have demanded an equally high standard of efficiency in his household management. As well as the immediate family, there were many other dependants in his care, apprentices, servants, grooms, and their families, and of course the families who were tenants on his holdings in villages outside the city.

Jane was no doubt brought up to these responsibilities, but hers certainly increased as time went on. It is hard for us to visualise the problems encountered when food arrived such as herrings or wine in barrels, or fresh fish in buckets, or flour in sacks. It all had to be stored with great care and made safe from rats, damp, or simply deterioration. When a pig or sheep was killed every part was used or salted down. Jane herself made the preserves, the comfits, and most of the medicinal aids in her stillroom. She also had to buy the linen, cloth, velvet, damask or silk needed for all their clothing, and see to the making up. She had to use her own initiative, keep good order, and 'rise while it was yet dark to look to the ways of her household'. Her many pregnancies wore down her health, but all women were in the same case, and no allowance was made for that.

One can only hope that, despite a hard life, Jane was able to share in some of the colour and pageantry when Richard reached the top of his various trees. She only survived to early middle age, but it is pleasant to imagine her receiving some of her due of admiration as she swept into a civic banquet, (perhaps even Archbishop Neville's great feast), wearing a sumptuously embroidered velvet gown, sparkling with jewels.

When Richard decided to make his living as a merchant, he applied for admission to the Freedom of the City.[7] This was required before engaging in trade, and if the applicant had not been born in the city, payment had to be made. We know that Richard did buy this freedom in 1456, and it is likely that his marriage took place about then. From this point he evidently put his shrewd brain and financial acumen to some effect, for information about his career follows rapidly. By 1460 he was sufficiently well known in the city to be chosen one of the Chamberlains. These were officers belonging to the Chamber of the City, or common sergeants to the Mayor. There were three or four Chamberlains and they were responsible for collecting fines and accounting for them to the Council, for enforcing certain rules, and paying out allowances granted by the Council.[8]

By this time the Wars of the Roses had begun in earnest. After the first blood had been shed at the battle of St Albans in 1455, the Yorkists succeeded in capturing Henry VI at Northampton in May, 1460. In December that year, at Wakefield, the Lancastrians surprised and routed the Yorkists, and no mercy was shown. The Duke of York's head, and that of Lord Salisbury, were hung on Micklegate Bar in York for all to see. Richard and his family must have gazed on the frightful sight with a feeling that the revered and rightful Henry VI had re-established himself. Only four months later however, after the massive defeat of the Lancastrians at Tadcaster, the nineteen year old Edward IV reached York, and removing his father's head, replaced it with several newly-congealing heads of Lancastrian nobles.

Although York was a Lancastrian stronghold, the feelings of the ordinary people were very divided. They abstained from joining either side in active warfare, and felt respect for the sanctity of Henry VI, as well as admiration for the moderation of Edward of York. As a Chamberlain of the city, Richard the merchant carried on his daily business and civic affairs as best he could in difficult and uncertain times.

The characteristics required by a merchant then were as now, enterprise, ambition, adaptability and shrewdness. He needed a quickness of mind and an ability to forecast future demands. Account books and ledgers took up a vital part of his time. There were inventories, salaries, deeds and contracts, and bills of lading to contend with. Sound judgement was required to appoint honest factors and agents to live abroad. For international trading, a knowledge of foreign currency, if not the language, rates of exchange, prices of conmmodities and market fluctuations was needed. The hazards of business included robbers, shipwreck, piracy, dishonest agents, closed ports, plague or simply the deterioration of the wares. No insurance was available.

It could take three and a half years from the first order for wool being received until the final sale of the finished cloth.

The Merchant's Guild included all the workers connected with the trade, although there were some subsidiary specialised guilds as well. Amongst the wool and clothworkers the first group were

The sorters, washers, pickers and dyers' of the wool.

Then came the woolcombers, who also greased the wool and put it on distaffs for spinning.

Next came the carders, spinners and men who measured it off the warp, and then the weavers.

The various stages of finishing followed: burling, scouring, fulling, tentering, teaseling, clipping, dyeing, napping, shearing, pressing and folding for packing.

When a man enrolled in a Guild he swore to submit to its laws, and to come to the assistance of any fellow craftsman. It was only through the guilds a man could hope to make his fortune or to be a full citizen. He was ruled by his Guild all his life. In earlier days masters and apprentices had worked alongside each other, and a complete identity of interests (even if not wealth) bound all the members together, but by this time there was a greater gulf. The officials of the guild settled disputes, imposed fines, judged standards of workmanship, and were responsible for correct measurement. Richard and his wife were made members of the Merchant's Guild in 1469.[9]

From the accounts of 'John Dey, Collector of the Customs and Subsidies of our Lord King in the Port of Kyngeston on Hull'[10] we learn that on

'November 16th 1464, The ship of John Porter called "Mayor of Hull", sailed, having on board 12 cloths without grain forwarded by Richard York, denizen.' A total of 144 cloths carried by the Mayor of Hull paid £8.8.0 customs, or 1s 2d each. (Cloth without grain meant the ordinary broad cloth – and not that dyed with the scarlet dye known as 'grain'.)

Such a ship carried the goods of several merchants who preferred not to risk too large a consignment to one vessel. The 'Mayor of Hull' was a stout wooden cog with sails, which held about twenty men. These were made up of the sailors, a sailmaker, two or three merchants and three or four soldiers for protection, and also 'victuals, tackle and the ablements of war'.

By 1465 Richard's capabilities were obviously held in considerable respect by his fellow citizens for he was made one of the two Sheriffs of York.[11] This increased his civic duties which included much time consuming work regulating weights, measures and prices, and fixing taxes and tolls.

One year later he was elected Mayor of the Staple at Calais.[12] The Staple was the very centre of the all important wool trade. The Company of the Staple oversaw all the custom and subsidy on wool sold, and in exchange, paid all the garrison wages in Calais, together with other expenses. The Company ran a mint in Calais, so there was no need to import cash from England. The Merchant Staplers were assured of a ready sale for their wool, and a safe sojourn for themselves under the protection of the garrison.

The duties of the Mayor were manifold, for he was head of the whole Company of ambitious thrusting English merchants and had to co-ordinate not only their regulations and demands with those of the Hanseatic, Italian and Spanish merchants, but also keep the political peace. The mutiny of the garrison soldiers in 1454 had greatly disturbed the trade. The garrison wages had continued heavily in arrears, and the men were aggrieved and discontented. After the Staplers had calmed matters down and had taken over the payment of the wages from the King, the differing loyalties of the civil war caused further altercation. The merchants of the staple were obliged to remain detached from the political and dynastic issues (as Professor Postan points out), and carried on their commercial activities, willing to deal with either party by necessity, or for the chance of gain.

When the Company had first been established in Calais in 1399, it had brought to a conclusion seventy or eighty years of disagreement. Staple towns had previously been set up, at various times, in York, Lincoln, London, Bristol, Bruges and Antwerp. The wool tax was the principal source of revenue early in the fourteenth century, when Parliament first appeared. After uneasy co-operation between the burgesses of the various towns, says Eileen Power, a compromise was reached, and the fixed site at Calais provided Edward III with a place on the continent to handle transactions, and a merchant company ready to bear his taxes from which he could finance his armies and allies. By 1466 however the financial appetites of the crown were less violent. The near monopoly of the Staple prevented great financiers from emerging, and established a large and substantial middle class.

Large landowners sold large amounts of wool by contracting directly with an export merchant in advance, and it seems that Richard's father was just such a one. He, and merchants like him, paid cash in advance, which the sheep owner needed, and, on the way, took interest in cash, or a sack or two of wool.

Some wool dealers who were burgesses in the local towns of pastoral districts, collected the wool from small farmers and passed it on to the exporters. Later some of these dealers themselves took to exporting, so it is quite possible that Richard's father started as a dealer. The line between middleman dealer and exporter was fluid.

As Mayor of the Staple, Richard travelled to the Continent many times, and was in close touch with the Flemish, Spanish and Italian wool merchants who traded there. He would certainly have known William Caxton, also a Stapler, who was described in one document as 'the Govenour beyonde the sea'. We do not know whether Richard usually travelled on one of the ships carrying his wool from Kingston on Hull, but it seems likely. Undoubtedly the journey, however made, was long and hazardous and involved considerable discomfort and danger. Travelling merchants often took their own food and cooking pots with them, as well as their lives in their hands.

As Mayor too, he attended meetings, dinners, feasts and religious services as part of his duties. George Neville, the brother of the Earls of Warwick and Northumberland and a very powerful man, held a feast in York as one of the ceremonies to mark his enthronement as Archbishop of York. Great entertainment was provided at Cawood Palace on January 16th 1466, and the feast was described as 'the greatest that ever subject made'.

Cawood Castle had a main hall and a low hall, and the new Archbishop presided over several hundred noble or gentle people sitting at seven tables in the huge raftered main hall. Here 'at the Fyffth Table in the Hall' were seated 'the Mayor of the Staple of Calais, the Mayor of York, and all the Worshipfulle men of the said Cite'. The thirteen year old Duke of Gloucester, brother of Edward IVth, presided over three tables of noblewomen and ladies in the chief chamber. Other guests were seated in two other chambers, and the household and servants were squeezed into the 'gallery'. Seven bishops, ten abbots, twenty eight peers, fifty nine knights and innumerable judges, lawyers, clergy, aldermen and great ladies travelled from all over the country to attend it. With their attendants they numbered around 2,500 people. The jewels on the silken and damask gowns, the scarlet, blue and gold embroidered robes of the nobles and dignitaries gleamed richly in the candle light. It must have been a dazzling sight. Liveried serving men ran in and out with great platters of steaming food, ornate silver and gold cups and flagons of wine were passed round, musicians and tumblers entertained the company, and the noise and feasting lasted all day and far into the night.[13]

Some of the food consumed included 113 oxen, 1,000 sheep, 6 wild bulls, 2,000 each of pigs, geese and chickens, 12 porpoises (or sea-pigs as they were called) and 4,000 cold venison pasties.

The coat of arms granted to Richard Yorke was a silver saltire on an azure ground. His crest was the head of a monkey[13a], and his motto, taken from Psalm 18, was 'Per meum deum transilio murum'. (With the help of God I can scale any wall.) Being a merchant and not a feudal landowner, it is likely that he received his arms during his lifetime. Shields were often devised from the arms of a patron or close associate, with a variation, and the Neville shield bore a simple silver saltire on a red ground. It is more than possible that Richard was granted permission to adapt this for his family by altering the colour of the background. Such a mark of favour from the Neville family would have been very significant, for at this period the three brothers held the reins of government in their power.

Edward IV was only nineteen years old when he was crowned, and when the fighting was over he was content to enjoy the pleasures of peace, and leave his counsellors to rule the country. However, when Edward married a widow, Elizabeth Woodville, for love, instead of a Princess chosen by his cousin Warwick, relations became strained. In 1469, after a masterly stroke by Warwick, King Edward was obliged to bow to his superior forces, and was restrained in Middleham Castle under Archbishop Neville's surveillance. His rival King Henry VI was also a prisoner of Warwick's, in the Tower at the same time. As Sir Winston Churchill commented, this was a remarkable achievement for any subject.

This same year, on February 3rd at the feast of St Blaise (the patron saint of wool combers), Ricardus de York was elected Lord Mayor of York.[14] He had become, like Robert Sturmey of Bristol, 'a full notable worshippful merchaunt'.

As Mayor, he took the chair at the City Council, assisted by twelve Aldermen, two Sheriffs and twenty four councillors. Proceedings at the meetings were kept strictly secret, with a huge fine of £10 imposed on anyone who broke this rule. A fine of 4d was payable for non attendance, and 2d for being late. Councillors received a fee of 20s per annum. They oversaw all the minutiae of medieval city life, from setting the price of bread and wine, or the exact place where a market should be held, arbitrating upon bills of complaint, or quarrels between customs officers and ship owners, to making fit preparations for a royal visit.[15] The position of Mayor, as head of the city, was one of great dignity and authority, and this was enhanced when men of strong character, such as Richard seems to have been, filled the post.

York commanded the route to the North and had been granted its charter in 1156, but its liberties had been established even earlier. It was a self governing entity held from the King at a fixed fee each year. The major element of city income were tolls paid for the right to have a stall in the market, or to use a warehouse or the weighing beam. Tolls were levied too to help in the upkeep of the city walls with their four great bars, six posterns and four towers, and its bridges and streets. The city corporation had to try to maintain public health and safety when streets were foul with refuse and open sewers, clean water was sold by the bucketful and houses were overcrowded.

Then there was the problem of the poor and the vagrants. St Peter's hospital made regular provision for two hundred poor men, but wandering travellers, beggars and lepers were sent outside the walls, and forbidden to lodge within. The sick or crippled were cared for by the monasteries, or like those in prison, depended entirely on charitable gifts from individuals. Every man of means gave regularly and frequently to charity for the good of his own soul. There were at least thirty nine parish churches in medieval York, as well as chapels, and the various religious houses included Dominican, Austin, Franciscan and Carmelite Friars.

In 1469 also, Richard joined the prestigious Corpus Christi Guild.[16] The great festival of Corpus Christi, held on the Thursday and Friday after Trinity Sunday, was the culmination of weeks of preparation by the thirty or forty city guilds. They had been rehearsing a cycle of thirty mystery plays known locally as the Pageant. The purpose of the plays was to dramatise a summary of the Bible from the Creation of the world to the Last Judgement, as a religious instruction for all the people in the city.

The night before, a proclamation ordered the citizens to go unarmed on the day, the guilds to provide 'good players, well arrayed and well speaking', and every player to be ready 'in his pageant at convenient time that is to say at mid hour betwixt 4 and 5 o'clock in the morning, and then all the other pageants fast following each one after the other as their course is, without tarrying.'

At 4.30 a.m. each pageant – on a decorated wheeled platform, with some basic scenery – trundled out from Pageant Green to begin the day's performance. One after another the plays were acted out at various fixed points around the city. The Fullers and the Coopers acted the Garden of Eden story; the Goldsmiths, the Epiphany; the Locksmiths, the Temptations and so on, ending with the Mercers portraying God and his angels on Judgement Day and some fearsome devils consigning the damned to a

3. The South East Prospect of the City of York 1745 By Sam'l and Nat'l Buck, Garden Court, Middle Temple (Micklegate Bar on extreme left)

fiery Hell. The combination of civic pride and theological teaching, sacred scenes and tender poetry with rough humour and low comedy seems strange to us, but was an instant success with the medieval audience, who were often quite carried away by the reality of it all.[17]

The first play was outside the gate of Holy Trinity Priory, Micklegate, then the Pageant wound through the city and ended up at the Pavement.

Any man paying enough for the privilege could ask for a play to be performed outside his house. Richard is listed as paying 6d 'for the Pageant Silver' so perhaps this enabled his household and children to watch from their own windows.

Later in the day the crowds watched the Lord Mayor's procession, with 'each man's servant with him bearing a Torch to the praise of God', going to the Minster for the special Mass. In his fur trimmed Mayoral robes of rich scarlet, with a golden girdle and chain of office, a black velvet hood on his head, preceded by his mace-bearer and followed by his Aldermen in scarlet, and twenty four city councillors in murray or crimson, Richard must have felt justly proud of his adopted city of York, and of his responsibilities in it.

In 1472, Richard Yorke and Thomas Wrangwyshe were the two burgesses elected by the city to attend the Parliament summoned by Edward IV at Westminster. This continued in session until 1475. They were paid eight shillings a day between them for two hundred and eight days, receiving £83.4.0, plus twelve day's extra pay for going and coming, and £10 for 'their riding and other expenses'. Six days were allowed for riding from York to London at a reasonable speed, and £2.10.0 each for all expenses on the way.[18]

The two elected members set off early in the morning on good horses, their short riding cloaks worn over fur-lined jerkins, and warm woollen hose, under leather riding hose and boots. Some armed retainers rode ahead, in case of danger and servants leading packhorses followed on behind. In those troubled times there were many marauding bands of Lancastrian supporters, or simply freelance malcontents, on the lookout for rich travellers. The roads in winter had deep muddy ruts, into which the horses stumbled, and in summer the riders were choked with dust. As they rode down England they saw men with oxen working the fields, shepherds guarding their flocks of small leggy sheep, and heavy wagons carrying their loads to market. A herd of cattle or sheep on the road could delay the journey, and when the weary riders eventually reached an inn, the beds were frequently infested with bugs, and the food tough and indifferent. Fortunately Richard was a seasoned traveller by land and sea, and no stranger to hardship. At first he knew few if any of the other elected members, and it was hard to understand some of the broad local dialects, but with his many mercantile connections he became a respected figure in Westminster, and had the ear of many influential people. The citizens of York felt, I hope, that they had chosen wisely when they elected him as their representative. He did not sit in the Parliament called in 1477, but he served in many lengthy sessions over the next eighteen years, in Parliaments summoned in turn by Edward IV, Richard III and Henry VI.

The political instability of this period must have made the last ten years of Richard's Parliamentary duties years of intense anxiety in the city of York. To retain the goodwill of the city with all its ancient rights and privileges was of importance to the rulers of England. Richard III was able to do this, but while he kept the City Council on his side he was thought less of by many of the commons.

Some tavern gossip is related in the city minutes – 'What might our lord of Gloucester do for the city then?' 'Nowt but grin at us!'[19]

In 1475 Yorke was made Master of the Mercers' Guild and of the Company of Merchants and Mercers. At this period the wool trade was in decline and the cloth trade on the increase, so the dominant interest of the English merchants was changing from wool to cloth. As E.M. Carus Wilson says, the wholesale export trade had become a career no less reputable than the church or the law, with prospects no less attractive and a training no less strict, first as apprentice, and then as factor. Those who professed it were an aristocracy of merchants. . . making or losing small fortunes in the markets of Europe.[20]

Shippers of cloth, unlike the staplers, were adventurers, or venturers, not bound to any one company or any one port. They risked their goods and sometimes their persons voyaging to Holland, Zeeland, Brabant and Flanders, and later to Spain, Prussia, the Baltic and even Iceland. As well as cloth they exported lead, iron, hides, fish, corn and salt, and tried to capture the foreign markets from their rivals. (Some of the venturers, like Richard, remained staplers as well.)

The oldest account book of The Mercers' Company mentions a levy on all the 'adventurers of the Mercery' as early as 1443. By 1478 there was talk of the 'northern adventurers' being closely associated with the Mercers' Company of York, of which Richard was Master. All these were part of the great group who, by the end of the fifteenth century, were known as 'The Merchant Adventurers of England'. They met together in their great hall, 89ft long and 40ft wide, with its huge central pillars and oak roof trusses. Four fireplaces had been built 'to make the hall more commodious for feasting'. These merchants imported oil, wax and wine, woad, and 'grain' for dyeing and alum for fixing the dyes, honey, sugar, almonds, saffron, spices and pepper, figs, raisins, and dates, vinegar and rice, and rosin and pitch, amongst their merchandise. Although the alliance with Spain and with France in 1478 had made the seaways safer, there were still frequent acts of piracy, and the hazards were very great.

A licence granted to Richard Yorke in 1484 'for a ship of Kingston on Hull called "Anthony of Hull" of the portage of 260 tons' shows us his

4. The Seal of the Mercers and Merchant Adventurers of York from 1435 onwards

affairs were prospering, for this is a very large ship for this period and would have required a crew of between forty and sixty men.

As Richard was so involved in both civic and parliamentary duties, his wife had to oversee and direct much of his business from home, sending letters to agents, receiving goods and money due to him, making gifts and benefactions to the church and the poor in his name, and arranging masses to be said for his safe and successful return. She also had to entertain his merchant associates and foreign traders, and see to the education and marriages of their ten children. In his will Richard made provision for two bastard sons, Giles and George, and it is quite possible that Jane Yorke may have cared for them also, especially if, as was quite common, they were born to maidservants in the household.

If their house stood in Ousegate End, one of the busier thoroughfares in medieval York, its chief distinction would have been its superior height of four storeys, its leaded windows, and the stables behind. The Mayor and his family may however have moved to a more fashionable and spacious house in Micklegate, set amongst gardens and meadows. In either case, the rooms were certainly large enough for entertaining, hung with brightly coloured cloth or tapestries, with imported carpets on the floor, and furnished with cushioned seats and trestle tables. For special occasions candelabra were used, and the family plate. . . perhaps a great silver salt cellar, some dishes and a large gilt cup. . . gleamed in the soft light.

The huge canopied beds in the bedchambers had sheets and feather mattresses and pillows. These were highly prized, and were frequently bequeathed in wills. They were surmounted by rich silk or tapestry coverlets, or by embroidered cloths of blue and white, yellow or green. Strong iron-bound presses and coffers held clothes or valuables, and in the corner stood a basin and ewer. Many merchants kept their leather bags of silver in a chest at the foot of their bed, but bags of gold or jewels were hidden in a recess behind the bed curtains.

Richard and his wife slept naked in their great curtained bed, but when they arose he would put on a linen undershirt, wide legged breeches or pantaloons, and even linen undersocks. Long black or blue woollen hose were topped by a short, tight fitting doublet, made of fine quilted cloth. Over this he wore a long gown of dark cloth, fur-trimmed and gathered at the waist by a belt. A rosary, a pouch or a small dagger hung from the belt. A hood buttoned on to his tunic covered his head and neck. When out of doors he added a wide brimmed merchant's hat, and a full cloak, which fastened at the neck and reached down to his feet. The latter were encased in pointed leather shoes, strapped across the instep.

My lady Yorke wore a shift of fine linen under a fur-lined warm cloth garment. Over this came a long, tight sleeved gown of purple, green or blue. Separate embroidered sleeves could be added for greater effect, and trimmings could be of velvet, damask, silk or ermine. On her head she wore a wimple drawn around under her chin, and over it, when she went out, a beaver hat in winter, or a straw one in summer. For special occasions she wore a heart shaped, or 'horned' head dress.

By 1476 Richard was named as Alderman which office was held for life. As such, and when not at Westminster, he continued to sit regularly in council, hearing such cases as these.

'A controversy and debate hanging between Thos. Nelson and a son of the one party, and William Scauseby of the other party, touching some property in Thursday Market was settled by the Mayor and Richard York, Alderman, Miles Metcalfe, Recorder, Will Todd and N. Pearson, late sheriffs, made a full end in all things depending betwixt the parties.'

'In September 1479 came John Fulford into the Council Chamber before William Welles, then being Mayor, and there and then it was said that master Richard York should, for maintenance of the said John against Christopher Bell, resave and take a scaffold. The said John, uncoerced, swore upon the holy Evangelist that the said master York bought the said scaffold from him for 10s, the which was paid, 6s of silver to himself and 4s to the chamber. . . .'

'On 26 March 1480, before Robert Amyas, Mayor, 10 of the 12, 2 Sheriffs, and 9 of the 24. . . a bill of complaint against Richard York, Alderman, Richard Burgh, John Spooned, and Thomas Baxter, by one Christopher Bentley made, was openly read, the which so read was understood by the parties abovesaid and answered in the manner following.

First the said Richard York in all things comprehend in the bill denied, and said in manner and form rehearsed in the bill that he was not culpable therein. Richard Burgh and John Spooned answered the same. Then Thomas Baxter examined upon the maim and hurt comprehended, (said) that he did not hurt him nor him strike. . . .'[21]

In March 1480, Edward IV asked the city for help against the Scots. At the council meeting it was decided to raise a force of 120 archers within the city. This offer was gladly accepted by the King, and on April 20th . . . 'Thos. Wrangwyshe was appointed Captain of the 120 archers of able men to do the King's service in his viage towards Scotland. Richard Yorke, Alderman, to be second in command.' Richard spent much time, energy and money helping to raise, equip and feed these archers. Each soldier was due for 6d a day and 2d a day for hire of a horse, to be paid fourteen days in advance, and the captains were to hold the next two weeks money for them. Three men said they wanted four week's wages in advance, or they refused to go, so the Council, in order to prevent a mutiny, paid up. On their return in August, the three were sent to prison to teach them a lesson. (29 August 1482.)[22]

The next year in June Richard is back in the army leading men to the 'right noble lord the Earl of Northumberland', head of the Neville family, at Newcastle to support him 'for certain causes touching certain towns of Ainstie, in going forth to Scotland'.

(At this time the Scots were much feared and hated. Several cases of proof of birth were heard in Council when a man had been defamed or slandered by being called a Scot.)

Sixteen years after his first term of office, Richard was once again elected Mayor of the Staple. This must have been the height of his mercantile career. He had by now invested some of his profits in land around villages near York, and also in houses in York and Hull. Gold and silver plate was another investment much favoured at this time, for there were few English banks such as the Medici bank in Italy. Various donations to local churches and chantries kept him reasonably at peace with the prospect of his end, even though the teaching of the church on usury caused feelings of great guilt amongst the merchants and capitalists of the day. The hardest headed of merchants led their lives within an intricate framework of religious observance, and believed that the true benefits of almsgiving were to the giver.

Richard was also re-elected Lord Mayor of York the same year, for the second time, and it seems there was quite a turmoil over the election. Maybe by then, he had made a few enemies, either political or in business.

It would be surprising if he had not, with so many factions to please, and so much arbitration to deal with. The length and detail of the three Minutes passed by the Council shows that it was necessary to make the issue very clear to all, and it was certified under the seal of the Corporation, that 'the plane and trewe election of the right wirshippful Richard York at St Blaise last passed, elect maiour of this wirshipful cite for this yere ensuing'. A deputation of 'the 24' was nominated to ride up to the King. . . 'upon Wednesday next coming'. . . . Suitable new clothing for the deputation was ordered by the Corporation, and provided by the Chamberlains. On March 12th 'the Kinge's gracious letters affirming the election of Richard Yorke, Mayor' were read.[23]

It seems to have been thought politic to seek the further support of the Duke of Gloucester, the King's brother, (later to become Richard III) as well as others to back up the new mayor. Handsome presents were authorised to be ready for the Duke at his impending visit to the city.

This visit took place in Easter week, as the Duke was on his way North. The Mayor presented him with gifts of two dozen rabbits, six pheasants, one dozen partridges, apples, wine, and 'mayn breid'. At the feast in his honour, the Aldermen wore their scarlet and the twenty four their murrey or crimson. For their consumption the city provided five shillings worth of Sunday bread, 14 gallons of wine, viz 4 red, 4 claret, 4 white, 2 sweet, and also six pike, six tench six bream, six eels and a barrel of sturgeon. (Being Holy Week only fish could be eaten.)

On September 4th letters came from the King requiring Richard Yorke to be at Newcastle 'for the conservation of the said town as hastily as he could conveniently be'. This was again to help with the problem of the Scots.

There are very many extracts from the minutes of the City Council which Richard chaired during his second mayoralty, and these are just a few. . . .

'22 March 1481   It is agreed that the offenders in ringing the common bell shall be punished by way of imprisonment, according to the King's high commandment and the Duke of Gloucester.

29 March 1482 Item.   It is agreed that all foreign butchers coming to this city to sell flesh from Thursday forward sell their flesh in Thursday market and go toll free and pageant and all other common charges.

12 April 1482   At the which day came into the Council Chamber Sir Raufe Assheton, Knyht, in the name of. . .the Duke of Gloucester. . . to correct and punish Thomas Redhead for his offence and commit him to prison.[24]

31 May 1482 Item.   It is agreed that a proclamation shall be made that all vagrants, that is to say poor people, coming to this City, that they

abide not within the city nor suburbs of the same, not over a night upon pain of imprisonment and other punishment according to the discretion of the Mayor.

1 July 1482 That the common women and other misgoverned women shall inhabit them in the suburbs without the walls of this City and not within.

That the brewsters from this day forward shall sell for 1 obulus (half penny) a gallon of the best.

15 November 1482 At the which day it was advised by the Council that as long as the price of beans be at 4s or above that the baxters of this City shall sell three 'hors lofys' (horse loaves?) for 1d and that every loaf shall weigh three pounds, and if the price be under 4s that then every baxter of this City shall sell three horse loaves for 1d and that every loaf shall weigh four pounds.'[25]

Richard may have been a strong Mayor but he meted out harsh treatment at times. Guy Rencliffe of Escrick owed Richard a debt of £40 which he would not pay. Rencliffe was declared an outlaw and was only pardoned seventeen years later after Yorke's death.

After the untimely death of Edward IV in April 1483, his heir Edward was escorted to London by his uncle Richard Gloucester, who had been appointed Lord Protector. He had taken a public oath of loyalty to the young Prince. They arrived in London on May 4th, and by June 5th, detailed instructions had been given for the boy's coronation on June 22nd. On June 8th it was revealed that the young Princes were bastards, from an illegal union, because Edward IV had already been married to Lady Eleanor Butler before he had married their mother. Parliament accepted their illegitimacy and gave the crown to Richard, in an Act called Titulus Regius. His magnificent coronation was attended by all the nobility, both Yorkist and Lancastrian, and hopes rose of an end to the stuggle between them.

In August King Richard rode to York with his Queen Anne and his son. Great preparations were made by the Mayor and Council to receive him with due honour, 'on horseback in fine scarlet gowns', and, (as strongly advised by the King's secretary), 'with Pageants, with such good speeches as can, this short warning considered, be devised, and with the streets decorated and hung with cloths of arras and tapestry'.[26] On arrival the King invested his own son as Prince of Wales at a ceremony in the Minster. Having established himself firmly upon the throne, he summoned Parliament in October to which Richard Yorke was sent as representative of York, once again, with Thomas Wrangwyshe.

With Richard Yorke's long experience as a City father, alderman, trader, traveller and soldier, the Council evidently felt he was the best man to represent them at that moment, to keep the affairs of the city calm, and to allow them time to restore their economy. The complaints they made of civic poverty were true, for the deficit for that year's accounts was £160 – a very large sum to make up.

King Richard III revived the power of Parliament and inaugurated a series of enlightened reforms in every sphere of government. Commerce was protected, and the Fellowship of the Merchant Adventurers of London formed. Attempts were made to please the clergy and the landowners, and a period of reconciliation followed. In April 1484 his ailing son died at Middleham. Richard proclaimed his nephew, Warwick, his heir, but many in England then turned towards Henry Tudor, Earl of Richmond, (a direct descendant of Edward III through his mother), who had lived in exile until now. During that year several prominent Englishmen quietly withdrew from London and joined Henry.

By August 1st 1485, he had landed in England and was proclaiming Richard a usurper and a rebel. The King marched from the Midlands, supported by loyal troops from the city of York and by the Earl of Northumberland, and met Henry at Bosworth Field on August 21st. After the fierce battle the crown of the defeated king was picked out of a bush and placed on Henry's head. Richard's body was stripped and flung over the back of a horse. So ended the Plantagenet line and began the Tudor dynasty.

The scrivener of the York City Records wrote, 'This day was our good King Richard piteously slain and murdered to the great heaviness of this city'. He was but thirty two years old.

For Richard Yorke the intense difficulties of keeping his city (and himself) loyal to King Richard and then, after Bosworth, to Henry VII, must have required considerable adroitness and finesse. Evidently he achieved this balancing act successfully. In fact, after Bosworth, certain affairs had to be conveniently forgotten. Even some documents implicating the Council too deeply with Richard III were tactfully omitted from the official record. (Included in these was the report that if Gloucester had approved of a man for mayor, the common people would exercise their ancient right to refuse him and choose one of their own.) (13 February 1483.)[27]

Yorke was again elected to go to Westminster in October 1483, although Parliament did not sit until January 1484.

On November 1st 1485... 'Robert Hancock, alderman rode to the Parliament, and eight days later Richard York, alderman rode to London to the Parliament. They returned on December 18th.' For the next sitting they sat from January 18th until March 10th 1486.[28]

Richard's wife Jane must have died in her late forties, for sometime after 1486 he married again. Joan was a comely widow, ten or more years younger than Richard. She had first been married to John Dalton, a prominent merchant stapler of Hull, and close friend of the noted Cely family of woolmerchants. Secondly she had married John Whitfield, another merchant and one time Mayor of Hull. She had at least one daughter, who married Henry Myndrum, and she owned some property in Hull. It appears that she got on well with Richard's children, and was a support to him in his latter years, but although she was included in his memorial window, in her own will of 1506 she asked to be buried beside John Whitfield in Hull. It seems that of her three husbands she was most fond of the second. Could she have felt that 'the better part of the affections' of her first and third husbands were, like the Merchant of Venice, 'with their hopes abroad'?

Having seen the strife of the Red and the White Roses end, and the Plantagenet line die out, Richard sat on in the first Parliament under the Tudors.

He was by no means alone in his anxieties. There was scarcely a man of standing whose family had not supported the losing side at some point or another during the civil wars. Henry VII had to calm and stabilise the powerful families as quickly as possible to prevent further strife, so he stated that all who gave their allegiance to the King upon the throne should be secure in their lives and property. However at the same time, he secretly and systematically eliminated all possible heirs. There is evidence that it was he who ordered the murder of the young Princes in the Tower. (In order to marry their sister he was obliged to make her legitimate, which in turn made the boys into possible heirs. He accused the late King of every possible crime, but never of their murder.) He gained popularity by securing favourable terms for the English merchants trading with the Netherlands.

In the North Richard III had been very popular, and in the wilder more remote areas the new King's authority was often ignored, if not flouted. Border warfare with the Scots and cattle raiding was still carried on, and much of the population was turbulent and lawless. Richard's sister in Burgundy stirred up plots against Henry and backed the insurrection when Lambert Simnel was put up as pretender to the throne. This caused further upheaval and York was in a ferment of apprehension from April till June. The Civic Records relate, 'upon the Sunday by three of the clock in the morning tidings came to my Lord Mayor from the field of battle how God had sent the King victory'.[29] The rebels had attacked Bootham Bar and been repulsed by the citizens.

That July, 'in the vigil of St Peter called Advincle', King Henry rode to York. Wisely, tremendous preparations were made for the King's reception. The Mayor and Council had recently refused the King's nominee as Recorder of the City and had chosen their own nominee, John Vavasour. They had written to the Archbishop of York thanking him for his help to the city and to Richard Yorke and Robert Hancock in particular, on behalf of the City. They also asked for advice over their preparations in view of the 'evident decay, povertie and ruine of the same citie', but wishing nevertheless to show that the inhabitants 'be gladded and joifull of the Kinge's commyng'.

The final arrangements made were for two Sheriffs with twenty horsemen and two Aldermen with forty horsemen to meet the King at Tadcaster Bridge. Two miles outside the City were assembled the Mayor and other Aldermen, clad in long gowns of scarlet, and members of the Council in violet, the Chamberlains in murrey, and many of the inhabitants in red, all on horseback. Other inhabitants on foot were to join in nearer the city with a certain number of children 'calling joyfully 'King Henrie' after the manner of children'.

At the first Bar of the city entrance stood a place 'craftilye conceyved in manner of a heaven', with trees, roses, and flowers, and a crown upon a cloud. The leader of a group of citizens presented the King with the Keys of the City and recited a poem of fulsome praise. As the King rode through the streets he saw fine cloths and draperies hanging everywhere in his honour, and 'if the weder be fair', rose water was to rain down on him.

On Ousebridge was placed a royal throne, with effigies of the six previous King Henrys. There another speech was made and a sceptre handed to the King. Further along the procession came a shower of sweetmeats like hailstones, then a player representing David presented the King with a sword of ivory. Finally actors representing Our Lady and her angels sang to him. After this the Royal party were feasted on 'six greate fatte oxen, and fifty greate fatt weders, (lambs) a ton of rose coloured wine and two hundred loaves of mayne bread'.[30]

It was quite as important for the King to have the loyal support of York as vice versa, and no efforts were spared on either side. After this great civic reception, the King 'wishing to reward the loyalty of the city and gain favour with the inhabitants, he dubbed my Lord Maier called William Todd and Richard York alderman, knights'.[31]

He may thereby have gained favour with some of the inhabitants but not all. Two years later a further uprising occurred in York. Leland says 'Fishergate was burnt down in Henry VII's time by the commons of Yorkshire, who would have beheaded Sir Richard York. It has ever since been blocked up.' Sir Richard may have been a marked man after he had supported the Crown during Simnel's rebellion, (as Professor Gwyther Moore suggests), and been held a symbol of Henry's detested rule by the malcontents. Or he may have been unpopular on another score for failing to achieve favourable terms with the embassy from the Emperor Maximilian, who was supporting the Burgundians and frustrating the export activities of the local merchants.[32] The Duke of Burgundy and his wife, (Richard III's sister), aided the two pretenders to the English throne, Lambert Simnel and Perkin Warbeck, who plotted and schemed for seven years. Henry VII forbade all trade with them and the Netherlands from 1493–1496. The Emperor Maximilian joined with the Burgundians and forbade all importation of cloth or yarn into his vast dominions. After many years of talks, the favourable commercial treaty of Magnus Intercursus was drawn up in 1496. This granted reciprocal freedom of trade to the merchants of both England and the Habsburg Empire. (It was renewed in 1497, the year before Richard Yorke died, with special clauses exempting English cloth from any new tolls.)[33]

The interruption of trade with the Netherlands had reacted on the German merchants of the Hanse, and feelings ran high. Fights broke out in London in 1493 with English merchants attacking the Hanseatic groups. At one point Richard Yorke was sent out as ambassador to treat with the Hanse.[34]

This is the last public record of Richard's many and varied efforts as negotiator and arbiter over his long and full life, but as his mind was perfectly clear up to the day of his death, he probably continued to sit in council as Alderman for several more years. He must have been keenly interested in Cabot's discovery of Newfoundland in 1497, with all its implications for the merchants.

If we assume that he was born around 1435, he was nearing sixty five when he died in April 1498. This was a great age for that period and is evidence of his stamina and excellent general health. Despite constant long and arduous journeys by land and sea, and countless years of the responsibilities of public office and settling disputes, his mind remained sound and clear to the end. His will, so characteristic of the man, reveals his thoroughness and meticulous care for his soul, his family, his land, his possessions, his church and even his ancestors.

We can picture him in his last months, growing daily more frail and arthritic, his limbs more shrunken. Despite that, his piercing eye and commanding presence could still reduce his five grown sons to silence, and his grip on his affairs was as strong as ever.

In the solemn presence of the Lord Prior of St Mary's Abbey, two Doctors, and fellow monks, he drew up the main part of his will in Latin, on April 8th. Then after reflection, he added a codicil on 10th, also in Latin. One can imagine his active mind going over and over his affairs, as he lay in his great bed, growing daily weaker. Finally two days later, he again summons his scrivener, Master Bryan Palmys, with his parchment sheet, his sandbox for drying the ink, and his wax for seals. He asks him to alter the wording about his sons being taken in hand and reformed should they disagree, and instead allows them, if in agreement, to be his sole executors.

The Will of Sir Richard York, Knight, Alderman of York, 8 April 1498 (Translation from the Latin.)

Richard York, Knight, and alderman of the City of York. To be buried in the Church of St John the Evangelist, near Ouse Bridge in front of the image of the Trinity, in my own tomb which I have caused to be made there.

I will that that chantry, which once upon a time I began to found in the Church of St John the Baptist in Hungate, shall now be founded and endowed at the discretion of my executors, and that it shall be increased to make up one whole and sufficient chantry, from my tenements in Bowdon and Popylton, and that Sir Thomas Gripthorpe my chaplain, shall have it for the term of his life.

I will that the repairing of the roof of the choir of the said church shall be done at my expense, according to an agreement made in certain indentures, made hereon between me and the carpenters hired to do the work.

I leave to the aforesaid church 20 ells of purple cloth for copes: and one fringe of gold on a cloth of gold containing in its embroideries the image of Our Lord's Passion; with this express condition that the parishioners at their own cost shall buy for themselves one suitable cope, under a bond of £100.

But if not I leave the said gold fringe to the Minster at York

To the said Minster I leave 6 marks for forgotten tithes.

I leave to the Bedryns one silver and gold cup.

To Sir Robert Langlandes, the parson of my parish, ten shillings to pray for my soul.

To the poor on the day of my burial £10. To Joan, my wife, all my tenements, etc., at Kyngston upon Hull, for the terme of her life, with remainder to my younger sons; and the mansion in which I live for the terme of her life, with remainder to Richard my son of my lands in Barwyk (Berwick on Tweed), Newcastell, Sledmar, Normanby and Donnynton.

To my younger sons, viz: master Christopher doctor of laws, to Thomas, William and John, and their heirs, land held in copyhold in the townships of Holtby, Morton, Heslyngton, Flaxby, Barnby-super-Moram, Rynghowse and Bissopthorp; and to each of them one tenement in the city of York, at the discretion of my executors.

To master Christopher my son, ten marks per annum for ten years.

To Joan York my sister and Elizabeth York my sister, but only if they survive me, 40/- each.

The residue to Lord William Senvois, Bishop of Carlisle, abbot of St Mary's Monastery at York, to Sir Reginald Bray, knight, to master Christopher York doctor of laws, to Richard and William York, my sons, and to John York if it is justified by his behaviour and habits; that especially, as in all things, I leave to the ingenuity and will of the said father bishop of the church, and of Reginald Bray whom I appoint my executors.

Before these witnesses – The Lord Prior of St Marys Doctor Thurkylby and Suffell, his fellow monks, etc.

Codicil 10 April 1498 – To master Christopher York, my son, my terms concerning the release of the rectory of the church at Rybe, in the diocese of Lincoln.

For lights of the glorious Virgin Mary of the Parish Church of St John the Evangelist, 200lbs of wax.

To Doctor Suffell one old noble (a gold coin value 6/8).

I will that if my sons are unwilling to agree among themselves, or deviate in any way from the path of justice and equity, that the said venerable men, the lord Bishop of Carlisle and Reginald Bray, shall take them in hand and reform them.

I will that all my goods shall remain in the house I usually live in. I will that my sons shall have free ingress to my house, which I leave to my wife.

To Edmund Tayliour one fother of lead (Fodder of lead = 2,352lbs, approx.)

To the reverend Bishop of Carlisle, a ring with a sapphire.

The second codicil (as in the original) –

Md that hereafter folowith the wyll of me, Sir Richard York, Knyght, of myn wyll and mocion, for the well of myne owne soule; and thus I charge myn sones. Chr. doctor, Thomas, William and John, my executors, dischargyng me and chargyng them as they wyll awnswere to me at the day of dome that they fulfyll my mynd.

I wyll that my cosyn Guy Foster have the pece (of land) that was my cosyns his fader.

I wyll that Roclyff have myn yeres in the land at Scarburght. (These are the years left of his leasehold.)

I wyll that they make an almehowse of the Trinitie for vj men and vj women.

Item. That my lady of Clemthorpe have that that I gaffe hir in the bylle, as appiereth by hir bylle.

Item. That they found oure Lady-mess in my parishe Church, and I geve unto it vjs. viijd. to be taken out of the howse that Sir Richard Flynt hath.

To my sone Doctor Christofer my cramsyn cloke lyned wt sarsnett.

To Robert Person a furryd gowne.

To Agnes Barker a cramsyn gowne furryd.

To William a gowne.

I wyll that they agre wt the child daughter, the smyth, for his howse, or elles she to have hir howse to hir and hir heirs.

I wyll that my sone Richard make a memor(ial) for me and my awnsystors at Barwyk, in the chapell of Seynt Kateryn.

I wyll that there be a vestment geven unto the churche of the Trinitie in the towne of Barwyck upon Twete.

I wyll that if my sonnes can agre amonges themself, than the right reverend fader in God, bysshop of Karlell, and Sir Reynold Bray shall have noon administration of my goodes but oonly my sonnes.

Moreover, the yere above written, the xijth day of Aprill, that is to say on Shyer Thursday, Sir Richard York knyght, holl of mynd, as it wele appiereth, in the presens of the persons whose names are after wreten, at x of the clock afore nonne of the said day, herying the contentes above writen red by Maister Bryan Palmys, said and declared that it was and is my last wyll in theis wordes 'Haec est ultima voluntas mea. And for more strength of the same writting myn own name wt owne hande as appiereth herein, and to the same sett my seall. And I say theis wordes, Sum compos mentis et sanae memoriae.'

The will was proved at York, 17 July 1498.

We cannot know whether he designed his own memorial, but even if he did not, his wife and his sons knew his wishes well enough to include in it every facet of his long and distinguished career.

The glass from the original window in St John's, Ousebridge end was removed bodily when that church was closed down in 1947, and placed in the Minster. It was taken from a 'Perpendicular' window of four lights, and put into an 'Early English Lancet', so, in effect, the glass had to be reframed within the Lancet upon a general field of plain glass.

During the removal, the figures of Sir Richard's two wives were mislaid and were thought to be part of a small Trinity, but their original figures are confirmed by Drake's researches, and he described the Mauleverer arms on the skirt of the first wife. The figures are still incomplete.

The eight tracery lights each contain an angel holding an escutcheon or heraldic shield. The first is the arms of the Merchants of the Staple, commemorating Richard's mercantile career. The second, the arms of Foster – a friend, or even a relative. The third, the arms of Stapleton impaling Gascoigne, the connection of which is uncertain. The fourth is the Yorke family's coat of arms. The fifth, Yorke impaling Mauleverer – his first wife. The sixth, Yorke impaling d'Arcy – Richard's eldest son, Richard, married a d'Arcy. The seventh, Yorke impaling an unknown family, who may have had a connection with a younger son. The eighth is the arms of the City of York, in which and for which Richard worked for so many years.

The four religious panels represent the Trinity – Richard wished his tomb to be built as near the image of the Trinity as possible: St George (and St Nicholas) – a Guild of St George was important in Kingston on Hull: a procession of Corpus Christi – of which Guild Richard was a member: and St Christopher – the patron saint of travellers, of which Richard was certainly one.

The six sons and four daughters kneeling with their father all wear simple robes of blue, which lend a richness to the whole, and although it is a tragedy that the figures of the wives are damaged, the memorial still bears witness to a notable man.

5. Memorial window to Sir Richard York as it was in St John's, Ousebridge end.

Chapter III

JOHN YORKE 1460? – ?
OF
GOUTHWAITE
(Styled thus in Dugdale's Visitation)

Of the five remaining sons who mourned Sir Richard only a few details are known.

The eldest, Richard, who inherited the lion's share of his father's lands, married a daughter of Lord Darcy and Meynill. (The Darcys, an old Norman family, de Arci, were fellow members of the Corpus Christi Guild, and lived in style. Lord Darcy kept a household of eighty people.) This Richard's death is recorded in 1508, when he was described as Sir Richard, and he was buried in the church of St John, in Ousegate.

Master Christopher, doctor of law, in his crimson cloak, is only once mentioned as his step mother's executor in 1509, and nothing further is known of William. It is Thomas who seems to have followed in his father's footsteps. Described as 'gentleman and merchant', he was admitted to the freedom of the City of York in 1497, and served in the office of Chamberlain in 1502. However, he too had died by 1515, only seventeen years after his father.

John, the youngest son, must have been born between 1460 and 1470. We know that 'his behaviour and habits' were a cause of anxiety to his elderly father, so he may have been a wild headstrong lad, who felt unable to fit into the family ways.

He was married in his late teens to Katherine Patterdale, (whose family may have come from Cumbria), who bore him three sons and a daughter. They had inherited a house in York but there is no record of his life there.

When John's two brothers died at a relatively early age, he may have inherited some more money, for it appears that he later rented or bought an old monastic farm called Goulthwaite, or Gouthwaite, in Nidderdale. A family of this name had farmed the land since the twelfth century, and Thomas Gouldthwaite had been keeper of the sheep at Dacre for the Abbot of Fountain's Abbey in 1456.[1] At that time Nidderdale was dominated by three great lordships, the Honour of Knaresborough, the Liberty of Ripon, and the sprawling empire of Fountain's Abbey.

Gouthwaite lay in the wild moorland township of Stonebeck Down, at the head of Nidderdale, and had been a 'waste' in the possession of a Norman knight, Roger de Mowbray, from 1150. Over the next century the Mowbray family had granted the land and mineral rights to the monks of Byland Abbey, reserving only the rights of chase and access. They made other grants of land and minerals (including Bewerley and Dacre), to Fountains Abbey in return for a donation towards Roger's journey to the Crusades.[2]

The monks farmed the area with lay brothers settled in scattered granges, grazed their huge flocks and worked the lead and iron mines. As time went on the Cistercian system of granges was superseded by one of leases and tenancies. By the time of the dissolution, many of the gentry who bought monastic land had, in fact, been stewards of that same land for years before.

The old farmhouse stood in a peaceful and secluded part of the dale, beside Burn Gill. The sides of the valley were deeply cut by narrow wooded gills, and in some places they rose in precipitous slopes of bare rock. A small beck ran down on the north side of the dwelling into the lake below.

The house was an oblong two storey building of grey stone roofed in slate, facing south, with an entrance near the south east corner. The main hall, with huge oak beams, had a chimney four yards wide. In former days, master and men had lived, dined and slept in the hall, with their weary dogs stretched out beside them on the rush strewn floor. John Yorke may have altered and enlarged the house somewhat, but it would have been his son who added the six foot wide oak staircase, which led to the raftered upper chamber.

This chamber was the best room in the house, being lighted by several narrow windows on two sides, and later, divided from the staircase by a panelling of carved oak. The outbuildings of the farm lay to the west of the house, and a corn mill was powered by the water from the beck.[3]

Perhaps John and Katherine found that this remote spot provided the tranquillity they wanted after life in a crowded medieval city. The hardy kindly dalesmen became their neighbours and friends, and their children grew up in peaceful surroundings.

John, their eldest son, died young. Christopher married Joan Milward from Shropshire, and later went to live in that county, near Pontesbury. The third son, the second John, became his father's heir. Their daughter married Bernard Frobisher, and her son Martin spent much of his youth in his uncle John's household.

No more is known of John or Katherine, not even the date of their deaths, but although John led his life entirely out of the public eye, he passed on to his third son all the seeds of enterprise and ambition, together with the business acumen that his own father had possessed.

Chapter IV

SIR JOHN YORKE 1490? – 1568
OF
LONDON

THIS PORTRAIT OF A MERCHANT HOLDING A ROSE, the first of the Yorke collection, is clearly dated 1518, and is believed to be of John and Katherine's third son John, later known as Sir John Yorke of London. As it appears to be of a man between twenty and thirty, he must have been born around 1490, at about the same time as Henry VII's second son, the future Henry VIII.

John grew up therefore when Henry VII's shrewd political judgement was bringing peace and stability, especially in his dealings with Scotland, France and Spain. The excellence of his foreign intelligence was admired by his enemies as well as his friends. At home, the King was the embodiment of direct government and was probably the best business man ever to sit on the English throne.

Due to the discovery of the New World by the efforts of the Portuguese and Spaniards, new wealth was flowing into Europe, gold, silver, spices, tobacco, potatoes and sugar. It was an age of opportunity for merchants, traders and bankers.

John Yorke was certainly familiar with his grandfather's trading interests and connections. It is most likely that he was apprenticed to his uncle Thomas in the family firm, for we know that John, too, became a merchant who spent much time in Calais and Antwerp. It was in the latter town that he sat for his portrait, held to have been painted by Hendrik van Wueluwe, (otherwise known as the Master of Frankfurt).[1] The hard clever face and shrewd calculating eyes of the sitter indicate characteristics which are confirmed by the details of John's life and career. The merchant's hat and fur trimmed gown show him to be a man of standing. His uncle had died in 1515 so John had been well established in the family business, as apprentice, factor and heir.

He married Anne, daughter of Robert Smyth of London, and young widow of one Paget, by whom he had a large family of eleven sons and five daughters. They made their home in London.

Tudor London was small, not extending far beyond the walls, and a man could easily be familiar with every part. It only differed marginally from medieval York, in its larger population, and greater houses, and in certain improvements such as conduits of piped fresh water. The colourful Court of Henry VIII drew many foreign visitors of course, and

6. The Man with a rose

provided pomp and ceremony in the City. The Parliament at Westminster was a meeting place for the knights and burgesses from all the shires, so a well travelled merchant, such as John, felt more at the hub of affairs in London than in York.

As in York, the four great city gates, Aldgate to the east, Aldersgate to the north, Ludgate to the west and Bridgegate by London Bridge to the south were the main entrances, but several other postern gates such as

Moorgate, Cripplegate and Newgate had been added 'for the ease of citizens and passengers'. Outside the walls ran roads and lanes which soon led to gardens, fields and farms, interspersed by suburbs and villages like Chelsea and Knight's Bridge.

Inside the City the street names indicated the goods offered for sale, Milk Street, Wood Street, Oat Lane, Honey Lane, Cornhill, The Poultry, and so on. In the Stocks Market, (where the present Mansion House stands), were stalls for twenty five fishmongers and eighteen butchers, some of which had living quarters above. Poulterers and rabbit sellers sold in The Poultry which was over against the Stocks Market, and the fowls were scalded and dressed in Scalding Wike street. South of these noisy and noisome streets lay St Mary Wool Church where the great bales of wool used to be weighed on a huge beam in the Churchyard. South of that lay the parish church of St Stephen's Walbrook.

By 1546 John Yorke was able to buy a fine house in Wallbrook, (the main street in Wallbrook ward), adjacent and to the south of St Stephen's. It had formerly belonged to Sir Thomas Pope, Treasurer of the Court of Augmentations, (said to have made himself one of the richest commoners in England), and stood 'amongst divers fair houses' with gardens. The Wall Brook ran from north to south through the heart of the City, into the Fleet and on into the Thames. As the population had increased so all the fresh waters of the city had become fouled, and despite constant edicts to the parishioners 'to scowre their watercourse' it grew worse. At last the landowners beside the Brook were made to vault and pave it over with brick, then houses and roads were built over it.

John's house had a large upper chamber and was half timbered, the first floor being built of brick and the roof tiled. By law no house could be made all of wood because of the risk of fire. In spite of this law terrible fires did occur, as when Sir John William's house caught fire one Christmas Eve at seven o'clock. (He was the master of the King's jewels.) It 'burned so sore... that it was seen all the city over and was hardly quenched, whereby many of the King's jewels were burnt and more were embezzled (so it was said)'.[2]

Some of the great nobles and prelates kept immense households even in London. The Bishop of Ely had one hundred indoor servants, paying each 53s 4d per annum, and giving him four yards of broad cloth for his winter gown, and three and a half yards for his summer coat. He provided bread, ale, and warm meat for two hundred poor people every day at his gate. Thomas Cromwell, for all his own rapacity, also fed two hundred poor people at his gate each day.

As John went about his business in the City, carts, drays and coaches crowded the narrow streets, and although by law the fore horse of every carriage had to be led by hand, 'some coachmen lasheth their horses and looketh not behind them, and the drayman sitteth and sleepeth on his dray and letteth his horse lead him home'. On all sides John heard the raucous cries of the street vendors, 'Cheap cloth for sale!' 'Hot ribs of beef well roasted!' 'Pies well baked!' The frequenters of the many taverns hung about the open doorways, tankards in hand, and apprentices ducked in and out of the crowd on errands for their masters. In certain places John might pass a poor wretch in a pillory, spattered with refuse, or an iron cage in which stocks were set. Bawds, scolds, 'nightwalkers' or thievish millers and bakers were locked in these to make them mend their ways. The constables or watchmen, (of whom Wallbrook ward had nine), kept a lookout for rogues and felons, but every man carried a small dagger, if not a sword, against sudden attack. Life was hard and rough, and it was a case of each man for himself.

The sports and games were rough too, and bloodthirsty. Cockfighting, where the losing bird was torn into a gory mess by the sharp steel tips on the spurs of the winner, was immensely popular with all ages and classes. So was the baiting of bears and bulls by savage mastiffs. The bear gardens were scaffolded round with benches for on lookers. An execution was considered first class entertainment.

Leaping, cudgel playing, archery, wrestling and ball games exercised the youths, and the maidens danced with garlands across the streets to the music of the timbrel. John Stow, the tailor antiquary, who described the contemporary scene so vividly in his 'Survey of London', adds darkly, 'these open pastimes of my youth being now suppressed, worser practises within doors are to be feared'. Stow advised his friends that if 'they were disposed to be merrie they went not to sup and dine in Tavernes but to the cooks (market) where they called for meat which they liked and found it ready dressed at a reasonable rate'. In taverns they would turn to dicing, gaming or cards and risk losing money.

On feast days and holy days masques, plays and pageants were performed in the streets. Church processions with banners led the people to celebrate the great festivals, and highlights of the year, like the Midsummer Watch, were marked with bonfires. The houses were garlanded with green boughs and white lilies, and bands of fifes and drums played, with trumpeters on horseback.

In everyday life, however, even that of a successful merchant, cold, hardship, pain, disease and death were never far away. The Merrie England we read of had a harsh background.

By 1518 the learned, handsome vigorous Henry VIII had married Catherine of Aragon, (widow of his brother Arthur, and daughter of the King of Spain,) had been on the throne for nine years, and had already set his stamp on his kingdom. With his close advisers Thomas Wolsey, then Thomas Cromwell and Thomas Cranmer, he developed the principles of centralised and arbitary government. He also taught the local unpaid Justices of the Peace to govern and administer all small local matters. He was popular and his good humour appealed to the crowd, although his sudden rages were terrible to behold. His successes in routing the French, and the English victory over the Scots at Flodden Field in 1513 had increased his popularity.

By 1529 however, Wolsey was disgraced and the King enamoured of Anne Boleyn. He longed for a son, and feared that Catherine, who had lost three in infancy, would bear no more. The winter of 1531 saw the tensest crisis of Henry's reign. Queen Catherine was banished from court with her daughter Mary, and within two years, Henry had divorced her and married Anne. In March 1534, every person of legal age was made to swear allegiance to the Acts of Supremacy and Succession, declaring the King Supreme Head of the Church in England, instead of the Pope, and vesting the succession in Anne's daughter Elizabeth, instead of in Catherine's legitimate daughter Mary.

Bishop Fisher and the Lord Chancellor, Sir Thomas More, rightly and heroically refused and after a long imprisonment, were both executed, under the Treason Act. Henry was excommunicated by the Pope shortly afterwards, in 1535.

It was in this year that the first mention of John Yorke is made. He had arrived in Calais from Antwerp and reported on a sermon he had heard in Antwerp against the English King. This report was conveyed to Thomas Cromwell, by the Lord Deputy of Calais, Lord Lisle. – 'Three merchants of London have arrived who told me strange news concerning the "mallyshos" intent of the bishop of Rome (the Pope), and the behaviour of a lewd friar openly in the pulpit at Antwerp. The men's names are Richard Lencolne, John York and John Dene.' All three received a reward for their report.[3]

Thomas Cromwell, a former wool merchant and money lender, had risen to be Lord Great Chamberlain. His eyes and ears were everywhere. He had built up his superb intelligence service by having a paid 'friend' or spy in every great man's household. (Most great men at that time, it seems, followed the same practice.) We know from the letters of John Husee, steward to Lord Lisle, that the closest possible ear was kept on every whisper of political change. He tells also of the staggering traffic in 'gifts', or sweeteners, as we should call them. Copious and regular supplies of game, wine, sturgeon, hawks, hunting dogs and even home made marmalade were sent to influential officials to incline their favours towards the senders. No doubt visiting merchants like John were sometimes asked to convey these gifts, which in turn brought them into contact with the men of power.[4]

At the command of the King, who sought relief from his acute financial straits, Cromwell organised the dissolution of the wealthy monasteries with cold blooded efficiency. He started with the smaller houses, then suppressed the friaries, nunneries and priories. In the North this aroused fierce resistance, for the poor and ailing had always depended on the monks' care.

Local needs too were pressing. A special plea was made to retain the extra chapels with priests around Nidderdale, for 'the paroch is of grete circuyte withe one grete ryver called Nydde runninge and passing through the same, so that many times the curate being forth on visitation in some part of the said paroch cannot come home to the said church by the space of two days, by reason of the lett of the said ryver at suche times when there be grete flude.'[5] No more notice was taken of this plea than of many others made by people on behalf of the monks and clergy. Widespread resentment grew and wild rumours increased it.

An uprising began in Lincolnshire and spread up into Yorkshire. Led by Robert Aske, this Pilgrimage of Grace mustered thirty thousand 'tall men and well horsed' who gathered near Doncaster demanding a reunion with Rome, the restoration of Mary's rights and the downfall of Cromwell. Nicholas Tempest of Broughton and Stephen Hamerton of Hellifield Peel, (both of whom were well known to John Yorke), together with Lord Darcy (a relative by marriage), took active parts, and 'the commons of Nidderdale' marched with them. No doubt John's sympathies were with them, but perhaps his business affairs or his political astuteness kept him away in the south. He was, after all, in favour with the all powerful Cromwell at this time. The rebels were offered a free pardon for all who disarmed, together with other promises by the Duke of Norfolk, so they dispersed. A few months later, a fresh uprising gave Henry the opportunity to break the Duke's promises. The rebel leaders were captured. Aske was hanged alive in iron chains from the top of the keep of York castle, to twist and turn in the wind and to die an agonisingly slow death by cold and starvation. The Abbots of Fountains, Whalley and Salley Abbeys, together with two hundred others including Lord Darcy, were executed.[6]

These savage punishments engendered such fear that all the larger abbeys, along with Fountains and Byland, were emptied and stripped of all their possessions by 1540, with no more resistance.

This same year Queen Catherine died, and four months later Anne Boleyn was sent to the block. Only ten days after that, Henry married

Jane Seymour, but she died in childbed giving birth to her son, Edward, after only eighteen months. By 1540, Henry had married Anne of Cleves for political purposes, and divorced her, executed Cromwell for treason and heresy, and married Catherine Howard. She also was to die upon the block before the next two years were out. Henry's health and temper were in a poor state. He had become suspicious and ruthless, and his ulcerated leg made him even more capricious than before.

The death of James V of Scotland had left his daughter Mary, of only one week old, as Queen of the Scots, a tiny pawn in the religious and political struggles. Her French Catholic mother naturally opposed Henry's wishes.

By 1544, Henry found himself without an ally, faced with possible invasion by France and Scotland. He desperately needed money and demanded loans and subsidies from all classes of people.

John Yorke had rendered considerable service to the Crown by raising loans through exploiting his position as a merchant trading abroad. He also enjoyed the patronage of the Earl of Warwick, with whom he shared a common interest in former abbey lands in Yorkshire. It was at this juncture that he was appointed to the responsible post of assay master to the Mint.[7]

He continued in this post for the next three years, through the death of Henry VIII and the accession of the boy king Edward VI. He was promoted to being master of the mint at Southwark in 1547, where he was given an official residence. 'This was a large and most sumptuous house. . . called Suffolk House. . . then afterwards called Southwarke Place, where a mint of coynage was there kept for the King.'[8] In this position he became even closer to the powerful men in the City, and to the Protector and guardian of the young King, his uncle, the Duke of Somerset.

Southwark, across London Bridge, on the south bank of the Thames, was one of the two 'wards without' or outside the city walls. (There were twenty six wards within.) It contained several notable houses belonging to the Bishops of Winchester, and of Rochester, the Abbot of Hyde, the Prior of Lewis and the Bridge House as well as Southwark Place. There were four parish churches, St Thomas' Hospital, a leper hospital and five gaols, one of which was called The Clinke on the Bank.

Being outside the walls, Southwark provided 'many fair inns for the receipt of travellers', one of which, The Tabard, was the most famous and was mentioned in 'The Canterbury Tales'. The bear gardens drew many visitors, and next them lay the Stewes, or Bordello 'for the repair of incontinent men to the like women'. These brothels were controlled by strict rules, and although named The Boar's Head, The Cross Keys, The

Swan, and so on, were not allowed to sell any ale or victuals. The administration of Southwark ward was carried out by its own Alderman, three deputies, a bailiff, sixteen constables and six scavengers. Yorke was appointed one of the two Sheriffs of London in 1549, the other being John Turke. This office carried considerable responsibility, as well as personal expense. The Sheriff had to make regular attendances at the two sheriffs courts held in the Guildhall, to hear cases under his jurisdiction. Each Sheriff had ten clerks, an under sheriff, stewards, butlers, porters etc., and sixteen sergeants with yeomen. The various guilds gave money each year towards the city liveries, and the guild to which a Sheriff belonged, (in John's case the Merchant Taylors), contributed towards the cost of the broadcloth and satin to clothe his officers. He himself needed a scarlet hooded and furred gown, and 'a round flat cap of scarlet or velvet with a brooch and a feather' for special processions and occasions. No doubt he also had to distribute a good deal of largesse during his year of office.

However he had enriched himself as a mint official by providing bullion at prices higher than those generally in force, and also in the course of his foreign trading. The demand for wool was limitless and the prices high at that time. He acquired some land called Gallyons Farm in Woolwich, Barking and East Ham in the counties of Kent and Essex.[10]

In 1547 John had purchased the former Byland estates of Stonebeck Up and Down, (including Gouthwaite) which became known subsequently as the manor of Ramsgill in Nidderdale, (or the manor of Netherdale) paying about £2,200 for it over the next ten years. This included all the valuable rights of minerals, chase and warren.

He had also purchased the manor of Kilnsey, which had belonged to Fountains. Two years later he added the manor of Appletreewick.[11-12] The latter comprised nearly 4,000 acres and included a village with outlying farms, the grant of the privilege of holding 'a fair each year for four days duration', and the rights of mining for lead and iron, free warren and chase. It cost Yorke £2,000.[13]

The Protector Somerset by now had a rival for power in the Earl of Warwick, an able soldier but self seeking. Discontent in the countryside was growing over the land enclosures and rising rents, and Warwick was given charge of the army in order to suppress it. Somerset feared that Warwick's confederates were plotting for power over the King and asked the city for troops for Edward's protection. Warwick came to the city and on October 6th went to stay in John Yorke's house in Wallbrook. It was here that Warwick persuaded the city leaders and the 'lords in London' to take sides with him, and over dinner together on October 8th, they drew up a summons for aid and troops from the common council. This was granted. Somerset was quietly deposed and sent to the Tower.

As a reward for his help and hospitality, Edward VI visited John Yorke at his official residence, and there dined with him on October 17th.[14] The pale eleven year old King, wearing a colourful doublet with slashed sleeves, surmounted by the fashionable starched ruff of the age, sat amongst his elegantly dressed, bearded and be-ruffed statesmen, nobles and advisers. Dish after dish of delicacies were brought in by the richly liveried serving men – roast swan, baked guinea fowl, quails, snipe and larks' tongues, syllabubs and tansy pies, marchpane and comfits, together with plenty of Gascon claret and sack to wash it down. John Yorke's acute mind and sound judgement had helped him to avoid the political pitfalls of the last years of Edward's father. Now they had served him well again in a delicate situation, and he must have felt both relieved and honoured to have the King grace his table. His wife Anne, too, had followed every twist of fortune, and had had had many anxious days of preparation. On this evening she wore her most ornate gown and her finest jewels.

At the end of dinner, the King called John to his side and thanked him. He bade him kneel. Then to John's pleasure he drew out his sword, tapped John on the shoulder and said, 'I dub thee knight. Arise Sir John.'

The following February, Somerset was brought to Sir John's private house in Wallbrook from the Tower and there released on his recognisance.[15] Two days later the Privy Council met there also and the now powerless Somerset was allowed to join them.

At this time Sir John was employed on secret missions abroad, one of which was smuggling arms from the Netherlands. To prevent information about this reaching the Netherlands government, the Privy Council forbade the customs officers at Calais to search 'such provisiones of the Kinge's as Sir John Yorke shall from tyme to tyme bringe thider'.[16] At this time Yorke also held office in the Admiralty, where he was ordered to sell a consignment of prize sugar.[17]

The famous Fugger family of merchants and moneylenders, who owned silver mines in Austria, had lent the King 127,000 florins the previous June. Sir John was commissioned to repay that sum in February 1551, and in that summer he repaid a further debt to them of £23,279.[18] In return for these services he received a licence to export 800 fodders of lead, (about 840 tons). Some of this certainly came from his mines in Nidderdale.

He was also made under treasurer of the Mint in the Tower, for which he received 200 marks a year. His successor there, with whom he worked closely, was Sir Nicholas Throckmorton with his sharp foxy face and cunning eyes. (He was an able and impetuous man, a schemer with an eye to the main chance, but a great favourite with the boy King.) Later Sir John was promoted to Master of the Mint.[19]

In 1551 he and Sir Nicholas handled the beginning of the revaluation of the coinage, and many of the coins then issued were stamped with Y, one of Yorke's mint marks.[20] New coins were made for 5s, 2s 6d, 12d, and 6d. A 1d bore a double rose, a ½d a single rose, and a farthing a portcullis. In fine gold a sovereign was 30s in value, an angel 10s, and an angelet 5s. In crown gold, a sovereign was 20s and a half sovereign 10s.

It was about this time that the manor of Austwick, in Yorkshire, and eleven other neighbouring manors were conveyed to him for £1,100 by the Duke of Suffolk, the father of Lady Jane Grey. It seems that the Yorkes may have lived at Austwick for a period, possibly at Lawkland

7. Edward VI coin showing the 'Y' mint mark

Hall.[21] It was not uncommon in those days for a landowner, on hearing of the downfall of an erstwhile friend, to try to get the grant of his confiscated lands even before his trial. This cannot have been so in this case however, as Suffolk was not imprisoned until 1553.

Sir John kept on close terms with the leaders of the two rival factions in the Privy Council — Warwick and Somerset. He had aided Warwick against Somerset, but a year or so later he lent Somerset the enormous sum of £2,500.

The reign of Henry VIII, (1509–47), is widely remembered for its executions, and the hideous brutality of the rack, the stake, the scaffold and the block continued throughout the century. No prominent man or woman was safe from the accusation of heresy or treason. Queens, bishops, abbots and ministers were beheaded. Many a man was despatched to ache and shiver in a freezing and insanitary cell in the Tower, where the foul river water and the fog combined to bring on consumption and rheumatics, while his wife and family awaited in daily dread.

The Duke of Somerset was such a one, and after his earlier release and return to the Tower, he was executed on Tower Hill in 1552. After his death Sir John had produced the Duke's note of hand for the £2,500 for the Council's inspection, but it had somehow been mislaid. Warwick however,(recently promoted to Duke of Northumberland), himself intervened to procure an order for payment to Yorke.[22]

Just before Edward VI's death there was evidently trouble at the Mint, for a pardon was received from the King for John Yorke and Nicholas Throckmorton, and for two of the controllers, three of the assay masters, a haberdasher and an auditor for 'all transgressions concerning the coinage'.[23] As well as this pardon, Yorke also received another from the King for killing one of the royal deer in Bardon Chase. (This is the first record we have of the family love of hunting.)

Sir John's mercantile affairs were prospering for in May 1553 he became one of the 'merchant adventurers to Moscovy', the company sailing through the Arctic waters to trade with Russia.[24] This had the backing of the government and was incorporated under a charter of Edward VI. Its Governor was Sebastian Cabot, son of the famous explorer, John.

The type of ship used by this company was far larger than that in which old Sir Richard Yorke had sailed. The tallest of the three masts was over a hundred feet high and their great wooden sides looked like the walls of a house. Two wooden 'castles' stood on the deck, one at the bow, one at the stern, and through openings could be seen the glistening muzzles of the cannon. A richly carved and painted balcony opened out from the captain's cabin, but the sailors off watch lay down to sleep where they could in the cramped, dark, airless lower decks. Many of the men had been to sea since they were lads and knew the channel ports well, but only those with a real taste for adventure signed on for the voyages to Russia. The journey of 2,250 miles to Archangel could take from eight to ten weeks, in every sort of weather, often bitter cold, but the furs they exchanged for the bales of cloth were valuable and the merchants paid well. This Russian trade helped the English merchants to replace that lost by the monopoly of the Hanseatic towns.

Sir John's father by now had died so, when he could, he spent more time at Gouthwaite. He added on to the house and reorganised it considerably, probably adding the great oak staircase, and making more use of the upper chambers. His London household had increased in size considerably, and room for more indoor servants at Gouthwaite was needed too.

As well as the fertile farmland in the valley of the river Nidd, there were extensive areas of moorland for sheep grazing, and woodland. Lead, coal, slate, ironstone and limestone were all available to be mined or quarried. There were considerable difficulties over fixing and keeping the boundaries in the wilder areas which can be seen by the numerous boundary disputes in the legal documents of the Yorke family. In one, Peacock, Beckwith and Hall sued Yorke and Topham, but in 1553, the Duchy Council ordered that Yorke could occupy a piece of ground called Monugill (Mungo gill) which, it has been decided lies in Appletreewick not in Knaresborough Forest.[25]

In other respects 1553 was not a good year for Yorke. He seems to have overreached himself, for, following the alleged transgressions against the coinage, he had apparently seized thirty six loads of lead ore which properly belonged to Uvedale, a mining tenant of the late Abbey of Byland. He had also refused the same man the right to cut timber to use in his mine. The Recorder of London ordered Yorke to return the lead and supply the timber but the issue remained unresolved.

It was one of the innumerable and lengthy wrangles over the mining rights which carried on over the next four hundred years.[26]

The Duke of Northumberland's three years of powerful government proved to be altogether too close to Sir Thomas More's definition – 'a conspiracy of rich men procuring their own commodities under the name and title of a common wealth'. The rich men of the day certainly lined their pockets a good deal, but, if Yorke was one of them, at least he had the enterprise to venture into the new trade with Russia, and to expand the markets. He also assisted his nephew Martin Frobisher on his voyages of exploration, particularly the one to Guinea.

Northumberland felt that the succession of the Catholic, half Spanish Princess Mary would be a disaster, so, seeing that the young King was an invalid, he married his own son, Guildford Dudley, to Lady Jane Grey. As Henry VII's great grandchild, this sixteen year old girl was in the direct line of succession after Henry VIII's children.

Yorke supported Northumberland in his ambition. On July 6th when Edward V1 expired, Yorke was present at the proclamation of Lady Jane as Queen. He threw his jewelled cap up in the air and shouted 'God save the Queen!' with the loudest, but this time he had made the wrong choice. After many years of keeping his balance on the political see-saw, Yorke went down with his patron, with a resounding crash.

The common people saw through Northumberland's intrigue, and supported Mary as the rightful heir. Their support swayed the Privy Councillors and the City. Northumberland was abandoned, put under arrest and sent to the Tower.

Two days later, Yorke was also put under arrest in his own house by the Lord Mayor.[27] On July 27th a warrant was issued for his committal to the Tower. 'The Duke of Suffolk, Maister Cheke, the Kinge's schoolmaster, Maister Coke and Sir John Yorke to the Tower'. An inventory of his goods was ordered and they were seized for the Queen's use.

That day was a terrible one for John and Anne. They and their children fully realised the fearful possibilities which could lie ahead. Guards surrounded the house. Carpets, furnishings, gold and silver plate had all been seized. John walked along the dreaded route to the Tower and entered his cell. Lady Jane and her husband had also been imprisoned for some time.

Mary entered London with Princess Elizabeth at her side, and was proclaimed Queen. In vain Northumberland pleaded and begged, but nothing could save him. After an agonising wait of three weeks, he, John's former friend and protector, was led to the scaffold on Tower Hill. As his crime was treason his sentence was, 'You shall be drawn upon a hurdle through the open streets to the place of execution, there to be hanged and cut down alive and your body shall be opened and disembowelled. . . your head stricken off from your body and your body divided into four quarters to be disposed of at the Queen's pleasure. And God have mercy on your soul.' And so it was carried out.

John was incarcerated in the Bell Tower and closely confined at first. The conditions of everyday life in those days were spartan by present standards, and John's life had entailed much travel and hardship. He was then in his late fifties but his suffering was probably as much mental as physical. The gnawing uncertainty, the dread of the Queen's displeasure, the daily news of the executions of his friends and colleagues, and the distress of his wife wore him down in his dank cell. One day he heard that sixty cloths of his which were being exported had been stopped at Dover.[28] Fear of financial ruin for his family grew, and he dreaded to hear of the loss of his Yorkshire estates, and fretted for news. To add to his worries, his tenants in Whitby took the opportunity of his being in prison to bring an action against him in court. The tenants claimed that their rents had been increased by 122% on average, and also fines had been exacted upon the change of lordship. As their previous lord had been Northumberland, who was not noted for clemency or fair dealing, this action does not speak well for Yorke, and when it was heard on October 24th, the court gave judgement against him. Many of the landowners in the West Riding had indeed, in response to high inflation, raised their rents by as much as 400%, so he was not alone.

However, it seems that Sir John had not wholly lost the art of keeping his head above political waters. At all events, by 14th September he was allowed 'the liberty of the leades'. The joy of breathing fresh air and feeling the sun on his face again as he walked the leaded parapets, raised his spirits, and his natural optimism returned. The efforts of his City friends outside who had supported Anne, and of his sons, combined to gain his release. A pardon was granted on October 18th. 'Pardon to John Yorke of London, knight, alias John Yorke of Marks in Essex, knight, alias John Yorke, knight, late sheriff of London, alias John Yorke, knight, late Treasurer of the Mint in Southwark for all offences committed before 1 October I Mary'.[29]

What a homecoming he must have had and what a narrow escape it had been. He was still an Alderman of the City, and still an influential figure. At that period the tightrope of the monarch's pleasure or displeasure had to be walked by all, and disgrace did not cling for long. Nevertheless he made sure he conformed closely to Queen Mary's new order. He attended his parish church, St Stephen's, in November to hear the sermon of one John Feckenham, the Queen's private chaplain and confessor. The Catholic Mass had been brought back and those Tudor magnates who feared to lose their possessions and even their lives, went obediently to the rites they had forsworn seventeen years before. In fact this was not hard for the Yorkes, for, along with many northerners, they had secretly remained faithful to Catholicism.

One record that tells us that John and Anne were safely back in favour with the Queen again is the account of a christening. Robert, the infant son of Sir Gilbert Dethick, had Queen Mary as his sponsor. 'My Lady Sakefield was deputy for the Queen, and after wafers and epocrasse in great plenty, and much pepull there, my Ladye Yorke bare my Lady deputy's train, and so home to her place and had a bankett (banquet).'[30]

Over the next five years of Bloody Mary's reign, (unlike his friend Throckmorton, who was tried, acquitted and then sent to the Tower for a year in 1554), Sir John kept out of the public eye and occupied himself with his Muscovy ventures, his northern estates and mining enterprises.

His eldest son was his steward in Yorkshire, but his other numerous and adventurous sons were growing up fast, and marriages had to be arranged for his daughters. His wife, Anne, evidently had astonishing stamina for she bore sixteen children, lost several, endured the distaff side of all her husband's city and commercial activities, and yet survived him at the last.

In 1558 the unhappy childless Queen Mary died. Sir John must have joined with many men of cautious good judgement in welcoming Elizabeth as Queen, the undoubted daughter of bluff King Hal. Her auburn hair, high courage, natural dignity and fiery temper were at first a refreshing change from Mary's sallow face and bitter, disappointed mien. Elizabeth I inspired devotion in her people, but plots and conspiracies surrounded her on all sides from France, Spain and Scotland. Religious peace at home and safety from her foes were the needs of the realm.

John lived through ten years of this his fifth sovereign's rule, and although he was loath to renounce the Catholic faith again, he was covert in his religious behaviour, and made himself useful to the government.

In 1559 he was nominated, possibly by Sir Ambrose Cave, Chancellor of the Duchy of Lancaster, to stand for Parliament for Boroughbridge. He was duly elected but only served for one year.[31]

The following year Sir John was buying gunpowder and salt petre in Antwerp, and earning the unfavourable attention of Sir Thomas Gresham, the Queen's best financier, who was trying to monopolise the English trade in these commodities.

A project for re-coinage was then under consideration. Sir John wrote to the Secretary of State, Robert Cecil, recommending that foreign refiners should be employed, as having greater skill. He thought they could save the Queen £20,000 at least. He also requested Cecil's interest in his favour.[32] Cecil presumably felt that with Gresham's services at his command, he could ignore Yorke. (Throckmorton had been restored to favour as the Queen's ambassador in France, and was trying to regain Calais for England.)

In 1560, Yorke sold his farm and land in Woolwich. His eldest son, Peter, married Elizabeth, daughter of Sir William Ingilby of Ripley Castle, a close neighbour down the dale. This forged an alliance between the two major land-owning families in the area, and the young couple went to live at Parcevall Hall in Appletreewick, from where Peter could run his father's estates.[33]

Concerning the remaining seven years of Sir John's life, little information is known, but he certainly would have continued to oversee his business, and keep abreast of all the latest proposals for the Queen's marriage, the marriages of Mary, Queen of Scots, and the ensuing murders.

As a freeman of the Merchant Taylors, he contributed £6.13.4d towards the building of the Royal Exchange in 1566.[34]

Over the last few years of his life he may have spent more time at Gouthwaite, but, fond as he was of Nidderdale, I feel that the City was where his heart really lay. It was there in the end that he died, his faithful wife at his side, in Wallbrook in 1568.

His body would have lain for a week or more in the main great chamber of his house, encircled by many lighted candles, before the stately funeral procession, led by an elaborate four posted hearse, wound its way to St Stephen's, where he was buried. The entrance to the house, the staircase and the great chamber were all draped with black cloth garnished with escutcheons of arms. A man carrying a painted banner followed behind the chief mourners, his sad Anne, leaning heavily on the arm of her son Peter. The church was also draped in black cloth, and was filled with a large number of prominent people.

Many of these were entertained afterwards at the funeral feast, and quantities of bread, ale and money were distributed to the poor.

He had drawn up his will in 1562, and had made his wife the sole executrix.

His eldest son Peter inherited the former monastic estates bought by his father including the west side of upper Nidderdale, and the adjacent manor of Appletreewick, both of which contained valuable lead mines. His father's main houses in York and London were also bequeathed to Peter and 'his greate pounzed basone and ewer of silver duble gylded, and his greate crosse of goulde sette with diamonds, and his chaine of goulde and ring and signet to be delivered after the death of his wife or before if she thinks good'. Peter was bound in the sum of 500 marks to treat them as heirlooms.

To his son William, the whole manor of Pedderthorpe, co. York. To his son Edmund, the manor of Sledmere, and all his lands in Marton and Bishopshill.

To his sons Rowland and Edward, each a moiety of the manor of Rudston.

To his son Henry, all his lands and messuages in Heselthorpe, Sherburne and Leigh, co. York, and a mansion house in Soper Lane, London with all cellars, shops, etc. thereto belonging.

To his son Edmund, 'his best agget set in goulde and his second best ewer and bason'.

To his daughter Jane, 1,000 marks and 'his second crosse of dyamond', for preferment of her marriage.

To his son-in-law William Hylton, 'a button of gould with a pointed dyamond for a ring'.

To his daughter Hylton (Anne), 'an agget sett in gould with four dyamonds'.

All the residue of his goods he left to his wife. She made her will in 1575, and died shortly after. She left Peter her 'greate table dyamond'. She mentioned her daughters Hylton, Elizabeth and Fanshawe, her sons William, and Roland to whom she left £200 and her diamond 'with many cuttes'. She mentions William Paget and others, and directs William, her executor, to sell her house in Pancake Lane for the performance of her will.

CHAPTER V

PETER YORKE 1525? – 1589
OF
GOUTHWAITE

PETER WAS THE SECOND, BUT FIRST SURVIVING, son of John and Anne. He was just a few years older than his contemporary, Queen Elizabeth I, and came to his inheritance at about the same age as she did. While she trod a cautious path during her first quarter century, through the court and political intrigues of three reigns, he grew up in a large and secure family in York and London. Nevertheless his life too was shaped by the religious turmoil and royal upheavals.

His father was frequently away from home seeing to his business, so the responsibilities of the eldest son fell to Peter at an early age, with so many younger brothers and sisters By the time he was ten, his parents had a permanent home in London, and he was educated at one of the four great schools of the day, St Paul's at Westminster, or St Thomas of Acon's Hospital, St Peter's, or St Anthony's Hospital. All these schools had been founded early in the century for poor scholars, under Henry VII. Each year the masters and scholars held a 'disputation'.

'Under a bank boarded about under a tree one scholar stepped up and there hath answered till he were by some better scholar overcome and put down, and in the end the best opposers and answerers had rewards. . . a garland or a silver pen,' or some such.

There was a long standing rivalry between St Paul's and St Anthony's scholars. They provoked each other, calling out 'Pigs!' to the St Anthony's boys, or 'Pigeons!' to the boys from St Paul's, and 'fell to blows with their satchels full of books, many times in great heapes that they troubled the streets and passengers'.[1] [Peter's younger brothers probably went to the Merchant Taylor's free Grammar School after it opened in 1561.]

From school, Peter went on to university at Peterhouse, Cambridge, (which had been founded in the late thirteenth century). The college system provided academic homes for undergraduates. It had greatly improved the morals and discipline in the universities, compared to the lawless and licentious lives of the students in medieval times. After Cambridge Peter went on to the Middle Temple in 1557, the normal course to follow in his day. Here, as John Stow says, 'was a whole university as it were, but by private maintenance, for apprentices at law,

58

... where students, practisers, judges of the law of the realm and sons of gentlemen studied'.[2] As well as the study of the law this was a centre of culture from which sprang some of the best poets and dramatists of the age. This legal training undoubtedly proved invaluable to Peter in the many transactions, agreements, disputes and court cases in which he was involved during his years as landowner and estate administrator. He inherited the former monastic estates bought by his father, including the west side of upper Nidderdale and the adjacent manor of Appletreewick, both of which contained valuable lead mines. He saw the property he had inherited from his father as a commercial asset, and looked after it well.[3]

Peter seems to have taken after his grandfather in his preference for a country life for, as soon as he left the Middle Temple, he made no attempt to establish himself in his father's mercantile and financial affairs, but went back to Nidderdale and settled there to manage the estates and the mining enterprises for the rest of his life.

In Nidderdale at that time, the typical Dales farmer was a small holder with between fifteen to twenty acres and common rights, but only a few sheep and cattle. It was the gentry who were the great graziers, as the monks had been before them. The larger landowners (like the Ingilbys), kept flocks of over a thousand sheep on the rough moors and fells. These followed the ancient tracks to summer pasturage over in Craven around Malham. In winter the sheep were brought down to the lower pastures, and in snow, or if feed grew scarce, holly was a valuable addition. An extra payment for the use of the holly was often included in the tenancy agreement. Huge droves of Scottish cattle grazed on their way southwards to market too, contributing manure to the land.

Some smallholders and cottagers were customary, or copyhold, tenants, and these were tenants for life. After the sale of the monastic estates, the legal complications of inheritances, leases, rents and fines were endless.

There was often further confusion when manor boundaries were disputed, or when local measurements such as 'Forest acres' differed widely from statute measure. (One surveyor found a holding described as 20 Forest acres was actually 72 statute acres.) All these issues were normally settled by appeal to custom followed from time immemorial at the manor courts. The major courts were held half yearly before the lord, (or his steward), the reeve or bailiff, and three or four local men of standing. Every detail of land management and social justice was considered and rules were laid down by common agreement for every conceivable eventuality. Especial care was taken to regulate grazing in the cow pastures, and to prevent overstocking the common land. A specific number only, or stint, of sheep or cattle were permitted. There were bye laws and penalties against putting unringed swine, or diseased animals, or stallions, bulls or tups on common land. Fines were imposed for dogging stock unnecessarily, for driving off geese, or allowing animals to stray, failing to scour ditches or mend fences. (The large lordships such as the Honour and Forest of Knaresborough held a court every three weeks.)

Living at Gouthwaite, Peter waited until he was over thirty before he chose a wife. His choice was Elizabeth Ingilby, who lived a fourteen mile ride away down the dale at Ripley Castle. Her father, Sir William Ingilby, was one of the longest established and largest landowners in the area. He had known Peter since childhood and watched his progress as a neighbouring landlord. He evidently considered Peter a suitable match for his daughter, and, after the careful discussions necessary for the arrangement of the marriage settlement, they were married in 1560. The Ingilbys were a devoutly Catholic family, and although Peter had later to go through the motions of conforming to the Church of England to protect his estates, he too was Catholic at heart.

About the time of Peter and Elizabeth's marriage, the population was growing and more tenants were seeking holdings. Rents rose and so did the 'entry fines' paid by incoming tenants. The Yorkes tended to raise the fines but leave the ancient rents unchanged in the dale.[3a]

Farmers like these kept between twenty and thirty head of cattle, thirty to fifty sheep, a horse, two plough oxen, pigs, poultry and bees, and grew enough corn and rye for their own needs. Richard Waite, a yeoman, left in his will, one sheep to each of his twenty three grandchildren, so each could start a flock.[4]

The smaller tenants, like Christopher Wheelhouse, had perhaps three cows, three lambs, one horse, one heifer, two stirks, one calf, two swine, eight geese, one cock and two hens. They eked out their livelihood by weaving woollen, linen or hemp harden cloth, using the same loom but with different 'gears'. There were fewer weavers at the head of the dale than lower down, but several fulling mills were kept busy. In these mills the cloth was 'felted' by being beaten or trodden under water, and dues had to be paid to the landowner for use of the mill. Some small holders knitted coarse stockings, or were employed in spinning yarn and wool. Others mined the veins of lead and iron ore, which had been worked since Roman times around Grassington and Greenhow.[5]

These people needed oats and corn for their bread, but there had been no common arable fields in the monastic system. Some of the shared meadow land had therefore to be turned into arable fields, as the occupiers wished. The common moor lands had also to provide peat and turf for fuel, rushes and heather for thatch, bracken for cattle bedding, stone for building and limestone for burning to till the soil. On the huge moorland areas the farmers 'hoofed' or 'hefted' their cattle and sheep on to particular stretches of ground by 'dogging' them back for as long as they tended to stray. Leland, writing in the middle of the 16th century describes the moors as 'baren ground. . . forest ground ful of lynge, mores and mosses with stony hills'. He noted that the dalesmen cut heather and turf or peat for fuel.

William Grainge describes these farmers: 'The Nidderdale dalesman is tall and athletic with considerable length of limb, and plenty of bone and muscle. His countenance is fair, generally florid, the freshness of the colour being retained, even to old age; he has great strength and agility, and he is kind and sociable, shrewd and intelligent. He speaks his genuine thoughts freely, with little duplicity. Masters and men mingle on equal terms, all sitting and eating at one table. They are hospitable and welcoming, and have a great love of music, both vocal and instrumental. (This love was also noted by Gerald of Wales in the twelfth century.) They have considerable knowledge of cattle and sheep. . . and very rarely do you meet a farmer without his dog.'

In 1588, James Ryder also praised their drive, adaptability, resilience and industry.[6]

Their houses were strongly built of stone, but were mostly of one storey, in the Norse tradition, often thatched with reeds or ling. Animals were frequently kept at the 'low end' of the building, for convenience in tending, and for extra warmth. A wooden table, and some bench seats, stools and a coffer made up the only furniture standing on the stone flagged floor, the beds being palliasses filled with straw or heather. A log served as a pillow.

Much of the bread eaten in the upper part of the dale was made of oatmeal, beaten out by hand into thin flat circles, then baked. (These were called clapcakes, from the Danish, klappe brod.) They and the coarse rye bread were eaten with cheese and onions and washed down with broth or milk.

Their speech contained very many words of Danish origin, such as addle, flit, bield, fettle, throng, flay, gang, gate, lish, teem or shippon, as it still does. The shepherds counted their sheep however in a far earlier tongue, most probably used by the Celts, for its base is Welsh. Fishermen and knitters also counted like this, in scores, 'Yan, tan, eddero, peddero, pitts', and so on. When they reached twenty they 'scored' a mark and started again.[7]

The great Northern lords like Henry Clifford of Skipton Castle, the 1st Earl of Cumberland, wielded enormous power over their own estates, but, although they increasingly emphasised rents and profits, the ancient concept of the service and obligations of lordship remained.

In 1560 most of the county's five hundred and fifty seven gentlemen resided on their estates and were influential people in their own districts, often sitting as Justices of the Peace. I like to think that Peter Yorke followed the advice of his neighbour Henry Tempest, 'Oppress not thy tenants, but let them live comfortably of thy handes as thou desirest to live of their labour, that their soules may bless thee and that it may go well with thy seed after thee'.[8]

But there were plenty of tales heard in the Court of the Star Chamber of violence between ruthless lords and men who tried to defend their rights. Knowing how provincial juries could be intimidated by their former masters, serious charges were sent to this court set up by the King.

Peter's father-in-law had a reputation for fair dealing,[9] and so had the Yorkes. Over the next thirty to forty years both families gave many of their tenants, in return for a capital sum, long term security of rent and tenure with extensive leases of between 1,300 – 3,000 years. This enabled substantial yeoman families like the Baynes and Horners in Stonebeck Up to have a secure economic and social position. The value of their land had risen through inflation.[10]

The Ingilbys farmed over 500 acres themselves, and let the rest. Both families owned huge expanses of moorland on which the tenants had both common grazing rights, as well as ancient unwritten mining laws and traditions.

After the dissolution, each one of the monastic mines was assigned to a lord of the field, who was usually also the lord of the manor, and dues were paid to him in proportion. (In Bewerley however, these rights had become separated.) These ancient rights and laws of the moors were extremely powerful.[11]

The lord of the field appointed a Bergh or Barrmaster to be 'an indifferent (i.e. impartial) man between the lord and the miners', and also between the miners and the merchant. Individual miners had the liberty to sink shafts and explore for lead ore. Upon finding a vein, the miner was granted two meers. One meer equalled thirty yards in length and seven and a half yards on either side of the vein. This was the measure in Grassington, and the system was as follows:

No person was to work a mine until the vein had been booked, measured by the Barrmaster, and paid for, with one shilling.

The ore had to be smelted at the lord's mill, upon a fine of forfeiture. It was smelted in the order in which it was brought to the mill, not exceeding twenty tons, then the next amount was taken, in order.

The Barrmaster had to provide just and lawful weights. Using these, the lord took every fifth piece of lead 'as is justly and customarily paid'. For this royalty the miners 'ought to have wood from the lord's woods to. . . smelt their Oar withal'. The Barrmaster informed the miners where the wood could be cut, and a heavy fine was imposed for cutting wood unlawfully.

A series of laws governed every aspect of work, tools, absence, concealment, hindrance, water misuse, intrusion into another's workings, fraud, waste, fines, claims and arrests. All of these matters were dealt with at the two Barmoot Courts, one held about Easter time, and the other about Michaelmas. These were organised in a similar way to the manor courts. Meerstones carrying the initials of the miner often marked individual meers.

The ancient Tribute system was based on a 'Bargain' offered by a promoter to a group or partnership of miners for an agreed amount of eight cwts of ore, which the partnership would produce. The miners were paid a proportion of their 50% share monthly, and the rest at the year's end. This system benefited both parties, and engendered a spirit of enterprise.

In early medieval times, the ore was dressed near the mine. The 'bouse', when brought out of the mine, had to be cleaned of all worthless matter by being picked over, hammered and roughly graded. Boys and women did this work, then the results were 'washed' in great tubs. The richest deposit of ore was found at the bottom of the tub, and was given a final washing on a hair sieve. A strong water supply was essential for the dressing and washing, and production could be severely held up in the dales by frost and snow in the winter and by droughts in the summer.

The earliest smelting places were hearths made on the brows of hills facing into the direction of the prevailing winds. A low stone wall was built, about two feet high, with openings for draughts on the south side. Inside was a bowl shaped hollow with a base of puddled clay. Faggots, peat and crushed ore were placed in the hollow, and when burnt, the melted lead was run off into a clay hollow at one side. (Much later, some form of bellows was invented to increase the heat.) The molten lead was ladled from the hollow and poured into moulds called 'pigs'. The weight of a pig varied, but was approximately one sixteenth of a fodder, that is about 170lbs.

By the time Peter Yorke was lord of the field in Greenhow, the design of the hearth furnaces had much improved. Four sets of bellows were operated from an overhead horizontal shaft, powered by two waterwheels. The whole structure was protected by a pitched roof, with some form of chimney to carry away the fumes. Peat, coal, charcoal and cinders were used, but chiefly peat. The smelters worked in pairs, one stirring and drawing up the 'bouse', and the other stoking the fire and keeping the muzzles of the bellows clear. This type of hearth was beginning to be used but the smaller hearths were still better for the small partnerships of miners, who used mixed fuels and had to work close to the mine.

In 1564 The Company of Mines Royal had been founded by Queen Elizabeth I with Thomas Thurland and Daniel Hechstetter. This company employed German miners from the Augsberg area who brought with them equipment far more advanced than any then used in England. They worked at Richmond, so their methods would have been closely noted by the Nidderdale miners, especially their drainage techniques.

The smelting hearths were in isolated positions up steep sided gills branching out from the main valley, so the lead had to be transported over the moorland tracks. It was placed in slotted bags slung over the backs of pack, or 'jagger' ponies. These ponies walked in trains of about twenty five, led by a bell mare or leading pony. They passed in single file down the narrow stony paths until they reached roadways fit for carts to use. The carts then conveyed the lead to boats on the rivers. The men walking with the ponies and the miners tramping the long distances to the mines often knitted as they went, to earn a few more pence for their families.[12]

Appletreewick, to which Peter and Elizabeth moved after their marriage, was a tiny hamlet consisting of a single street with a few cottages on both sides, a smithy, a bakehouse and an inn. Like most of the local villages it was a centre for the families living on the outlying farms around, and it was self sufficient, with its own miller, carpenter, butcher, shoemaker, tailor, weavers and baker. Close to the inn, The Craven Arms, the village stocks complete with hand cuffs stood as a warning to the unruly.

The lord of the manor had been granted a charter in 1311 to hold an annual fair, from October 26th to 29th. This was of great value both to the lord, through tolls, and to the inhabitants, through trade.[13] Ponies, Highland cattle and black faced sheep were brought down from Scotland in large numbers, and found ready purchasers. Onions were an important local product. These were hung for sale in long strings on the walls of Onion Lane. Dalesmen and their families walked from Skipton, Malham, Kilnsey and Kettlewell, Grassington, Ramsgill, Middlesmore and Pateley, Dacre, Coverdale, Swaledale and Wensleydale to attend the fair, with their cattle and their cloth, their leather and their knitted stockings. These tireless hardy people knew how to enjoy themselves when there was a chance, and music and dancing, sports and cockfighting were their entertainments during the two days. Peter and his family joined in and enjoyed themselves as much as any, finishing up at the alehouse with all comers. Pedlars sold ribbons and fairings, pins and knives, and there were always one or two glib tongued salesmen with potions and remedies for every ill, human or animal. After the fair, the beasts were driven away and groups of people set off home again. The village returned to its normal seasonal hard working life.

Parcevall Hall, where Peter and Elizabeth spent their early married years, stood a mile or two out of the village and half a mile from Skyreholme, (then another large farm). It was a grey rectangular stone house similar to Gouthwaite, but smaller, and it stood with its back to the hillside in a hollow facing a great sweep of moorland. This was topped by a huge rocky outcrop called Simon's Seat. Farm buildings stood near the house, and a garden with apple trees led down to the gate opening on to the track which was their only roadway. From the narrow windows Peter and Elizabeth looked out directly on to the dark brown and purple moors. There were few trees for shelter, and no sign of any other habitation. At the back of the house, over the hill, ran the deep cleft of Troller's Gill where lead had been worked for centuries. Fearsome stories of trolls and spirits which had appeared to miners in the darkness underground were handed down to each generation. It was an isolated spot compared to Ripley Castle, or even Gouthwaite, where pasture and cultivated land ran down the sides of the river valley, but it had a wild beauty of its own, and the house was strongly built against the elements.

The great central hall, open to the oak rafters above, was warmed by a huge peat fire in an arched stone fireplace fully fifteen feet across. This had deep within it the stone hearth and low benches that ran on either side of it. A long trestle and a few bench seats filled the rest of the room.

The low stone flagged kitchen, the hub of the house, led out from the hall. Over the blazing heart of the fire hung a great iron pot attached by three chains to a smoke blackened hook above. Smaller pots hung from smaller hooks and wisps of steam joined the smoke from the outer logs. An outsize oak dresser took the whole of one side of the room, and on the table lay pewter dishes and wooden platters, with heavy iron spoons and ladles, and some sharp knives. Into this kitchen came haunches of venison, hares, rabbits, curlews, and gamecocks to be skinned, plucked and dressed. Local cheeses, onions, oatmeal in sacks, hogsheads of ale and vats of wine all had to be stored for months ahead.

From Parcevall Hall it was a rough ride of nearly two hours across the steep open moorland to Pateley Bridge, and over an hour just to reach the neighbouring village of Burnsall. In good weather there was no lovelier place to ride, with only the sounds of the little racing becks, the bleating of sheep, the call of a curlew or the harsh 'G'back, g'back' of a grouse. Good horses were essential and Peter took a great pride and interest in his. (He would have had to pay from £5 to £7 for a well bred riding nag.)

The area around the Vale of York had acquired a reputation for rearing fine horses, and Leland noted that Ripon Fair was much celebrated for its

8. Parcevall Hall

horse sales. Ripon colts were known throughout England by 1600, and Peter makes special mention in his will of two favourites.

'One colte called Christopher' was left to his brother William, and 'one colte called Bald Jackson' to Thomas Spence. Two of his 'best nags' were bequeathed to his brother Edmund, and to his brother-in-law, William Ingilby.

As Peter rode across to Gouthwaite or Ripley he saw the same stretches and sweeps of the moors that we can see today. As now, parts of the ground were filled with treacherous spongy bogs, and parts of it had stony outcrops. The winding tracks he followed had been made by the cattle and sheep. These linked up with the old packhorse track or droveway from Pateley, along which the flocks and herds had been driven for centuries to their summer grazing on the sweet Craven grass. Tall upright stones acted as guide posts along the way, in mist or fog.

Peter must have ridden many a weary mile in all weathers to visit his farms and tenants, his family and in-laws, the local fairs and markets, the local courts and the scenes of his mining operations.[14] When his horse clattered into the cobbled stable yard at home, Elizabeth was ready to greet him. He came in stiff, wet and cold, but his boots were soon pulled off and dry clothes were ready beside a huge roaring fire in the raftered hall. The smell of newly baked bread taken from the beehive oven beside the kitchen fire wafted to him, and preparations were made for a hearty meal of venison pasty, local cheese and ale.

Some days he would spend long hours over his estate books, entering up the details of crops, acreages, repairs, wages, rents and sales to show to his father on his next visit. He and his steward would pore over the ancient yellowing parchment scrolls on which were written the title deeds, leases and charters. These detailed his rights and dues, and were his only legal record. The seals were carefully laid flat when the scrolls had been rerolled, tied with tape, and placed very safely in an iron bound coffer. There were no banks or safe deposits then and on these documents depended his inheritance.

In the evening, being a cultured and scholarly man he would take down a book from the well filled shelves of his library. The works of Luther, Calvin, and Beza, Jewel's 'Apology' and Harding's 'Reply', Ptolemy's 'Geography', Garceus' 'De Tempore', Euclid, Horace, Suetonius, Piccolomini, Vitruvius on Architecture, Cicero, Livy's 'Decades', Decameron, William English Herbal', Lives of the Philosophers, Plato, in Greek, Amyntus, in Latin, and of course Thomas Tusser's up to date advice on farming, and Georgius Agricola's work on mining, 'De Re Metallica' all had their place, but, as yet, a separate library was a rarety.

Often the family would make music together, composing both tune and verse in the free and joyful manner of the age, and sometimes some of the servants would also join in. Ballads and lovesongs were popular everywhere.

Elizabeth had quite a household to manage but, having been brought up in the dale, she had learnt all the skills necessary to run a self contained and isolated manor house in a harsh climate. It was up to her to make sure there was always a plentiful supply of fuel, food and warm garments, not only for her household but also for any visitors. In winter they could be snowed in for days or even weeks.

Their diet was varied as the meticulous observations of Fynes Morison relates:

'They had an abundance of white meats, of all kinds of flesh, fowl and fish. In the season of the yeare they eate fallow deer plentifully, as bucks in summer and as does in winter, which they bake in pasties, and this venison pasty is a dainty rarely found in any other kingdom.' A good deal of their other meat came from hares and rabbits, and fatted geese and

9. Notification by Symon the dean and Hamo the treasurer of York of the settlement of a dispute between Sir William de Molbrai and the abbot and monks of Byland about the forest of Middlesmoor in Nidderdale 1204, 4th August

poultry. Few vegetables were eaten, but instead, bread made from wheat or rye. The chief meal was eaten at eleven or twelve o'clock, and supper followed about five hours later.

John, their eldest son, was baptised at Burnsall in 1566, and altogether Elizabeth reared four sons and a daughter, but it is more than likely several other children would have died in infancy. The hazards of childbearing in her remote home were many. A neighbour wrote, 'My wife's delivery was with such violence, as the child dyed within half an hour, and but for God's wonderful mercie, more than human reason could expect, shee had dyed. But he spared her a while longer to mee and took the childe to his mercie.'

At least one hopes Elizabeth's mother was able to advise and help her, and that she did not have to endure the treatment recommended to Arthur Throckmorton's unfortunate wife at that date, whose first infant had died at a month old. 'My wife had. . . a double cloth laid upon her belly. . . dipped in plaintain water and vinegar of roses in equal quantities. Both her arms must be tied very hard, and sometimes loosed and tied again. . . . To open a vein on her arm two or three days, and to let her sit from her buttocks up to her navel in a deep bowl of cold water. . . .' (This was the advice of Dr Atslow, a Fellow of New College, Oxford.)[15]

Elizabeth also took responsibility for Gouthwaite Hall, as Peter's parents spent the greater part of their life in London. As well as her care of her children, servants and neighbours she had to oversee the purchase of materials for their clothing. The fantastical fashions of the day demanded yards and yards of cloth, purple and yellow for liveries, taffeta and sarcenet, white and tawny velvets and satin for dresses and doublets, cloaks and sleeves. Silk ribbon, gold buttons, and jewelled caps may not have been needed at Parcevall Hall, as they were at court, (where it was said, many a courtier wore an estate upon his back), but neverthelss the Yorkes had a position to keep up. Mourning was another costly item. In Throckmorton's diary he entered, 'Blacks for mourning – £77.18.6', which was for when his mother died and their household had to be suitably attired. After the funeral of the head of the household, the upper servants might each be given a gown and kirtle, and the men servants each a gelding, or a gift of similar value.

From all we can gather, Elizabeth and Peter's marriage was as happy as it was prudent, and in his will he refers to her as 'his dear and loving wife'.

Compared to his father's busy public life in London, and the adventurous exploits of his several younger brothers, Peter may seem to have been unremarkable, but it is his attachment to the land and his qualities of stewardship and public service which have been handed down strongly through the generations. The methodical and meticulous care for his land and the people living on it, their dwellings and their stock, and their mining operations occupied his days. The routine of the shearing of his sheep, attendance at his manor courts and barmoot courts, dinners for the village people at Christmas, provisioning his house and balancing his books in the days before banks, filled the year. Like his neighbouring landowners, his relaxation and enjoyment was with his horses, hounds and hawks, and much time was taken up with their selection and training. Great herds of red deer roamed over the Pennines, and these were hunted by the gentry and their ladies, but everyone, on foot and on horseback, hunted the hare. [When a fox was killed, the churchwarden paid a shilling for it and nailed the mask to the church door.] Wildfowling with hawks or bows, for which trained dogs were essential, brought variety to the diet and provided further sport. A letter to Sir Thomas Danby J.P. of Swinton, dated July 1580, has been preserved. It is in Peter's own scholarly hand with its curlicued flourishes and careful script.

'To the Right Worshippful Sir Thomas Danby Knight'
'My hertye commendacions etc.,
I doubt not but you do well remember a taulk had at York at my Lord President's at Lamas last past, when I told you that upon reasonable considerations and usage, you should find me a good neighbour towards your game in Mashamshire . . . so that I marveille much why your servants should so use bad neighbourhood upon my spaniells, which may not cum but to be taken up, for my man was within my bounders. But I persuade myself that it rather was the rashness of your lewd servants than your commandement. But if you mean to have good neighbourhood I am willing. . . if not you must understand that your servants shall not do as they have done, for I would you well know, I have within me as free chace as you have, and as large bounders as you can shew. . . I will offer as much right and curtesie as may be and because I am not able to travel to you, if you would take the paynes as to come hither, wee should soon conclude. . . . if I had been such an enemy to your game as your servants report, the deare should not have been so long (a time) at the New House (at the head of the dale) and other places. . . in such quiet confidence. I pray you send me my spaniell by my servant for I have none other to serve me withall. Thus I bid you farewell.
Your friend yff you so account,
Peter Yorke.'[16]

In one particular Peter shared his father's anxieties and that was in the observance of religious matters, with the changes in administration. The progress of the Reformation was halted when Mary ascended the throne, and in the North, this news had been received with joy. . . 'Tholle commonaltie in all places in the northe parttes grettlie rejoicde, makynge grett fyers, drinkyng wyne and aylle and prayssing God.' wrote Robert Parkyn, but when Elizabeth brought in a new religious settlement in 1559, it caused no great stir at first. The fervent recusant Catholics around

Ripon and in Nidderdale continued to hear Mass together, said secretly by a priest housed in one of the local manor houses. A fine of one shilling was payable for failure to attend divine service on Sundays or Holy Days, and in the churches, the images and Latin service books were removed. Over the next ten years however, the Protestant Archbishop of York seemed to be content with securing quietness and a modicum of external obedience by church going. Certain priests in prominent positions, like the headmaster of Skipton Grammar School, were deprived of their livings for greater publicity.

This quiet period ended in 1569 with the rebellion by the Earls of Northumberland and Westmoreland, aimed at restoring the old religion and possibly putting Mary, Queen of Scots, (then imprisoned in Bolton Castle in nearby Wensleydale) on the throne. Northumberland's tenants and relatives in the West Riding supported this, but it soon collapsed.

In 1571, after the See of York had been vacant for two years, the new Puritan Archbishop, Edmund Grindal, began a far more thorough and determined assault on Catholicism. Priests were hunted and rounded up. All the older clergy were suspect. Fines and gaol sentences were increased, and Catholics were executed, not for heresy, but for high treason.

Peter and Elizabeth Yorke were faced with severe problems. Elizabeth was determined not to forsake her deeply held and loved convictions, and was supported by her own parents and family. Peter, like all the other estate owners, realised that he could risk losing his land by flouting the law. However, like many of his Catholic neighbours, he was in a position of considerable influence in the area. He could put pressure on the churchwardens and local clergy, and help both to protect his Catholic tenants, and to mitigate the severity of the persecution. He could, and probably did, shelter priests, without whose ministrations Catholicism would have died out. He and his father in law conformed outwardly, but their wives and children were determined recusants, and some fines had to be paid. Peter gave long leases on land in Arncliffe and Kilnsey in 1571 to raise some ready money.[17]

The case of Elizabeth's mother, Anne Ingilby, was remarkable. She was first summoned before the High Commission in 1572, but failed to appear. Over the next nine years she was summoned a further twenty seven times, but each time sent an excuse, which each time was accepted. In 1581 her son undertook to produce her in court, but she was not called again until 1585. She never did in fact appear before the Commission, and survived with impunity till her death in 1589.

Between 1580 and 1582, under the Presidency of the Earl of Huntingdon, there was a great round up of between 1,500–2,000 recusants and 'mislikers' in the West Riding. (The latter were alienated from the established church but not totally against it.) Just over a third conformed promptly. The rest paid fines, or in some cases went to prison in York. One hundred and twenty gentry families and four J.P.s were presented, and the districts of Ripon, Claro and Craven contained the highest number.

The interlacing branches of the Ingilby family accounted for some of the complications of administering the law in Nidderdale and around. One of Sir William's daughters was married to William Byrnand, Recorder of York, and a member of the High Commission in 1580. Known Catholics like Sir John Mallory, (Lady Ingilby's brother), and Lord Darcy sat on the Council of the North, which was set up to track down and fine recusants. The landed gentry were long practised in legal devices, as David Hey says, and resorted to delaying tactics over payment of fines, such as constant moving to another house or property, pleas of ill health and so on, with great success. It was up to the churchwardens and constables to swear to the presentations of offenders, but as these were their neighbours and often their landlords too, it was unwise to upset them.

In the next decade the 'mislikers' gradually accepted the established religion, but the die-hards grew stronger in numbers and determination, despite heavy fines. Long series of wearisome attendances at court were also imposed, intended to wear down resistance. To have to pay £260 per annum for each recusant in the household was a huge penalty. After 1586 two thirds of a man's land could be seized for persistant recusancy, and the ultimate sanction, excommunication, meant no church burial was allowed.

The strength of the support for the old religion in Nidderdale is understandable. The dale was off the beaten track far from the danger of Spain, and strongly conservative. Archbishop Sandys (1577–88), described as 'a learned and vigorous man, keen in his many quarrels', said, 'A more stiff necked wilful obstinate people did I ever know or hear of', but the comments of those who opposed him were equally downright.

John Hamerton of Hellifield Peel said 'that they were all heretics that are of the religion that is now preached'.[18]

Agnes Hunter, a farmer's wife from the dale said, 'the service that is read and taught in the church now is not God's word but the devil's word. . .'. Others called the Puritans liars and deceivers. One obstinate 'misliker', Thomas Beckwith of Thornton in Craven, argued reasonably enough (considering all he had been through), 'What if the world change as it did in King Henry's time and in Queen Mary's time? Shall we still stand bound to perform these conditions?' The perplexity and anger of these people was very real. They felt it wholly unreasonable to be uprooted from their deeply loved rituals and deeply held beliefs, and doubly so to be punished and fined as well.

It was accounted a crime to own a rosary, (the most treasured possession of many), or a crucifix or a Latin prayer book. It was forbidden to kneel and pray where the ancient crosses had stood along the moorland tracks. William Adcock of Bilton was presented for 'he kneels whenever corpses he accompanies to burial pass places where standing crosses once stood'. Latin texts on gravestones were prohibited, but this could be overcome by the fortunate coincidence that R.I.P. stood both for Requiescat in Pace or Rest in Peace.

Infuriated by these rules one 'misliker' went to church 'wearing a woman's white cap in derision', and another said openly he would buy his own bread and wine, and bring it with him next time for that was all it was now.[19]

The Vicar of Nidd was still following the Catholic rite in 1586, when he was charged with mumbling the new service incorrectly, crossing the sacramental bread, and saying the old Latin service every day. The curate of Pateley was sent to prison in York Castle for being unwilling to yield his opinion on 'Tu es Petrus', and 'Hoc est corpus meum' – the very basis of Roman Catholic teaching on papal authority and transubstantiation. These two men had clearly upheld the local people completely.

The recusant gentry families were often supported from overseas. Their sons travelled on the Continent and also came in fresh contact with instructed Catholic believers at the universities or the Inns of Court. Priests came over from France on secret visits to the bigger houses. Families like the Mallorys, Yorkes, Tempests of Broughton, Talbots of Long Preston, Danbys of Farnley, Arthingtons of Spofforth, Nortons of Boroughbridge, Hamertons of Hellifield, Trappes of Nidd, Vavasours of Kirkby Overblow, Peels and Pudseys of Bolton by Bowland, Paslews of Burnsall, and the Listers of Gisburn all played their part.[20]

The persecutions coloured the whole of Peter and Elizabeth's married life, varying from constant nagging anxieties to a very serious financial drain. It is hard to know the spirit in which they viewed it all. Although their feelings were strong and genuine, perhaps because of their abilities and connections, some of the law evading could have become almost a sport. Tales of success against the canting predestinating Puritans may have made prime entertainment around a dinner table far away up the dale.

However, judging by some of the transactions, Peter certainly suffered financially. Although he purchased the manor of Middlesmoor in 1581, with forty cottages, out buildings and lands in Stean Pasture, Angram, Westhouses, Woodall and Newhouse, this was a wild area at the head of the dale and of no great value.

He sold some of his property around Austwick, in eight or nine transactions over twenty years, to his in-laws. In 1592, his son John seems to have mortgaged or sold some of the Appletreewick property, with twenty messuages and ten cottages but kept the mining rights. This property was restored to the family again within a few years.[21]

Amongst those who conformed to the new Protestant doctrine, the lawyers, yeomen, merchants and gentry were men of the new age. Unlike the diehard recusants, they felt that the emphasis on Bible reading, family prayers and work dedicated to God suited their way of life. Many, like Sandys, endowed schools to improve the education of the parish clergy and to encourage learning from the Scriptures.[22]

While the northern pocket of Catholic resistance was hardening, Peter's younger brothers took up arms and travelled overseas. In 1578 Don John of Austria (Philip of Spain's half-brother), attacked and routed the Dutch States army. Queen Elizabeth sent an English regiment under Henry Cavendish with 'ten pieces of great ordnance' to help the Dutch. Owing to the great fighting qualities of the English, the Spaniards were beaten back, and Roland Yorke was one who shared in the pride and the spoils of that victory. They 'fought from eight o'clock before noon until four at night and we drove them to the flight', wrote Arthur Throckmorton, and Roland 'made challenge against that French that made the letter that was sent to St Aldegonde speaking in dishonour of us Englishmen'. 'Booty of kine, mares and horses from the enemy' was taken and five spies put to death. Throckmorton also mentions a quarrel between officers 'being at dinner' when two young swordsmen 'thrust through the bodies' of two others. (It was said that Roland had introduced rapier fighting into England.)

Roland, who was the ninth son, joined the Rising of the Northern Earls in support of Mary, Queen of Scots, and was obliged to leave the country after the rebellion's collapse. He volunteered to fight in the complex situation in the Netherlands, where he served under Captain Thomas Morgan in 1572.[23] He took part in the attack on Goes under Sir Humphrey Gilbert, a close friend of Roland's first cousin, Martin Frobisher.[24]

Although Roland was a bold soldier, as a Catholic he was distrusted by the Calvinist States and in October 1580, he was reported by Herle to Walsingham as having been arrested on a charge of felony.[25] Four years later he was detected in a plot to betray Ghent to the Duke of Parma.[26] He was imprisoned in Brussels, but released when Parma captured the city in 1586.

His brother Peter must have dreaded what news he would hear of him next. In 1586 however, Roland joined the Earl of Leicester's expedition to the Netherlands, where he was given command at the battle of Zutphen. (It was here that Sir Philip Sidney received his mortal wound.) The Earl wrote to Secretary Walsingham, 'There were at the last I think I may saye the most notable encounter that hath been in our age, and wich remain to our posterity famous, the day's flight I meane, when our son was hurt, when those gentlemen were driven to serve a fort, and sett themselves in the first rank with Mr Roland Yorke, who had the charge of that companie. They went in.'[27] It appears though that Roland bore some grudge against Leicester, for later he surrendered Zutphen to the Spaniards, and induced Sir William Stanley to do the same for Deventer.

After this treachery, he was known to be a 'bold and determined villain',[28] and it was said the Spaniards, fearing a double treachery, poisoned him. He died in February 1588, of either poison or smallpox.[29] Three years after, his body was exhumed and gibbeted by order of the Dutch States. Roland's nephew and heir, Edmund, was executed at Tyburn for attempting to assassinate Queen Elizabeth.

Three of Peter's other brothers, Richard, Edmund and Edward also served in the army as young men, and Richard was knighted. In 1591 Edmund and Edward, a Lieutenant of the Cornet of Horse, were both knighted on the field at Roane sur Loire by the Earl of Essex, the Queen's new favourite. The scandal of Raleigh and Bess Throckmorton, the Queen's maid in waiting, was just breaking then and both young soldiers no doubt took a lively interest in the court tales of Raleigh's fall from grace.

Edmund was made Captain of Duncannon Fort in Waterford, and later served in France as Master of Ordnance under Lord Leicester. He died in 1592.[30]

Younger sons were not always at a disadvantage. They did not have the obligations or the upkeep to maintain as did the head of the family. Edward, the youngest of the ten surviving sons, was very near in age to Peter's eldest son, John. Both from their boyhood days had admired their cousin Martin Frobisher, who was more than twenty five years older than they were. He was a huge man of great strength and bravery but not much culture. He was however, a superb navigator. His exploits at sea had long fascinated Edward, who had sat for hours listening to his tales. Martin himself had been inspired by Humphrey Gilbert's 'Discourse to prove a passage by the North West to Cathay and the East Indies, 1576'. The Queen had granted Frobisher a licence to explore in 1576 and gave him £100. In his day a chronicler wrote, 'Ships are mighty foul and stink withal', but the City and Court financed him sufficiently to be able to afford some unusual comforts to alleviate this, including 'duck upholstery for his bedding', and 'a bottell of aquavite'. As well as the ship's biscuits he had raisins, prunes, oatmeal, salt beef and pork, wine and beer. (One day's ration for an ordinary sailor was one pound of biscuit, two pounds of salt beef and one gallon of beer.)

As his three ships passed the Royal Palace at Greenwich on June 7th, they fired a smoky cannonade. 'Her Majesty, beholding the same, commended it and bade us farewell with shaking her hand at us out of the window.' He charted the bleak coasts round Hudson Strait, 'tossed up and down with foul weather, snows and unconstant winds', opposed by 'heaps of ice like mountains' and 'Eskimo with black hair, broad faces, flat noses, swarthy coloured, apparelled in seal calves skins. . . the women painted about the eyes and cheeks with a blue colour like the Ancient Britons'.[31]

He was in search of gold, and brought back some black ore. Two metallurgists pronounced that the ore contained gold. Frobisher was promoted to Lord High Admiral in 1577. With a charter to establish the Cathay Company, £1,000, three new ships and twelve dozen Cornish miners he set forth again. He returned home in twenty days with 200 tons of ore. In 1578, with fifteen ships and four hundred men he sailed off again, and nearly 2,000 tons of ore were dug. In the end it proved worthless. He presented the Queen with an Eskimo, a kayak and a narwhal tusk, and she gave him a gold chain, the only gold from the whole enterprise. Frobisher Bay, named after him in Canada, remains as a memorial to his efforts.[32]

Martin served as Vice Admiral under Drake in 1586, and took command of H.M.S. Triumph against the Spanish Armada. Only fifty out of one hundred and fifty Spanish ships returned home, and 10,000 out of 30,000 soldiers perished.

Two years later he served with Sir John Hawkins and was knighted. He was a passionate explorer but, lacking the popularity of those other 'sons of Neptune', Drake and Raleigh, he had difficulty in recruiting men for his expeditions.

In 1592 and 1593 he undertook a voyage to Guinea with Hawkins. Edward Yorke commanded one of the ships, the 'Bonaventure', under Frobisher, thereby realising one of his own longest held ambitions.

After this Sir Edward was accepted as a servant of the Queen, 'as trustworthy as any of his degree', and occupied himself with naval and military affairs. He was made a Vice Admiral in the Navy, and there is a splendid portrait of him in dark blue armour and a yellow sash, his wise kind eyes set off by his trim, pointed Elizabethan beard and starched ruff. The portrait of his brother Richard, in black armour, is not so good, nor does he look so fine a man.

To Edward's great sorrow, Sir Martin, the Queen's white hope for the Navy, died of wounds after storming the Spanish naval base on Brest Water in 1594.

Edward married a Miss Worley and made his home near Ripon. By the reign of King James he had become Muster Master for Ripon, and Justice

10. Sir Edward Yorke

of the Peace for the district. The multifarious business of a J.P was not only a matter of prestige but of necessity. Society was held together and law and order maintained by the structure of local public service. The village constable and churchwardens carried much responsibility, and depended on the justices to back them up at Quarter Sessions. Much time was taken up in imposing the Oath of Allegiance, and by rounding up and certifying recusants. If however, the families involved were close relatives and neighbours, the justices might send the case up to Westminster to be heard. Other crimes of robbery, violence and so forth, were dealt with through the Sheriff and Justices, overseen by the Judge of Assize.

To be Muster Master involved calling together and overseeing the musters of men from each hundred, or wapentake.[33] These men were taken to be armed and trained as soldiers under regular army officers, for King James was at pains to keep his armed forces in good shape. The leading gentry were obliged to contribute horsemen, and a levy was made on each parish, in proportion to its population, for the supply of arms and ammunition. Ten hundreds together were responsible for raising three hundred foot and fifty horse. (The ancient system was that a hundred comprised a hundred families, who had to provide a hundred fighting men. They were used in an emergency rather than kept as a standing army.)

Much travelling and considerable personal expense fell upon the Muster Master and he often, in addition, took command of a troop of horse himself.

In his will in 1621 Edward asked for '. . . my body to be buried in St Wilfride in Ripon . . . give to my vere kind friend Sir Thomas Fairfax of Denton, Knight, in token of my love, the pickture of myself and two hampers . . . to the poor in Ripon £5 . . . one carpitt cloth with gold fringe for the use of the Collegiate Church of Ripon. . .'.

Peter Yorke had been returned to Parliament repesenting Ripon in 1589.[34] The high steward of the borough, Sir William Mallory, probably put him forward, though with his strong Catholic connections it seems strange his nomination was accepted. Nevertheless he had conformed for many years, and brother Edward's loyal service to the Crown may have counted in his favour. At any rate he was appointed to the subsidy committee in the House of Commons on February 11, 1589.[35] By the following April he was dead, in his mid-sixties. Although he had spent by far the greater part of his life in Yorkshire, his wish was to be buried beside his father and mother in St Stephen's Walbrook.

In Peter's will, proved 4 July 1589, he leaves his eldest son, John, his Austwick, Kilnsey, Appletreewick and Nidderdale estates, and entreats him to have a special care for his 'mynes of lead'.[36] To his second son,

Thomas, he leaves 'Percevalle ferme now in my occupacion', and another holding, once granted to the Abbot and Convent of Bolton. He also leaves £200 each to Thomas, William and Richard, to be paid out of the profits of 'his mynes of lead orer'. Ten of the £200 left to Thomas shall be 'towards a tombe to be made for my Father Sir John Yorke and me'.

Thomas Spence, who received the colt called Bald Jackson, also had all Peter's apparel which he had in London, excepting his best cloak for his eldest son, John, and a ruby ring for his wife Elizabeth. His 'best saddle with the furniture' went to Sir William Mallory.

His sorrowing widow lost her mother the same year. We know Elizabeth lived on at least five more years, for she is listed as a recusant between 1590–95 in the Liberty of Ripon, and also in Ripley and Burnsall. She steadfastly refused to conform, and also kept her children unwavering in the Catholic faith.

CHAPTER VI

SIR JOHN YORKE 1566? – 1634
OF
GOUTHWAITE

JOHN SUCCEEDED HIS FATHER at about the age of twenty three and was knighted at Windsor the same year. I can only assume that this was in reward for service to his country in the army, but the reason is not recorded. His widowed mother continued to take an active part in local affairs and lived at Gouthwaite with him till her death.

John had been brought up first at Parcevall Hall and later Gouthwaite, and his early years had been coloured both by his influential Ingilby cousins, and by his much travelled and venturesome Yorke uncles. His youngest uncle, Edward, and he were very much of an age. His father, Peter, would have wished him to have a good education so it is quite likely John may have lodged with his grandparents in Wallbrook for a time, and attended the Merchant Taylor's school along with Edward. They probably went through university together, where like a contemporary, they were each 'sometime a too much careless and negligent student'.

Like Arthur Throckmorton, John may have made a continental tour to complete his education in order, as A.L. Rowse puts it, 'to polish his northern barbarism at the fount of sixteenth century culture in Renaissance Italy'. Unlike Throckmorton, John had few connections at Court, and fewer leanings in that direction, being a known Catholic. However, his network of relations gave him good scope for travelling around this country. There were houses in plenty to visit for hunting and hawking, from north to south.

John lived through stirring times in his late teens and early twenties. The exploits of his uncle Roland in the Netherlands in 1578, in the battle against Don John of Austria, was the talk of the family. Roland had had to fly the country after the collapse of the northern Earls' rebellion, which had made him a hero in the eyes of eight year old John. Uncle Edward and John also greatly admired Richard and Edmund and Martin Frobisher, and awaited every despatch in particular those concerning the Triumph's success in the Armada.

As a young gentleman of the day, John's other interest would have been in fine clothes, and no doubt he wrote to his father for money to buy the required velvets, satins, bands and ruffs, silver buttons and beaver hats then in fashion. Like his friends he longed for 'a new jerkin well bordered and not too short, the collar falling somewhat down, and the ruff well stiffened and brisky'.[1] Whether any money was forthcoming depended on the Nidderdale woolclip, and the lead sales. Peter had three other sons to clothe and educate, and was also paying increasingly heavy recusancy fees for the family, and incurring other expenses for his brothers.

Sadly, no diary of John's is left to reveal the details of his life but his contemporary, Nicholas Assheton of Downham in Lancashire, wrote a journal of which some fragments remain.[2]

The date of John's marriage is not known but it may have been before his father's death. [It was not uncommon then for a marriage to take place between a seventeen year old and a thirteen year old.] At any rate he chose a Yorkshire girl, Juliana, daughter and co-heiress of Sir Ralph Hansby of Beverley and Tickhill. I feel sure Elizabeth had selected his bride with care, a devout Catholic with a useful dowry, and that she herself was able to spend the last years of her life as the benevolent matriarch in the household.

John and Juliana set about making improvements to the old house at Gouthwaite in the way each succeeding generation tries to do. They added more fireplaces, chimneys and chimneystacks, and elaborately carved oak screens and banisters. They may even have put in wainscotting or panelling, tapestries and a plaster ceiling. Extra glazed and mullioned windows gave more light to the great chamber and to the other rooms. Gradually the house became more comfortable and considerably better furnished and equipped than in the days of John's grandfather. The elaborately carved bedposts of English oak were ornamented with grotesque figures and dates, as in similar houses. Turkey carpets costing between £8–£16 were used as table covers in the main rooms and bulrush matting, at 9d a yard, was an improvement on the old loose strewn rushes which harboured fleas in the other chambers.

In the garden too, changes were made. Gravelled walks and paving led to secluded seats, one overlooking a bowling green. Palings lined the driveway, and John planted fruit trees including some, perhaps, of the new apricots recently introduced from America. He laid out flower beds, and added to the plants in Elizabeth's herb garden, surrounding them with little clipped box hedges to make formal patterns.

Between twelve and fifteen servants were employed indoors and out. Two or three maidservants helped Dame Julian in the stillroom and the laundry, and with the making of clothes, but the kitchen and other staff were usually men. An upper servant such as Hodgson, the cook, was paid 10s a year, and received his keep and uniform for the year also. Workmen,

11. Goulthwaite Hall 1837, by Mary Yorke (drawing)

such as carpenters, shepherds and so on earned about 10d a day from March till October, (working from 5 a.m.–7 p.m., with a half hour for breakfast and one and a half hours for dinner), and 8d a day for the shorter winter days. A boy could earn 4d to 6d a day. One at least of the shepherds, was responsible for the 500 sheep pastured at Conistone, and John certainly owned many more sheep in Nidderdale.[3]

In the years between 1594 to 1597, very bad harvests lowered the peoples resistance to a severe outbreak of plague which occurred in the

Richmond area in 1597. There were even some deaths from starvation recorded, but the servants in the large houses fared better than many.

By the time John was overseeing his mines, a neighbour, Thomas Proctor, had been granted a patent (in 1589), for his process of mixing coal with peat for smelting. This could have made a great saving on charcoal, and thereby on timber, which was needed for shipbuilding, but there is no evidence that his results were successful.[4]

Proctor's son, Stephen, bought the Fountains Abbey estate and later built a mansion on the site of the Abbot's lodging. He also built the first recorded smelting mill on Greenhow and laid the foundations of the mining village there. He was litigious in the extreme, even by sixteenth century standards. He claimed the lordship of the field of Bewerley, and waged a complicated legal battle for his mining rights and for permission to enclose the commons in Pateley Bridge and Kirkby Malzeard, against the Ingilbys, Yorkes and Armitages. Ingilby aided the excluded villagers in tearing down Proctor's enclosures, and filling in his coal pits.

The case dragged on in the Star Chamber for seven years. Proctor's bill accused his opponents of five attempts to murder him, and riots against him and his servants with guns, pistols, bows and arrows, but the case was eventually settled peacefully.[5]

Proctor had strong Puritan sympathies, and took it upon himself to try to crush recusancy in Nidderdale, so on neither count was he popular with his neighbours. He had one seminary priest, Christopher Wharton, seized in Ripley Park, and another, Father Harrison, at the house of one of John Yorke's servants. Both priests and their shelterers were put to death about 1598.[6]

At this date John received permission to carry lead ore over Bewerley common. He was planning to build his new mill at Heathfield, which would serve both his Appletreewick and his Stonebeck Down mines, and was situated in the direction of the nearest navigable water at Boroughbridge.[7] Throughout John's life extensive explorations of the mineral veins went on, mostly still in the upper horizons of the ground. The productivity of these remained high, but over the next hundred years these upper veins were gradually worked out.

The two dominating issues in the country at the turn of the century were the question of the succession to the throne and peace with Spain. There was a feeling of disenchantment, and, at the top, almost anyone would betray anyone for personal advancement. The state treason trials were like those in Stalinist Russia today – the prisoner had to prove his own innocence. When the fearful sentence was finally carried out on Essex, the Queen's ex-favourite in 1601, many close to him trembled.

Two years later the great Queen's amazing vitality slowly ebbed away in her Palace at Sheen, bringing the Tudor dynasty to an end.

As the Calvinist reared King James rode south, thinking himself at last rich and all powerful, he was met and greeted by nobles and gentlemen anxious to gain his favour. His fixed view of kingship had not taken in the concept of Parliamentary privilege, and he soon irritated his first Parliament by demands for money, as well as by his religious views. The Puritan element was disappointed that James would not stiffen the Elizabethan Church Settlement. They represented only a large, able and noisy minority within the Church, but they enlisted support from many squires in the east, the Midlands and the south, as well as many merchants. Few sermons were preached owing to the lack of learning amongst the clergy, but the most effective preachers were of Puritan persuasion.

The Catholics were hopeful, (his mother having been their champion), that, if the Pope would allow them to give their secular allegiance to the King, he might let them follow their own religion. The Pope refused. James entered the argument. The Jesuits attacked his right to the throne. The air was charged with plots.

Between 1583 and 1604 there were over two hundred recusant gentry families in North West Yorkshire, and some fifty priests, (including five or six Jesuits), travelling around. Catholic books, letters and sermons were regularly smuggled in and out of England in bales of cloth. By the end of 1604 however, forty seven Yorkshire priests had been executed as traitors, and others were in gaol. In 1603–04 there were 1,136 presentments made in the West Riding.

In 1605 a small group of Catholic gentry became so filled with disappointment and despair that they conceived a desperate plan. Robert Catesby, Guy Fawkes, (whose father was the Archbishop's registrar on the High Commission), Robert Winter, whose cousin had married Jane Ingilby, (John Yorke's first cousin), and others decided to blow up the King and his whole Parliament with gunpowder while in session. They hoped this would be followed by a Catholic uprising and that a Catholic regime might be re established with Spanish help, in the resulting confusion. One of their followers, horrified by the plan, warned a relative who was a Catholic peer. The story reached Cecil and the cellars of Westminster were searched. Thirty six barrels of gunpowder were found, and Fawkes was arrested on the spot. The charges brought against them were that 'they. . . did conclude and agree. . . to blow up and tear to pieces. . . our sovereign Lord and King. . . and all of them. . . most barbarously and more than beastly, traitorously and suddenly to destroy and swallow up'. All the conspirators were hunted down, horribly tortured and executed. Fawkes himself, who had once been 'a very tall and desperate fellow' was so broken on the rack he could not mount the ladder to the scaffold. His signature on his confession trails off down the page in an agonised scrawl.

John Ingilby was arrested, but released after questioning, and both Thomas and Richard Yorke, John's brothers, were implicated but not charged.[8]

The agitation of the Gunpowder Plot gave James the fright of his life, made an indelible impression on the country and finally strengthened Cecil's hand in dealing with the Catholic community. The persecutions increased greatly. Avowed Puritans and concealed Catholics sheltered under the umbrella of the official Church . However, new ideas were flowing in from the continent. Professional theologians were divided over the literal interpretation of the Bible and the impact of new scientific argument. Much of the fine literature of the seventeenth century, written by John Donne, Beaumont, Fletcher, George Herbert, Ben Jonson, and Jeremy Taylor, as well as Spenser, Milton, Bunyan and Pope dealt with the conflict between science and religion.

Sir Stephen Proctor joined with two other new landowners in the Ripon and Nidderdale districts and stepped up his own vendetta against his recusant neighbours, especially the Ingilbys and Yorkes. First these three tried to enclose common land, which angered the neighbours who would like to have done the same. (In one incident a certain Dorothy Bayne led thirty one women of Kirkby Malzeard to the moor, tore down Proctor's fences and pastured their cattle there as they had always done.)

Then Proctor issued a shower of law suits contesting rival claims to land and mining rights, before the Star Chamber and the Council of the North. Naturally accusations of treason and recusancy came in useful as weapons in his battle. He used every means in his power to harry and punish the Catholics, but had considerable difficulty in succeeding.

The witness in court of the curate of Middlesmoor, George Manson, was that out of 400–500 people in his chapelry, only three or four, and sometimes none, attended his services. When the locals were compelled to attend 'they wolde spitt owt or convey the bread owt of their mówthes into their handkicheves or aprons'. He further related how Sir John's servants would bring a piper to the churchyard and 'make there with their piping and revelling such a noyse in time of praier as the mynyster colde not well be hearde'.[9]

On another occasion when he ordered the people to come to prayer they said 'it wolde hinder the aylewyff and all went into the aylehouse'.

When Manson was ordered to draw up a list of recusants to take the new Oath of Allegiance in 1606, Sir John sent for the list and crossed some names off. Manson rewrote it, but no one was summoned. (Sir John finally took the Oath himself in 1621. He evidently tempered religion with a sense of economic reality, for it was said of him, 'He did soe goe to the church for the saving of his goodes'.)[10]

Manson depended on Sir John for his salary, (which was only £8 to £10 per year,) but frequently was not paid. Other witnesses said that no sermon had been preached at Pateley Bridge for twenty years. The Yorke's grip on their own area was strong.

Proctor did achieve some success against them in the end, however, and this came about in an unexpected way.

Christmas was celebrated in the North with much entertainment and merriment and during the twelve days there was always some form of mumming or drama arranged to follow the feasting. There were many travelling companies of actors at that period. In 1609 the Yorkes invited one remarkable company of amateur Catholic actors to come to Gouthwaite. They came from Egton Bridge near Whitby and had been acting Shakespeare's and other traditional plays in houses around the county over the previous eight years, with great success. Their performances had thereby 'no doubt provided fellow Catholics with a legitimate cover for meeting together for Mass and the Sacraments', says Aveling.

That year at Gouthwaite, they performed King Lear, and, as an entr'acte, they put on 'St Christopher'. This contained a supposed dialogue between a Catholic priest and an Anglican minister, in which the latter, having of course been vanquished, was carried off by the devil to Hell, while angels bore away the former.

Symonds, the employer of one of the actors, gave this testimony in court. 'The part of the popish priest was to convict the English minister upon which conviction the devells, with thundering and with lightning and with great noyse compassed the minister about and carryed him away as it were to hell. Then the Angell. . . came in and took the popish priest by the hand and led him away. . . with harmony and music as if he were to have been transferred to some heavenly place.'[11]

Although only the family and their household and tenants were present, (about a hundred in all), Elizabeth (a former servant who had married the new and unpopular clerk at Pateley Bridge, William Stubbs), gave the story away to Proctor, no doubt for an ample reward. While Proctor was trying to bring charges against Yorke, he himself fell foul of authority over collecting fines, and was imprisoned in the Tower. As a result of Proctor's absence, neither Sir John nor Sir William Ingilby were arrested until 1611. They were first charged with implication in the Gunpowder Plot. Ingilby was released but Sir John was charged with 'countenancing a seditious disputation' and imprisoned in the Fleet prison with four of his household.

He was kept in solitary confinement for a time, by order of George Abbot, the Archbishop. As time went on, however, his friends were allowed to see him, and he could conduct his business from his chamber. The system was that each prisoner paid rent for his room, fees to the prison officers, his own expenses for food, fuel, laundry and so on, and could have his own servant to look after him.

The slowness of the court procedure was partly due to the fact that the more serious charges of implication in the Gunpowder Plot, and of harbouring a priest named Father Gerard, could not be sustained. The difficulties of finding and transporting to London a large number of witnesses scattered across Yorkshire, was the other factor. Many were unwilling to come at all.

Sir John was released on bail in October 1613. He must have been thankful to smell the sweet moorland air again after the stink of gaol, as he rode home on his favourite mare White Friar.

The public hearing began on July 1st 1614. The description of Proctor's servants searching in the hay in Yorke's shippon and finding 'two popish vestures, one of velvet embroidered with gold. . . a chalice of pewter, the picture of Christe in brasse', brings the scene vividly to mind.

The accounts of the taunts and threats made to Elizabeth and William Stubbs by their neighbours, the Yorke tenants, are very real. . . 'Your husband shall have his nose slit, his eares cut off and preach at Paul's Cross with a paper on his head!' On his way to church the people shouted at Stubbs and reviled him. 'Out black coat! Out villaine thiefe! The Divell goe with thee and all black cotes!'

Gossip, rumour and downright lies were used to support Proctor's charges, but in the end the Yorkes stood trial simply on the score of permitting an act or interlude by which the established religion was brought into derision.

John and his wife were both fined £1,000 each, and his three brothers, £500 each, by the Star Chamber for deriding the established religion. This was the longest case about a theatrical performance ever heard in the Star Chamber, and the fines were enormous. Richard Yorke was imprisoned in the Gatehouse to the Fleet, probably as surety, but no payment was made for three years. Evidently they were not able (or willing) to raise the huge sum at once, for both John and Julian were forced to spend some time in the Fleet prison for debtors. So many of their friends were in the same case from paying recusancy fines that it was scarcely a disgrace, indeed it may even have been a matter for pride.

By February 1617 they were released, had had their fines reduced to £1,200 in all, and been allowed to pay them by instalments.[12] Richard was released later.

In order to raise this money, John was obliged to grant very long leases, (for as much as five thousand years – or in effect, for ever), to fourteen or more tenants. In exchange for an ancient yearly rent of 33s 4d and a down payment of £33 one tenant, (Robert Wade of Riggs) received one of these leases for which he paid £4.2.0. a year. Another, John Servand of Middlesmoor, was raised from 40s to £13.[13] These leases of course gave long term security to the tenants and their families. In each case John reserved the rights to all minerals and the right of 'Fishing, Hunting, Hawking and Fowling', and the right to hold a fair. John continued to pay off the fines by instalments until 1631, but three quarters of Julian's and Richard's fines were still unpaid in 1640. (It is said some of the money was used to drain the Fens.)

Sir William Ingilby also granted leases of up to 1,000 years to twenty two Dacre tenants at about this period, and also sold the freehold of eight other farms. Some tenants agreed to pay a fixed annual sum in lieu of tithes in kind, corn, hay, wool or lambs etc. This benefited both parties, and was possible because wool was fetching a good price, so the farmers had some available cash. The Ingilby family had to pay a good deal out in recusancy fines, so were glad to receive cash.

Like his father, John enjoyed every form of sport, and regularly hunted the fox, otter, badger, rabbit, hare and deer. Shooting over spaniels, the day's bag might include mallard, moorcock, water ousel, pigeons and even a thrush. He fished, both with rod and line and with nets. Like Nicholas Assheton he could have written in his diary, 'Shot a stagg at top of dale. The keeper's two hounds cast off, brave sport, killed him at the boundary. Broke him up. Eat the chine and the liver.' Like Nicholas too, he 'could drink a bout with every farmer present' at the ale house and thoroughly enjoy the company.

John, despite many trials, was clearly ready to defend his rights against all comers. He was a J.P. and well versed in the law. The Earl of Cumberland, Francis Clifford of Skipton Castle, was involved in a lengthy litigation with John in 1611, concerning Free Chase and Warren in the manor of Appletreewick. The Earl claimed this manor lay in the Forest of Skipton, and that since the time of the Prior of Bolton, the inhabitants had paid 'foster oats and foster hens, as well as castle hens' to the Bow Bearer of the Forester of Skipton. He also said that his Keepers had always been able to range and view the deer at their will within the Town Fields of Appletreewick, and set courses and make general huntings on the commons. He maintained that neither Sir John nor his ancestors had ever hunted there except by courtesy of the Earl, or when he or his servants had stolen deer in the night time.

From words this dispute came to blows. Some of Cumberland's shepherds went to Appletreewick fair for the purpose of buying lean sheep 'to be fatted in the parks of Skipton Castle'. They knew of the animosity between their master and the lord of the manor of Appletreewick, and thought it a good opportunity to refuse to pay the accustomed tolls at the town end. These rough sturdy men used strong language in their refusal, well scattered no doubt with pithy allusions to Sir John and all his family. This was more than Sir John's loyal servants would stand for, and his bailiffs and men fell on the shepherds and beat them soundly. It must have been a bloody battle for it led to the whole matter being brought before the Star Chamber. As John was already in deep trouble there, this did not help matters. The Star Chamber looked with special severity at every instance of disrespect to a Nobleman. The record of the trial states that the defendant often gave directions to his keeper Fenton and his nephew John Yorke to kill deer in Appletreewick fields.[14] Accordingly they, with others, with guns, shot one of the Earl's stags and pursued it with a bloodhound. One John Hunt then said they would hunt and kill deer at their pleasure. At another time, in the presence of Sir John, Fenton shot at ten stags. When apprehended, the record goes on, 'Sir John, in a haughty manner, sent word to the Earl, that he would kill and hunt the deer there when he could'.

Curiously the Court did not try the title of the boundaries of the respective Chase and Manor, so there was no proof that the defendant was not hunting on his own free warren, and simply declaring his own rights. Instead, and probably because of the trouble Sir John was already in, he was fined for the hunting and the provoking speeches, and committed to the Fleet prison. Sir John was fined £200, Fenton £100 and nephew John, £50.

While these trials and tribulations were occupying the Yorke family, the social and agricultural changes in the rest of England were only very gradual, and life progressed peacefully.

Part of an agreement in Stonebeck Up in 1636 was for a bachelor called Will White to have half the west end of a cottage, a garden... and another garden 'with liberties to go to and from the oven in Wells House for Baking the said Bread and pies and other meate of the saide Will White'.[15] Neighbours gathered together in the local ale house to talk and drink freely. Horse races and cock fighting were very popular sports, and wagers were laid too on shooting at a mark with the long bow. Indoor games played included cards, dice, shovel board, tables, (backgammon), chess and billiards.[16]

Land ownership, opportunity and modest wealth was widely distributed in rural society, although the recent enclosures had driven many of the poorest off the land. National events included the printing of the Authorised Version of the Bible in 1611, (which gave further impetus to the Bible reading Puritans), and of Sir Walter Raleigh's History of the World. This vast work, written while he languished in the Tower, became a best seller, which Oliver Cromwell advised his son to read, and in which John Yorke would have taken the greatest interest.

The founding of the new colonies in Virginia, New England and the West Indies was the talk of the day. The settlers' reasons for emigrating arose partly from a desire for religious freedom and partly from land hunger. The capable and self sufficient settlers went of their own accord and were well equipped by their skills to be pioneers in a strange land. Somehow they overcame the fearful trials of the voyage, the disease and exposure which they encountered, and founded the strong stock on which America was based.

Another great chapter was the founding of the East India Company, to trade with India. Their 'goodly ships', some of which were as large as 1,100 tons, were heavily armed with expert mariners. They formed a private navy which added to the strength of England. They brought home salt petre, silk, and spices to flavour the salted and often rancid meat which most people had to eat. The East India Company was one side of the imperial coin of foreign trading policy, and later the Hudson's Bay Company became the other.[17]

In 1612, in the midst of the Yorke trials, young Prince Henry took a fever, and despite all efforts, he died. He was a far more promising youth than his handsome, stammering brother Charles, and few men felt hopeful of Charles' succession. The rivalries between Somerset and Buckingham, King James's two favourites, and between Coke, the Lord Chief Justice, and Bacon, the Lord Chancellor were the talk of the country in the years between 1612 and 1616.

A marriage was planned between Charles and the Infanta of Spain, in the hope of a handsome dowry. To please the Spaniards, Walter Raleigh, whose expedition to Guiana in search of gold had proved fruitless, was cruelly executed on a fourteen year old charge. But the Spaniards succeeded in driving the King's Protestant son-in-law, the Elector Palatine, out from his newly accepted throne of Bohemia. A wave of anti-Spanish and papist feeling swept the country, and the marriage plan failed.

King James died in 1625, and within two months Charles was married to the fifteen year old Catholic Henrietta Maria, sister of King Louis XIII of France. He secretly promised to help the English Catholics, which must have raised their by now very faint hopes considerably.

SIR JOHN YORKE OF GOUTHWAITE 1566?–1634

The Stuart landowners in Yorkshire and Lancashire were in far closer touch with each other than we imagine today, dependent as we are on cars and telephones. Not only did they ride long distances to meet for business and for sport, but the network of their stewards, keepers and servants from each great house enabled news to be passed on through relatives, markets and errands.

The journey to London from Nidderdale would be made in stages of between twenty to thirty five miles a day and take six to seven days, and clearly Sir John made the journey many times. Accustomed as he was to long hours in the saddle in all weathers, he made little of it. Nevertheless a man who had reached his sixties in those days was accounted a good age.

Early in the 1630s Sir John appears to have gone to live at Sleningford. This property lay about 15–20 miles from Gouthwaite and nearer to Ripon, where a physician could visit him more easily.

John and Julian had had no children, so he made the son of his brother Thomas, his heir. Thomas had first married Frances, daughter and co-heir of George Vavasour, a well known recusant from Spaldington in Yorkshire. She bore no children either, and died young. Secondly Thomas married Frances, daughter of Sir William Babthorpe, of Babthorpe. (Her sister was Mrs Nicholas Assheton of Downham, and her half sister was Mrs John Ingilby of Ripley.)[18]

Thomas and Frances brought up their eldest son John at Parcevall Hall in Appletreewick where his grandfather Peter had started his married life. Thomas died before his brother, so, on the death of Sir John, the estates passed to young John.

The will reads, 'I, Sir John Yorke of Sleningford, Kt. now grown with yeares, and being desirous in time of perfect memory (thoughe sicke in body) to settle and dispose of my temporall estate in such sorte, as may both give content to myselfe, and may make peace amongst my friends after my departure hence, I doe hereby make this my last will and testament'.[19]

He desires to be buried in the Chapel at Middlesmoor in Netherdale 'where divers of my ancestors are formerly layde', and 'that Julian now my wife shall first have her jointure of what shall be due to her'. He makes her his residuary legatee desiring her to see him honestly brought forth at his burial. His executors were Christopher Wandesford, Master of the Rolls in Ireland, W. Norton the younger of Sawley, gentleman, and Major Norton of Richmond, Esq. to each of whom he gave a piece of gold.

Then he asked his executors to sell a parcel of land and to give the money,

'To my servant Richard Beckwith, £30 and my old grey Barbary mare.

12. Middlesmoor Church

   To my servant Jane Hardcastle £3
To my servant Isobel Duffield 40/-
To my servant William Trees 50/-
To my servant Margaret Aromond 50/-
   To my servant Francis Bramage, the grey mare he rides, called the lame mare. To Richard Yorke, my black mare, and to each of my other servants 10/-.'

He left to his nephew the new suite of tables at Gouthwaite and the three Turkey carpets (after the decease of his wife).

'Lastly, my will and mind is that my servant William Radcliffe be kept at my house at Gouthwaite by my nephew, with meat, drink and clothes for life.' Sir John valued loyal service after his experiences of plots and informers.

Quite some time elapsed between a death and a large funeral to permit preparations to be made for the feast, and to allow the malt liquor to be brewed. Sir John's oak coffin was encased in Nidderdale lead, and, draped in black cloth, was laid in the hall at Gouthwaite so people could pay their respects.

On the day of the funeral two strong horses wearing black plumes drew the shrouded four wheeled hearse up the dale. Whole households tramped miles from the outlying moorland farms and cottages to gather by the roadside. The servants, grooms, keepers and shepherds walked in the slow procession with the family. The rough road wound steadily upwards. The last mile and a half is extremely steep and extra horses had to be hitched on to the hearse. Even so they had a struggle to climb the last hundred yards to the church gate, past the cluster of stone cottages which made up the tiny village of Middlesmoor. Young John, with his cousins, formed the bearer party, and after a solemn service, the old man was laid to rest with his ancestors. From the church door is the view of the length of Nidderdale in all its wild beauty, every inch of which he knew so well.

At his funeral feast there were many good tales told of him, mixed with respect, admiration and humour, for he knew his land and his people, and they knew him.

CHAPTER VII

JOHN YORKE 1592? – 1638
OF
GOUTHWAITE

THE FOURTH JOHN WAS BORN AROUND 1590 soon after his uncle Sir John had succeeded his father Peter. Whether Sir John and Dame Julian were childless, or had had children who died at birth is uncertain, but as his brother Thomas and his first wife had none either, there must have been considerable anxiety over the question of an heir. The second marriage of Thomas to Frances Babthorpe, and the arrival of a son was celebrated with great joy in Nidderdale, as it was too at Downham.

Young John was in the direct line of inheritance from a very early age. As he grew up at Parcevall Hall he came to know and love the moors and the Nidd valley, as well as the families who lived there. Gouthwaite was his second home, and Aunt Julian made him specially welcome for he brought life and laughter into their elderly household. His many cousins lived nearby so he did not lack for companions with whom he could hunt and hawk, fish or ferret, trap or shoot.

His father, Thomas, had remained an open recusant and was presented as such in 1603 at Ripley, and in 1615 at Burnsall. He was closely connected with all the Catholic struggles in the West Riding, and both his wives were from strongly Catholic families. By the time young John grew up however the persecutions had lessened, for the Stuart administration was never as efficient in these matters as its Elizabethan predecessor. Even the new Oath of Allegiance in 1606 was not enforced strongly. As Government policy later revolved around the possibility of Prince Charles' marriage to the Spanish Infanta, pressure against recusancy was reduced.

When Wentworth administered the system after 1628, the net tightened again but the priests were not harried. Recusants had to pay a high levy but in return they could lease back their lands which had been seized.

At about the age of twenty two, the fourth John Yorke married Florence Sharpe from Northumberland. Three daughters were born, but no son, and Florence died young. In 1632 John married a second wife, Katharine, the daughter of Sir Ingilby Daniel, of Beswick near Beverley. It was after this marriage that old Sir John moved to Sleningford Grange and made over the Nidderdale estates to his nephew, and we may assume that the couple then moved into Gouthwaite.[1]

A long awaited son was born, just in time for his ailing great uncle to know that the succession was assured. It was comparatively rare for people to live to see their children grow up and bear grandchildren at that date.

The baby was duly baptised John, and John and Katharine took up the reins of their new responsibilities with cheerful hearts. Aunt Julian advised them on many matters and saw the dear baby as often as possible. No doubt old William Radcliffe kept them straight on the old customs and the way things ought to be done. If Marmaduke Lupton stayed on as their steward too, they were well served.

The pattern of life had changed little in Nidderdale. Although King Charles had dissolved Parliament five years earlier and was ruling with only the advice of his ministers the country was, in general, enjoying peace and prosperity.

Many trees had been felled in Yorkshire in the previous fifty years, for use in ship building, house building, fuel for the smelting mills and bark for tanning hides. The denuded woodland had been converted to pasture and people had to burn peat, turves and sea coal in their homes. Some of the common arable land had been enclosed but the manor courts kept careful watch on the ancient rights. Mining operations continued apace.

The increasing trade amongst the weavers, wool sellers, cloth makers, stocking knitters, leather workers, tanners, cutlers and local miners meant that many more horses and vehicles were using the roads and bridges. New laws had been made for their maintenance but they were difficult to enforce.

John Taylor reported that 'the roads were so rocky, stony, boggy and mountainous that it was a day's journey to ride the short distance from Wortley to Halifax'. The Ripon to Skipton road, along which John Yorke had to travel frequently, was 'so fowle and moorish as sometimes the inhabitants cannot pass but with great danger'.[2]

In each parish it was the duty of the unpaid overseer to see that the unwilling householders were organised into groups to work their six statutory days a year on the local roads. In the Ramsgill manor court roll erring individuals are named.

'John Craven of Studfold to repair his part of the highway in Ealand before 25 March next so that his neighbours may pass with their carriages as has been accustomed. Pain of 1s fine.' 'Inhabitants of Ramsgill to repair their side of the ford over river Nidd between Bouthwaite and Ramsgill before Whitsuntide next on pain of £1 for every week unrepaired.' They were also threatened with a fine of 5s a month until the footbridge over Ramsgill beck was repaired.

The most important bridges were paid for out of county funds. and the Quarter Sessions saw to their upkeep. At the Weatherby Sessions, held in Jan. 1639 before five J.P.s and a jury, it was noted that 'a common bridge called Halton Bridge. . . over the River Rible, leading between the City of York and Preston. . . is now in greate decay for lack of repair, and that the inhabitants of the West Riding ought to repair the same'.

In July the same Court ordered that ten pounds be forthwith levied on the West Riding and a further eight shillings at the next sessions. 'If the works be deferred a farr greater summe will not be sufficient.'[3]

The overseer, the constable and the churchwardens saw to the smooth running of each parish, and the bailiff or steward of the lord collected rents and dealt with the tenants.

The thatched or slated timber framed houses of the average Nidderdale smallholder were well built, with three or four bays, and one or even two chambers.[4]

Life for the deserving poor was made tolerable by the system of parish relief, but wandering beggars and vagrants received short shrift and were often whipped, or even branded with the letter R for rogue. Bastard children were usually bound apprentices, but the punishment meted out

13. Halton Bridge over the River Ribble

to women of evil or lewd behaviour is chilling. 'Mary Walker (having several times before offended in same kinde) shall (on a specified day) betweene the houres of nine and twelve be stripped naked from the middle upwards, and tyde to the Taile of a Carte. And shall be openly whipped from the one end of Thornton to the other until her body be bloody.'

It was laid down in the Ramsgill court rolls that,

'On pain of a fine of £1.10.0 no one was to harbour any travellers, viz potters, razor grinders, chimney sweepers etc with their asses or galloways (which hath proved to be a very great nuisance to the neighbourhood) more than one night, and the same traveller not to return to the same place within a great space of time.' Another rule made to prevent misuse of parish funds was that 'no inhabitant of Stonebeck Up or Down shall take in any family, common woman or child. . . without ensuring sufficient security to the churchwardens and overseers.'

John and Katharine Yorke lived at Gouthwaite for six happy years, planning their future together and then disaster struck. There was an outbreak of plague in Richmond that year so it is just possible that this caused John's death, but whether by illness or accident, it left his four year old son as the heir.

Chapter VIII

JOHN YORKE   1633 – 1663
OF
GOUTHWAITE AND RICHMOND

THE YOUNG WIDOWED KATHARINE was left with John's three daughters from his first marriage, their little son to bring up, and all the administration of the Yorke estates. Fortunately William Yorke, (old Sir John's brother), and his executors, Christopher Wandesford and the two Nortons, Maulger and Welbury, helped her in every way they could, and proved to be trustworthy advisers and friends. A portrait of Major Maulger Norton reveals a dark, handsome man wearing the long hair fashionable in Stuart times, with an intelligent, sensitive face and fine hands. He holds a handsomely embroidered glove, worked with gold thread.

He held extensive properties in and around Richmond, including his house St Nicholas, (a former Hospital which was closed at the suppression), and land in Aske, Newton Morrell, Barton, Theakston, Cleasby, Burneston Armathwaite and Manfield. He had married Christopher Wandesford's sister, and they had one daughter.[1]

Katherine Yorke is one of those wives about whom little more is known than her name and parentage. Having produced the heir, she faced up to her ensuing long widowhood with courage. Her household at Gouthwaite provided opportunities for exercising a huge range of talents. The intricate pattern set by the self provisioning of such an establishment revolved around its head, and in this case she was in sole command.

We know from the hearth tax returns that the house had eight fireplaces. (Apart from Ripley Hall with twenty, this made it one of the larger houses in the area.) The central hall with its long tables, chairs and stools led to a huge kitchen. The old bread oven was built into the thickness of the stone wall. A parlour lay the other side of the hall, with a small table, chairs and cushions. Upstairs was the great chamber, then several chambers of varying size. Some had four poster beds, some truckle, and for the farm men in the loft, there were mattresses filled with heather. A buttery, brewhouse, larder and milkhouse adjoined the house. In these stood hogsheads of ale and bowls of skimmed milk.

The members of the household, which included those working in the stables, garden and home farm, bred, fed and slaughtered cattle, sheep, pigs, poultry and fish for their own use. They grew and milled their own

14. Maulger Norton of Richmond

corn, brewed their own beer, reared, broke and shod their horses, grew, felled and sawed their timber, planted, picked and stored their fruit and vegetables. They sheared their sheep, spun and wove their own wool and flax, made their own clothes, embroidered their own hangings, prepared their medicines from herbs, and distilled, cured, and preserved every possible article.

In addition to overseeing all this in due season, Katharine saw to her children's education, her tenants demands, and the needs of her neighbours in want. She had to confer long and often with her steward, her barr master, gamekeepers and shepherds. She kept up a correspondence with her own family, read and discussed the national and local affairs, ordered in such necessities as were not locally obtainable, and rode around John's estates with him as he grew older.

She had the companionship of her husband's many cousins and connections while she watched little John grow and mature, and she succeeded in making good matches for her three step-daughters.

Elizabeth was betrothed to James Leslie, Lord Lindores from Scotland; Frances to Thomas Barney of Dole Bank, Ripon; and the youngest, Jane, to General David Leslie, later Lord Newark, also a Scot.[2]

During John's early childhood King Charles became desperately in need of money for naval and military expenses and he was finally obliged to recall Parliament in 1640. The discontent felt in the country over the recent levies of ship money was growing, especially in the inland counties. Archbishop Laud's insistence on uniformity in the church was also vexing the more extreme religious groups.

In the new Parliament were many inexperienced members from the shires who although not afraid to oppose the King, respected him and regarded the sovereign as sacred. John Pym had had years of experience in the Commons, and although a moderate man at heart, he saw that pressure, even amounting to revolutionary pressure, must be brought to bear on the King and his ministers. Under his leadership an Act was passed so that taxes levelled without the consent of Parliament were declared illegal. Thomas Wentworth was impeached and sent to the scaffold. Pym and Hampden presented The Grand Remonstrance which was carried in the Commons by eleven votes. In January 1642, the King with 300 swordsmen entered Parliament and, taking the Speaker's chair, demanded the surrender of Pym, Hampden, Holles, Hazelrigg and Strode. These men, forewarned, were already safely in the City. The indignation at Charles's act knew no bounds, and from then on the City was lost to him.

Charles withdrew to York where, in June, he received an ultimatum from Parliament in the form of The Nineteen Propositions. When he rejected these, Parliament appointed a Committee of Safety and put the Earl of Essex in command of a force of ten thousand men. The Civil War had begun.

Little John Yorke's earliest memories must have been of the talk about King and Parliament, and by the time he was seven or eight, the country was dividing into Royalists and Parliamentarians, or Cavaliers and Roundheads. His great uncle William remembered that Walter Raleigh had argued back in 1615 that 'that the monarchy, if it were wise, would come to terms with the House of Commons, the organ of the gentry'.[3]

John's Catholic background put him among the Royalist supporters, who formed the large majority in the West Riding. Most of the Yorkshire gentry families were neutral at first, and many remained so throughout. Those who felt important issues of principle were at stake, however, put them before family loyalties, and in some cases the head of the family fought on one side, and his heir on the other. As Dr Cliffe shows there are no easy explanations for the choices made.[4] At first the Royalists, accustomed to the chase with their gamekeepers and huntsmen, had the military advantage over the Parliamentarians, but later the zeal and equipment of the Roundheads gave them the upper hand.

The Civil War was not social or economic but political and religious, and it was embarked upon most reluctantly. As John Yorke grew up the war news was part of his daily life. The Queen's arrival in York with fresh munitions was cheered to the echo by the local people. Reports of Prince Maurice's attack on the armed 'lobsters' of Waller's army, and Prince Rupert's capture of Bristol were breathlessly retailed by servants back from the market, or packmen from along the Dale. A lull during the winter of 1643, left the King with the larger part of the country behind him.

The whole of Yorkshire was under Royalist control, but the advancing Scots, who were being paid by Pym and had allied themselves to the Parliamentarians, surrounded York Castle and laid siege to it. There were 18,000 foot and 3,000 horse in the Scots army, (some of which were under the command of David Leslie who had married Jane Yorke).[5] Prince Rupert and his cavalry hastened from Wales to help the King, and saved York at its last gasp. But at the great battle of Marston Moor in July 1644, the Royalists, although they made a glorious fight, were soundly beaten by the combination of Cromwell's Ironsides and the Scots. 'God made them as stubble to our swords,' wrote Cromwell. Four thousand men were slain. The North was lost.[6]

The war caused substantial damage in Yorkshire with the general disorder and breakdown in administration, and the unruly skirmishes of the soldiers.. However the seasonal life in self-reliant Nidderdale cannot have altered greatly, and even after the shock of Marston Moor, ten year old John Yorke could still ride safely across his land, and hunt, fish and train his hawks as his father had done.

In June 1645 the last great trial of strength was made at the battle of Naseby where Cromwell drove all before him. By the spring of 1646 all armed resistance to the Parliamentary Army was finished. The King placed himself in the hands of the Scots, and General Leslie guarded him in Newcastle, more as a prisoner than as a guest.

By 1648 Cromwell was Dictator, and the only remaining fruit of victory to pluck was the head of the King. Preparations were made for Charles's trial, for which there was no precedent nor sanction in law.

John Yorke was fifteen when King Charles was tried. He may have already been studying at Queen's College, Cambridge, but Gouthwaite had a well stocked library and John would have had access to the serious literature of the day, both political, religious and poetic.

A stream of pamphlets and treatises were pouring from the presses. Chillingworth, Hales, Jeremy Taylor, Prynne, Lilburne, Winstanley as well as Milton, Marvell and Herrick all contributed to the ferment of ideas that swept the country then. Milton's passionate love of freedom may have influenced John, but whatever his own young views, his family were aghast at the prospect of the King's execution, as was almost the whole nation. When the deed was done, the groan of the watching throng was echoed everywhere. Most of his subjects considered his son now to be the rightful Charles II, as did most of Europe, but England was now a Republic, and was governed by a Council of State.

Although John grew to manhood under Puritan rule, his family retained their land and position. By and large the agricultural life in the Dales continued as before, but certain interferences with traditional customs greatly provoked the country people. The Puritans forbade bear baiting, cock fighting, sports and maypole dancing. All feasts, especially Christmas, were banned and even going for a walk on Sunday, unless it be to church, was punished. The independant Dalesmen, used to cheerful and rowdy celebrations, found this outrageous, and were as stubborn in their resistance as ever.

Owing to old Sir John's close association with Maulger Norton of Richmond, the two families knew each other well. Maulger visited Gouthwaite and John often stayed with Norton in his beautiful old house, with its two end gables, and a balcony running across the front of the first floor. He depended greatly on his wise counsel in the absence of his own father. Maulger's only daughter Mary grew up alongside John, and it seemed right and natural that a marriage should eventually be arranged between them.[7]

In the year that they were married, 1658, Cromwell, the Lord Protector died. In the confused year after his death, the young couple watched with alarm the Army contending for power with Parliament. General Lambert in England, and General Monk in Scotland, confronted each other, but it was Monk who had the confidence of the Scots and the sympathies of the Republicans.

The hopes of the whole country rose on hearing, on January 1st 1660, that Monk had received his long hoped for invitation from the House of

Commons to come to London. By then, after twelve years of constitutional experiments the people in England were longing for a return of the monarchy.

A newly elected House of Commons and the peers assembled. With Monk's sound advice and Chancellor Hyde's concern for Parliament and precedent, Charles II's manifesto was drawn up in which he promised to leave major problems to Parliament to settle.

This was drawn up about the same time as was the marriage settlement between John and Mary. It is dated 15 January 1659. John's Nidderdale and Appletreewick estates were to be held 'part to the use of John for life, Mary for life, Thomas, their eldest son, then younger children. . .'.

On his part Maulger Norton gave John forty acres of land in Bargate Green in Richmond, 'the decayed castelet called Hudswell pele and other premises', as part of his daughter's portion.[8] It was there on a delightful site on the banks of the river Swale that John began to build a large house. Sheltered by a steep grassy bank to the north, it lay below the clamour of the market place, and had the old castle walls in its view as well as the peaceful river.

Encouraged by the prospect of the King enjoying his own again, and the birth of his own son, John did not stint his resources. His father in law wished to see his daughter living in style. The result was an imposing mansion of three floors, with a large hall, parlour, and other rooms including a kitchen, workshop, buttery, brewhouse, milkhouse, passage and cellar, with adjoining stables. The upper floors had large well lit chambers, hung with 'painted cloths and hangings of red and green and gay with painted borders', floor carpets and even window curtains. On the walls were framed pictures and maps. A looking or seeing glass hung over the mantle in the parlour, on which stood a clock and candlesticks.

The Yorkes heard of the landing of the royal party at Dover on May 25th, 1660, with great joy. The King was met by General Monk and made a triumphal journey to London. It was only eight years since he had fled for his life from the very Army whose soldiers were now presenting arms in his honour. It was now firmly established that the Crown was the instrument of Parliament, and the King a servant of his people. The restoration achieved what Pym and Hampden had originally sought. A new concept of sovereignty had been born.

The country was impoverished by the ordeals it had been through. The King relinquished his feudal dues and was instead granted revenues for life by Parliament.

Some scapegoats had to be executed, though Charles strove hard for pardon for as many as possible. The corpses of Cromwell, Ireton and Bradshaw were pulled out of their coffins and hanged on a gibbet at

15. The South West Prospect of Richmond in the County of York Printed by Sam'l and Nat'l Buck, 1749, Garden Court, Middle Temple (showing The Green)

Tyburn. These ghoulish acts satisfied the ferocity of feeling amongst the public, and the country slowly settled down.

John Yorke also settled into his new life with his devoted Mary. She had produced a son and heir within the year, whom they had named Thomas, and they lived partly at Gouthwaite and partly in Richmond.

John was knighted at the Restoration court by Charles II in 1660, and was made a Justice of the Peace for the North Riding.[9] He was listed in the Wapentake of Claro at 'one horse and arms'.

Later, he was appointed commissioner for assessments for the North and West Ridings, and he therefore found himself spending more and more of his time in Richmond.

In 1089, Richmond had been planned as a new town around the imposing stone castle which the Norman knight, Count Alan Rufus, (son of Count Eudo de Ponthieve), had built. It stood in a commanding position above the river Swale, and was rightly named 'Strong hill'.[10]

The walls then enclosed eighteen acres, on half of which lay the castle. There were three main gates, Frenchgate, Finkel street gate and Bargate. Soon suburbs grew beside each gate and spread outwards.

About 1145, Count Alan's grandson granted his borough of Richmond to his burghers, or burgesses, confirming certain rights and privileges, customs and liberties. In return for an annual rent, the burgesses enjoyed their lord's protection free from all feudal obligations and interference. Some pasture land known as the Whitcliffe Common, was granted to them also later and their rent was raised.[11]

After a time, the term 'burgess' came to mean not only those who paid the rent, but those who held burgage properties. Later still it referred specifically to a select group of twenty four who represented all the burgesses, and who with four bailiffs, governed the town with the consent of the common people. From 1584 onwards, two representatives were sent to Parliament.

When John and Mary were married, Richmond was a busy market town, recovering from the violent outbreak of plague fifteen years earlier. Approximately 1,600 people lived in about three hundred and fifty houses, mostly stone built, and the castle, although almost in ruins, still dominated the scene. The river formed the southern and eastern boundary. St Mary's Church stood outside Frenchgate, with the grammar school nearby. Corn was ground at the three mills, the Green, Kirk and the Castle, and three fulling mills stood along the banks of the river. The wet cloths were stretched out on the tenter grounds beside them.

Two chapels, the Friary, and Hudswell Peel Tower were amongst the larger buildings, together with St Nicholas, Bowes Hall, Hill House and Mayor Wetwange's house. Half the ordinary houses were small dwellings with but one or two hearths, while another 45% had between two and four hearths.

The tradespeople were still mostly organised in the old medieval guild system, and there were thirteen guilds. The largest industry was that of the leather workers – the skinners, tanners, glovers, cordwainers, curriers, saddlers and bridle makers. (A pair of mens' shoes then cost three shillings).

The making and sale of knitted stockings and caps was an important industry too. (A dozen pairs of stockings cost six shillings, but the knitter only received less than half the price.) Cloth, metal working, building, milling, brewing and baking were all minor industries. Guild officials called searchers checked on the standards of work and reported any fault to the Guild. Apprentices were bound for seven years, and a watch was kept on their indentures to see fair usage between master and lad.

The goods were sold in open fronted shops on the ground floors of houses, or on stalls in the cobbled market. Richmond was a centre where corn, brought in from the Vale of York, was sold to Wensleydale, Dentdale and Craven, where conditions were not so suitable for its cultivation.

On market days each week the press and bustle of the crowded market square drew in scores of traders. Cattle driven in from the dales mixed with herds from Scotland, and sheep from the moors around were penned ready for auction and slaughter in the Shambles. The shepherds and drovers stood talking in small groups, the Scotsmen a little apart, their plaids over their shoulders. Heavy wagons filled with bales of wool, coal, iron, tar, timber, salt, and groceries rumbled over the bridge across the river, and their loads were hauled painfully up the steep hill. Lines of pack ponies, carrying lead from Swaledale wound their way in and out of the traffic, following the bell mare.

Shouts and curses, the clink of trace chains, the stamping of hooves and the rattle of cart wheels mingled with the cracking of whips and the bellowing and barking from the cattle pens.

Stout women, carrying butter, eggs and cheeses from the villages squeezed their way through the throng. Others brought dozens of pairs of stockings and woollen caps, knitted at home, to sell to the hosiers. Buckets full of live fish slopped water over the feet of unlucky passers by. Apprentices dodged the glancing blows bestowed on them and hastened on their errands.

At 11 a.m. the corn bell was rung, by which time all tolls and stall charges should be paid, and before which no corn should be sold. Crafty merchants avoided these bye laws by repairing to an inn and conducting their business there. (There were over thirty inns and taverns in the town, with stabling for 228 horses and beds for 100 guests.)

Three times a year, (on the Saturday before Palm Sunday, the first Saturday in July, and the Festival of the Holy Rood, September 14th), a fair was held, by royal charter. On those days the roads leading to the town were thronged. Farmers and their families in carts, merchants in gigs, droves of cattle and sheep, shepherds, packmen, pedlars, quacks, tumblers, rogues and vagabonds streamed into the town to take part in the festivities, and to buy, earn, beg or steal whatever fairings they could. The inns did a roaring trade. The bailiffs, constables and searchers were on constant call. In the days that followed, local Justices like Sir John Yorke, would be kept occupied dealing with cases brought before them, on charges of brawling, thieving, assault, forgery and many more.[12]

There were manor courts, and barmoot courts as well, and long and frequent discussions with his steward from Nidderdale for John to attend to, in addition to his duties in the Riding.

This was the life of the borough when John took up his responsibilities, and in 1661 he was one of the two people elected to represent it in the new Parliament. The Cavalier Parliament, as it was named, was the longest standing in English history. The many landed gentry in it who had lost fortunes in the royal cause had no intention of losing Parliamentary rights gained in the struggle. With the disbanding of the army, the control of the country had returned to the county families.

This Parliament recognised that there were religious groups definitely outside the National Church, but would not follow the King's preference for toleration. Instead the code drawn up under Lord Clarendon really destroyed all chance of a united National Church, by a series of statutes which succeeded in excluding the Presbyterians, the Catholics and the old Republicans from any municipal office. It demanded total assent to all and everything contained in the 1662 Prayer Book. Nearly two thousand ministers refused to comply and were deprived of their livings. They were also forbidden to preach within five miles of their previous parish. Because this confined municipal office and membership of Parliament to Royalist Anglicans, the lines were drawn up in political life between the Conservative and Radical traditions which still persist today.

Although John Yorke's Catholic connections were strong, he and Mary appear to have conformed to Puritan rule while it lasted, but were no doubt glad to see the pre-war church restored, with its bishops. In the Dales a few staunch Catholics held on to their beliefs, but many more dissented and joined the Quakers or Presbyterians. In the new and independent mining village of Greenhow, a strong dissenting congregation was formed by Richard Freeman, a former officer in Cromwell's army. Over the next twenty years, the non-conformists were persecuted in much the same way as the Catholics had been, and some of the pressure on the latter was relieved.

Through his marriage to Mary Norton, John had gained a right to burgage property in Richmond, and had bought in more also. The borough had returned two members to Parliament since 1576, elected by the mayor and burgesses. The latter held their ancient burgage rights and properties which gave them two votes each. They numbered about two hundred and seventy and were among the more prosperous of the inhabitants.

Local Members of Parliament were normally chosen from among the borough's more substantial citizens, or the local gentry up until 1645, several coming from the Bowes, Pepper, Wandesford and Wyvill families. Then two anti-royalist members were imposed, but after the Restoration, the seats reverted to local land owning families.

In 1661 when Sir John Yorke was elected, the market place resounded with the cheers of his supporters when the results were announced. Those wearing his 'favours' were liberally 'treated' in the local inns. As he rode off on the six day journey to Westminster he must have felt that he had achieved a good deal in the previous three years, and Dame Mary, though anxious for his wellbeing, was proud to see him go.

He knew she was capable of attending to his affairs in his absence, and her excellent parents were close at hand. Young Thomas was thriving and the plans for the house were well under way.

Lord Wharton, a powerful member of the Whig party, owned the manors of Aske, Healaugh and Muker as well as much land to the north of Richmond. He befriended John, who quickly gained attention in the House. He was appointed to serve on various committees, including that of elections and privileges. He was also nominated for committees for confirming public Acts and considering the shortfall in revenue.[13] At that time members sat from 8 a.m. to 2 p.m., on every day except Sundays, and used the afternoons for committee work. They disliked debates by candlelight. Members were not permitted 'to walk over the seats, or whisper or discourse during debate. . . to the disturbance of the House'. If they so offended they had 'to pay 12d to the box for the Use of the Poor'. [Today's problem of tolerable noise allowed in the House is not new.]

Among the more senior of John's fellow members was another of Lord Wharton's friends, Sir Ralph Assheton Bt. of Downham, who had been returned six times for the borough of Clitheroe.

Each time John rode the long journey back home, he saw 'all England as a planted garden, cornfields and hedgerows, villages and noble houses'. The roads were appalling, but the scenery 'all Nature' to an extent we can scarecely imagine. He found fresh developments at his new house. Mary proudly showed him the latest additions to the building, a gun room, a steward's room, a justice's room where wrong doers and witnesses could be interviewed, and some fine stabling.

The proportions of the house were very pleasing, in the style of Wren, and a fine formal garden was in the process of being laid out to enhance the whole. As well as the oversight of this enormous under taking, Mary, assisted in all things by her father, had kept her finger on the pulse of the Nidderdale estates and the lead mines, which were the vital sources of their income.

We can be sure that she arranged a splendid dinner for John's home coming, set out in the new dining room with its ornate plaster ceiling. A brace of stewed carps, a dish of fowl, (six pullets and two dozen larks all in one dish), a jowl of hot salmon, perhaps for the first course; then a neat's tongue, a dish of prawns, a tanzy, a great tart and cheese to finish. There was an ample supply of canary, (at 2s a quart), and claret, (at 14d a quart) with the dinner, and no shortage of pasties and the strong beer called 'mum' for the servants afterwards.

This meal was eaten at about 4 o'clock. The custom had grown up that the gentlemen remained in the dining room, while the ladies went to drink tea in the withdrawing room. Later in the evening the men rejoined them and card tables were set out.

By 1662 a little daughter was born and named Mary after her mother. Thomas enjoyed the company of his sister and the grandparents from St Nicholas visited them frequently.

Early in 1663, John was appointed to two new committees in the House of Commons. One was on bills against pluralities, and the other for the better observation of the Lord's day.[15] He had considerable experience of divided religious loyalties and confused congregations, and was not afraid to speak out about his electors' views. The Parliamentary sessions in his day were irregular in length and duration, and largely depended on the King's need of money.

Just before the Easter recess he was taken ill, and only in his twenty ninth year, on April 3rd he died, near London. The news reached Mary when a rain-soaked servant on a spent and muddied horse arrived at The Green with a letter. Utter disbelief numbed her, and it was some days before she could even grieve. Her parents hastened to her, and it was her father and brother who made all the complicated arrangements for John's body to be brought back home.

The tailor was sent for to measure the household for blacks. The carriage was put into mourning. A herald came to paint the hatchment for the outside of the house. Beer was brewed and preparations made for the feast. Two weeks later the coffin was conveyed into the house to lie under a black catafalque in the hall, surrounded by tall candles. All Mary's bright hopes seemed to be laid in it too.

Then came the last long journey to Middlesmoor, and the procession along the dale in which Maulger Norton had walked once, if not twice, before, following the bodies of John's great uncle and his father. This time as they reached the church, his twenty-five year old widowed daughter leaned on his arm and drew on his strength, while five year old Thomas and two year old Mary gazed uncomprehendingly at the solemn faces and sombre clothes.

The brass engraved in John's memory was in Latin. It reads,

'Here lies the body of Sir John Yorke of Gouthwaite, Knight, Member of Parliament for the ancient borough of Richmond, under the most illustrious King Charles II. He died near London when Parliament was assembled 3 April 1663 A.D. in the 29th year of his age, and was survived by one son Thomas Yorke and one daughter. This monument to his lasting memory was erected by his most faithful and sorrowing wife Mary. May he rest in peace.'[16]

CHAPTER IX

THOMAS YORKE 1658 – 1716
OF
RICHMOND, GOUTHWAITE AND BEWERLEY

After John's death, his young widow was helped in every way by her parents and advisers. In July the same year when the seasonal duty of riding the boundaries of each manor came up, it was not merely left to the steward, but carried out in person by Maulger Norton for his grandson Thomas.[1] On those wild moor lands it was essential to check the bounds regularly, for disputes could easily arise over veins of minerals or rights of chase, and marks or stones be shifted by ill disposed neighbours.

When Thomas was still only thirteen, Welbury Norton rode the boundaries of Appletreewick common and the Forests of Bardon and Knaresborough, and the moors of Hertlington, Hebden and the bordering towns on his behalf. This was no small undertaking and a long hard ride which took days to accomplish. Sometimes as many as fifty or more people took part on horseback, and others on foot. After such a day, an Ingilby steward wrote to his master, 'The good ale we had from (you at) Ripley made all the neighbours at a distance know our business, for we drank all upon the green swath, and laid several of the locals and fair foresters dead out upon the plain'.[1a]

Only two years after John's death, the news reached Richmond of a fierce naval battle against the Dutch. The next spring, horrifying tales were heard of the Great Plague raging in London. Richmond too had suffered this and the older townspeople shuddered, remembering their own trials. In London at its height 7,000 people died in one week. Mary must have known many who lost relatives that year.

In the autumn of 1666 came the Great Fire of London. Although terrible damage was done, it helped to extinguish the plague. Broadsheets and pamphlets described the terrors. The Puritans held both plague and fire to be a direct visitation from God on the immorality of the age, and the laxity of King Charles' Court in particular.

Whether Mary agreed with this view we cannot know, but there is evidence of her firm hand with her own family, as well as her competence in completing the huge house and gardens. (Celia Fiennes, in the diary of her travels, noted that 'Richmond had fallen into much decay, but there were two good houses, one being the Yorkes' mansion and the other the D'Arcys'.)

A letter from Mary's little daughter at a young age gives an indication of her strict and careful upbringing. It begins,

'Honoured Madam, Having nothing worthy your acceptance but the tender of my Duty I here offer you the firstfruits of my Pen. I should have been gone this day to the Dancing School if it had been fair weather. My Poyne (pony) is done and come home. Be pleased to honour her with a line from you who presents her humble duty, craving your blessing who is your dutiful daughter

Mary Yorke'

It is addressed 'These to my Honoured Mother The Lady Yorke at her house in Richmond', and sealed but not dated.[2]

Dame Mary was as determined as her own parents had been, to preserve and protect young Thomas' inheritance, and to further the education and careers of both her children to their very best advantage. Her efforts can be traced through the many legal documents in the family records. Leases, assignments, mortgages, and bonds brought in money for necessary expenses. She saw to it that suits were brought against miners who were defrauding their lord of his proper rights, and neighbours who disputed his boundaries.[3]

'Copy of the bill of Thomas Yorke, infant, by Dame Mary his mother, and copy of the answer of John Holmes and others in Chancery suit about the boundary between the manor of Appletreewick and the Forest of Knaresborough. . . 1673.'[4]

Not content simply to preserve the inheritance, Dame Mary added to it. In 1674 she purchased the manor of Bewerley near Pateley Bridge, formerly Fountain's Abbey land. The monks had had a grange, worth £16.16.8, with 'edifices, lands, medoos and pastors, moors and wastes and grounds called Bewerley Moor and Greenhow Moor, and . . . a sheep gate for a wether flock yearly from Michaelmas to St Ellen's Day'.[5]

This property included a chapel, (built by Abbot Huby in 1494) and chapel garth, several farms with pastures, and cottages, so it was a valuable addition.

As Bewerley lay only a mile or two south of Gouthwaite, the Yorke property now ran for a nine mile stretch from Middlesmoor down the dale. The smelt house, mill and lead mine and the rest of the 900 acres of moorland, (arranged for enclosure and improvement), were bought in at a later date.

Dame Mary had a concern for education beyond just that of her own children. This is clear from two of her actions on record. After acquiring Bewerley she found that there was no endowed school in the whole of

16. Abbot Huby's Chapel, Bewerley. Painted by Mary Yorke, 1837

Nidderdale, only a small private one at Dacre. Her family had taken an interest in Richmond Granmmar School and Mary at once saw the need. In 1678 she granted Bewerley Chapel and the chapel yard for the use of a school house and the convenience of a schoolmaster to teach 'English, Latin, Greek, (and if thereunto qualified) the Hebrew tongue, and such other Rudiments of Learning as are proper and necessary for a Schoolmaster to Teach and Profess in Order to the Advancement of Learning and Pious learned Education'.

The Trustees were Thomas Yorke, Welbury Norton and five local men, Samuel and Richard Taylor, John Beckwith, Robert Inman and Christopher Lowson.[6]

One can imagine the first twelve little farm lads in their leggings and clogs, trudging down the fellsides and clattering into the chapel yard as the school bell rang. What an onerous task the master had, first to shape their fingers round a slate pencil, then to teach them to form squeaky pot hook letters, then to read and reckon up by rote. The prospect of graduating to Latin, Greek or Hebrew seems daunting indeed. Crammed together on wooden forms, the boys did raise some body heat in the cold, high, stone-flagged chapel building, but they also jostled and jogged each other, which no doubt drew harsh punishments. But they were used to discipline and some of their parents jumped at the chance of an education. Others thought it a waste of good farming time, and kept the boys at home to work.

Dame Mary had thought for the children higher up the dale as well, for, after the assignment of Moor House Farm in Stean Pasture in 1684, she and her son gave the consideration money, amounting to £100, to the people in need in Stonebeck Up and Down, and 'to putting children out to a trade'.[7]

So the hard early years of her widowhood were filled with home and business affairs, and, as her children grew older, she spent much time and thought on possible marriage partners for them. She also received some advances herself, as a letter shows,

'Madam, When I had last not only ye honour but ye highest of satisfactions in waiting upon your Ladyshippe, I did then a little discourse with you concerning a small piece of land in Richmond. But I am affraid soo unwilling was yr Ladyshippe to thinke me serious in my other addresses. . . therefore I shall not untill I know how most ageeably to suitor your Ladyshippe's Mynd herein. Madam, my journey to London, unhappily as justly I call, occasions distancing me from your Ladyshippe unavoidably. . . (which) makes me repeatedly to wish that some indispensable (but pleasant) affair may also carry your Ladyshippe up this winter. Otherwise to me London will appear as far short of Richmond, as Richmond, by your Ladyshippe's presence, accords to all other places in my opinion, but probably you will believe this with as little faith as you used to do my personal protestations, those for which by more effectual proof I am able, I will give your Ladyshippe demonstrations that I am, if willing.

Madam, your Ladyshippe's most passionately
H. _larwood'   October 1st 1678[8]

Clearly Dame Mary froze off poor Mr _larwood. It is very likely she had plenty of practice in the art, being a well endowed young widow, with only two children.

As early as 1676, when her daughter Mary was not yet fifteen, Edward Blackett of Newby Hall expressed the wish to marry her. He had lost his first wife, and had no children. He wrote to his father, Sir William Blackett in Newcastle, a letter which reveals much of the current view on marriage arrangements and filial duty.

'9th September, 1676

In performance of my duty which I owe and shall ever pay you, these are to give you an account that last week I had some discourse with a Gent., who is a near relation to my Lady Yorke, and a very kind friend of mine, in reference to some overtures (from) me to my Lady's daughter, and I am assured my Ladie will make her equal to the best fortune in the countie, and further, there is only one brother belonging her, and 16 or 18 hundred pounds per annum, and ye Gentlewoman without all – my humble request is, you would please to make a journey to Richmond, where my Lady now is and will be this 14 days, and after some conference with my Lady, you will give me your advice in this great affair. I know I will undergo some censure in your opinion and of the world for this haysty proceeding, but I cannot avoyyd itt, for if I omitt this good opportunitie, am certainly informed there is a Gent. (Sir Christopher Wandesford's sonn) who intends to make his addresses there very shortlie. . . delay may be dangerous and. . . my lady. . . (The bottom of the letter has been torn off.)[9]

At about this time, two portraits were painted of Dame Mary and her daughter, in identical poses. They both wear elaborate dresses of silk, with low cut necks, and wide sleeves gathered in with beads, and long V shaped bodices. The mother's is a rich tawny colour, the daughter's pale green. Their faces resemble each other remarkably, with wide set intelligent eyes, straight noses and firm determined mouths. The artist has cleverly contrasted the youth of the girl and the maturity of her mother.

Dame Mary's plans bore fruit and 1680 turned out to be a triumphant year for her. At the end of October, Mary married Edward Blackett, and a magnificent wedding it was, with nothing spared in entertainment or feasting. Blackett settled £4,000 on his wife and in return received leases of land in Ramsgill as part of his marriage settlement.[10] He and Mary lived at first at old Newby Hall, but ten years later, under Dame Mary's influence (I feel sure), they pulled down the old house and built the present one, in the style of Wren, further from the river. It bore a very close resemblance to The Green, and is a most attractive and imposing house. The large formal garden was laid out with long axial vistas.

Sir Edward became M.P. for Ripon, and he and his wife lived in considerable style. They employed a butler, a cook, a cook's man, a brewer, three husbandmen, a coachman, a smith, a wheelwright, and two gardeners. Mary had a housekeeper, a lady's maid for herself, a maid for her eldest daughter, and another for the younger daughters. There

17. Dame Mary, wife of Sir John Yorke

were also two chambermaids, a dairy maid, a kitchen maid and a poultry maid. Their annual wages amounted to nearly one hundred pounds.

In one respect however the women of those days were sisters under the skin, whether rich or poor. They bore as many children as nature permitted, lost many and suffered much. Mary had six sons and six daughters, of whom several died young. Her husband died in 1718, aged sixty-nine, and they were both buried in Ripon Minster.

18. Mary, wife of Sir Edward Blackett

In November 1680, the final arrangements were also completed for Thomas's marriage. Katherine Lister was the daughter and heiress of Thomas Lister of Arnoldsbiggin near Gisburn in Lancashire. Her parents had both died when she was only three months old. She was brought up by her grandmother, the Widow Lister, who later married Sir John Assheton. Part of Katherine's inheritance was the manor of Worston, with the water driven corn mill and some cottages. She and Thomas

Yorke were married at Kirkby Malham church on December 7th 1680, and their marriage settlement was witnessed by an Assheton and a Yorke. This union drew the Yorke interests over towards Craven and Lancashire, although they continued to live in Richmond.[11]

Thomas, aged twenty two, had been well trained in his filial duties by his mother and grandfather and now, with his new wife, was ready to take up his inheritance. They moved into The Green and it seems that Dame Mary went to live with the Blacketts at Newby.

There are two oval portraits of Thomas and Katherine. His eyes have a look of his mother but his young face does not yet show much character.

Katherine's portrait may have been painted some time after their marriage for, although she was two years younger than Thomas, she appears older. She has a fine, rather narrow face and a long nose, but looks intelligent and alert.

For her it was a great change from living quietly near Gisburn with her grandmother, to moving into The Green, in a town of about 1,500 people. No doubt Lady Assheton had trained her well in household matters, but for Katherine to have to step into the shoes of her capable and commanding mother in law, and to manage her large staff, must have been extremely daunting. Thomas, accustomed to a matriarchal household, may have expected a great deal from his young bride, and their early years could have been difficult.

However, Dame Mary was both wise and welcoming to the wife she had chosen for her son, and she showed her the same care and affection that her own parents had given her. Yorkes, Nortons, Listers, Blacketts and Asshetons were now all connected by marriage. Their multiple interests in local government, politics, sport, business and kinship wove a fresh web into the network which joined Yorkshire and Lancashire.

Thomas and Katherine lived through the period known as the Age of Enlightenment, and through the reigns of five sovereigns. It was a vigorous age of growing wealth and civilisation, and of great achievements. As well as the great literary names of Defoe, Pope, Addison, Dryden and Swift, architects, painters and landscape gardeners had wide recognition. Together with interior decorators, furniture makers, china manufacturers, silversmiths and bookbinders, they were employed and encouraged by the owners of the spendid houses built in this era. The population of five and a half million grew, industry expanded, and Britain became a world power.

Although the Yorke family affairs were prospering in 1680, there was considerable agitation in the country over the succession to the throne. James, Duke of York, the brother of the King, was a confessed Catholic, and both the Anglicans and the Presbyterians were united in their fear of a

THOMAS YORKE OF RICHMOND, GOUTHWAITE, BEWERLEY 1658–1716

19. Thomas Yorke of Richmond

return of papacy. As the profligate Charles had fourteen bastards, but no son, his niece Mary was the heiress presumptive. When she married the Protestant William of Orange, and healed the breach between Holland and Britain, some people looked to him as the successor. Others however, hoped for the Duke of Monmouth, the King's loved but illegitimate son.

There was a real fear of civil war in 1682. A plot was laid to capture the King and his brother, but it failed. Three years later a sudden stroke

20. Katherine, wife of Thomas Yorke

carried off Charles II at the early age of fifty six, and, despite all the appalling struggles over the past eighty years, a Catholic was once again on the English throne.

From November 1685, when James II began to appoint Catholics to positions of power, the two groups in Parliament, who had begun to be known as Whigs and Tories, drew closer to each other against the King. By 1688 everything pointed to the outbreak of a civil war. William of

Orange was secretly invited over by the Whig leaders, but the King's army was large and well equipped. Then the Queen gave birth to a son and the whole country had a vision of a long line of Papist monarchs ahead. Rumour ran riot.

Finally, on December 23, 1688, James II fled from England to the French court and William of Orange ascended his father-in-law's throne. The whole nation had been in favour of expelling James but there was no lawful government, as Parliament had been prorogued. William immediately declared war on France. So it was that the event known as the English Revolution expelled the last Catholic king from the British Isles, and finally committed Britain to a long and fierce struggle with the French.

Britain was now divided by party instead of by creed. More than four hundred out of the five hundred M.P.s were mainly squires sitting for boroughs, whose constituents were townsmen.

The Convention Parliament was elected and Thomas Yorke, who held four burgage properties, was returned for the borough of Richmond as a Whig. His friend and neighbour, James Darcy, brother of Lord Holderness, was returned with him. Lord Wharton, said by some to have been 'an unequalled and unscrupulous adept in the art of electioneering', befriended Thomas as he had done his father.[12]

Wharton joined with the other Whig leaders, Lord Halifax and Lord Shrewsbury, in proposing that the crown be shared jointly between William and Mary. This was opposed by the Tory party, who had been largely created from the Anglican gentry and the Established Church by the Earl of Danby. They wanted Mary on the throne in her own right. Parliament eventually agreed to the Whigs' proposal, and William gained the throne for life. Mary's sister Anne, was persuaded to give up her right of succession to William, should Mary predecease him.

The disinherited James II, aided by the French King, landed in Ireland with a strong French Catholic army. His supporters, known as Jacobites, soon controlled the whole of southern Ireland.

William dissolved the Convention Parliament, and in 1690 the Tories won the hotly contested election and Thomas Yorke lost his seat. That year William drove James out of Ireland and refitted the English and Dutch fleets, thus regaining command of the sea. The war against France continued and was a heavy financial burden on the country. Fortunately, out of the newly organised Whig party, (containing amongst others Somers, Montagu, Orford and Wharton), Montagu proved to be a very able financier. He became Chancellor and, copying the Dutch National Bank, he started the Bank of England as a private corporation. He also reorganised the coinage and this enabled the burden of King William's wars to be borne.

The economic activity of the period between 1688 and 1720 was not equalled again for forty years. Amongst other industries, there was an upsurge in mineral working, and the ownership of mines and their working was not thought to be beneath the dignity of even great noblemen.

The Earl of Cumberland, Thomas Yorke's neighbouring landowner at Skipton Castle, was lord of the manor of Grassington. He had had a detailed document drawn up at his Barmoot Court in 1642.

'No man was to conceal any ore, lead or wood whereby to wrong the lord,' and equally, the Barmaster was not to alter the true and lawful weights at the mill to wrong the miners.

The lord was to provide timbers at 4d a dozen, and a good washing vat 'and a gallon to fill the same withal'.

'When there was a new workstone laid it shall have the pan filled at my lord's charge with lead according to former custom, and every man to leave it full as he finds it on pain of 6s 8d.'[13]

Each such barmoot court set out minutely stated rules so the barrmaster and jurors could judge the disputes and quarrels and keep the peace, for, wrote Defoe, 'the miners are of a strange, turbulent quarrelsome temper. . . very hard to be reconciled to one another. . . bold daring fellows in their search into the bowels of the earth'.

Like miners the world over, these miner farmers in the Dales were a hardy breed, independent, industrious, and satisfied with very little. The risk and chance of unexpected gain inspired their efforts. The uncertainty and danger they faced made them wary and alert, firm believers in the supernatural. Darkness, weird noises, and sudden accidents gave rise to tales of boggarts, spirits and knockings – lamps were blown out, ladders were thrown down, and rocks fell. 'Witch stones', with hollow centres, and lucky horseshoes were used as charms to keep the boggles at bay.[14]

Defoe, observant on his travels, and seeing the old world through sharp modern eyes, describes seeing a miner emerging out of a mine up a kind of iron ladder set in the angles of the shaft.

'He was clothed all in leather, had a cap of the same without brims, and some tools in a little basket he drew up with him. He was as lean as a skeleton, pale as a corpse, his hair and beard a deep black. . . very tall and lean. . . looking like an inhabitant of the dark regions below.'

He had been at work sixty fathoms below with five other men. If he had good luck he could earn about five pence a day. His wife and five children lived in a very poor but clean and neat house. Shelves contained earthenware, pewter and brass, and two whole sides of bacon hung in the chimney. A sow and piglets were running about at the door; a little lean cow was feeding on a grass place nearby, and some barley was growing on an enclosed piece of ground. The wife told Defoe that she could earn threepence a day washing the ore, and this made up all they had. Yet the children were 'plump. . . ruddy and wholesome' and the woman said she had a good husband and was content.

The miners were a sociable crowd and enjoyed drinking and singing together in the local pub, and telling stories of their exploits. Most households kept a hound, and hunting on foot was their sport all the year round.

Many of the Yorke family deeds of the period also reflect the increase in activity. Thomas received a warrant from the Archbishop of York to dig firestone on the moors in 1698.[15] He gave a lease to two yeomen to dig coal in Bradforddale for seven years at a rent of £12 a year,[16] and owned other coal mines in the area too.

He leased some of his lead mines in Appletreewick to three Richmond men for twenty one years at £3 a fother, to be smelted at his own mill.[17]

He brought lawsuits over many years against Lord Fairfax and John Holmes for digging lead unlawfully in Appletreewick.[18] On February 14th 1689, in a case of trespass,

'The defendants entered a close called Appletreewick Moor containing 200 acres, within the parish of Burnsall, broke the grass. . . and carried away eleven dishes of lead ore value 5/-. Trespass continued till June – damage 40/-.'

The witnesses called in such a case were the elder men of the village who had lived and worked there all their lives. This reliance on the memory of retired men meant that they were respected in the community, and still played an important part.

Between 1683 and 1685 Thomas gave several new leases on land in Nidderdale for rents varying from £1.10 to £15 per annum, reserving in each case the rights for wood, hunting and minerals. In one instance the tenant had to keep a dog or hound for Thomas.[19] One lease lays down a payment of '4 shillings instead of horse rakes and boons, 4 hens at Christmas and 35s to be paid on change of tenant'. All these tenants had a second occupation as well as farming.

At this time Thomas and Katherine between them owned land in Nidderdale, Appletreewick, Richmond, Armathwaite, Newton Morrell, Barton, Burneston, Manfield, Cleasby, Theakeston, Skeeby, Denholme, Ovenden and Worston.[20] Some of this had been inherited and some they had purchased over the years.

It would be extremely interesting to try to estimate the acreage of the Yorke lands at this time, but it is difficult for two reasons. One is that only

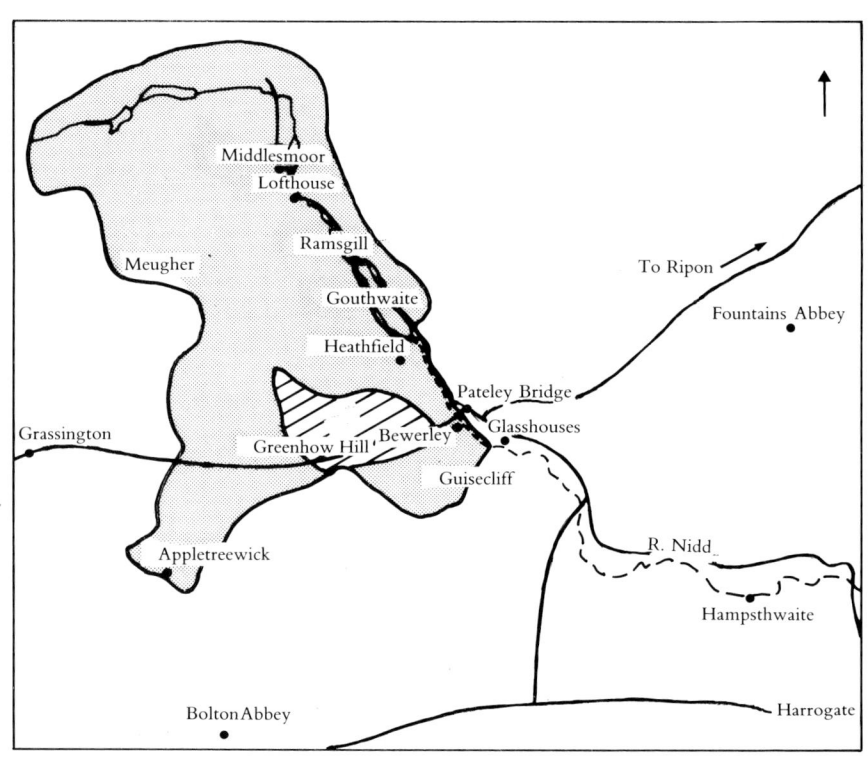

21. Map of Nidderdale showing the Bewerley estate

a handful of tenancy agreements remain, with no estate maps or terriers of the period. The other is that assessing the acreage of farms then is very difficult. Dales farming has always revolved around the extensive moorland grazing for cattle and sheep, but this was excluded from any written assessment of the size of the holdings.[22] Acreages stated usually refer only to arable, meadow or walled in pastures, so can be very misleading.

Some of the rent rolls remain however and show that Thomas's total rents for 1706 came to £1,651.19.0. From this he had to pay out over £576 in taxes, tithes, repair of buildings, relief of the poor for the constables in each of more than twenty parishes, (with highway repairs), and replacement of stock. This was before any personal or household expenses.[23]

A tenant could be listed as having a holding of just ten acres, but might be able to graze his stock over three hundred more acres, by common agreement. Some of the vast moors were 'stinted', or restricted as to numbers of stock. They were shared out in 'beast gates' or pasture gates, defining a specific number permitted, that number varying with the quality of the grazing. Others were unstinted. The custom varied from manor to manor.

Local knowledge of moorland boundaries was not lightly passed on to would-be surveyors or assessors. A Crown Commission in 1618 set out to survey land around Middleham. The tenants flatly refused to 'help or direct them in any way' saying 'Each man doe know his certain numbers of Gates, Joists or Stints and doe pay for the same by Ancient Tenement'.[24] Without local help it was impossible, and the Commissioners finally went discomfited away.

All this made life hard for an absentee landlord, or one with a steward he could not trust.

Thomas, however, had grown up to know the area and his tenants, and attended closely to local matters. When the manor court was opened with the customary call 'Oyez, oyez, all manner of persons who have suit or service to perform to the lord of this manor, draw near and give your attendance' Thomas was usually present. His concerns included the regular boundary riding,[25] a question on an exemption from tolls for men of Lancaster at the Appletreewick Fair,[26] and an agreement with the Vicar of Kirkby Malzeard about the stipend for the curate of Middlesmoor[27]. (This curate fared better than his predecessor under Thomas's great grandfather had done.)

His mother Dame Mary died in 1694, and part of her will reveals her strong family feelings,

'. . . to my dear daughter Dame Mary Blackett all my Silver Plate and what gold I shall have by me at Newby . . . and all my furniture, cloths and apparrell. To my dearly beloved son Thomas Yorke what goods or furniture I have at his house in Richmond, and . . . £1,200 to be divided between dearly beloved son Yorke and daughter Blackett. I to be buried at Ripon . . . not using any vain glory therein, and also my grave and my dearly beloved daughter's may be as near each other as they conveniently can.

I having ever an equall and dear Love and Affection for my said beloved son and daughter, I do earnestly desire that when it shall please God to take me from them, true and Intire Love and Affection may remain between them, and that we may all meet in the Joys of Heaven . . . .'[21]

At The Green, although the Yorkes lived in some style and kept a large staff, they were on much closer terms with their employees than was the case in the south. The grooms and menservants who rode alongside their master in all weathers, and the maids who dressed and tended their lady, comforting her through many weary times in childbed, were friends and confidants. They spoke their minds and were valued for it. The shepherds and keepers, the huntsmen and falconers were independent men of good sense and sound knowledge, if little or no book learning. Children in the household were strictly brought up and often beaten for misdemeanours, but they knew and trusted the members of the household from whom they often received more kindness and understanding than from their parents.

A craze for using china and Delft ware to decorate houses, and calicoes and chintzes for curtains, followed the fashion introduced by Queen Mary. The King delighted in gardening, especially in growing evergreens. He was also interested in fine paintings. Thomas and Katherine followed suit and enhanced The Green with new furnishings, china, plate and pictures.

One magnificent addition was made specially for Katherine in 1697.[28] It was a most beautiful dressing table set in silver, each piece being engraved with the Yorke and Lister coat of arms. She described it in her will,

'A large glass in a silver frame, two candlesticks, two salvers, one comb box, four powder boxes, two brushes and a pincushion,' but this gives no impression of the beauty of its design or the quality of the silver. A considerable quantity of other silver is listed too.

Katherine must have delighted in these lovely pieces. Four of their seven children died in infancy. Thomas was away from home a great deal. Her happiness had to be found in her home and her pleasure in adding to its treasures.

Another of these was a handsome leather bound Bible, containing the Prayer Book and a metrical version of the Psalms. In this Katherine kept the family records, (which have been continued down to the present day). She recorded the births and deaths of her babies, and also, sadly, the deaths of her two unmarried daughters at twenty one and twenty eight.

For the latter, Elizabeth, an inventory of all her possessions was made.[29] It is fascinating to know what clothes a young lady of that age was held to need. They included,

Five gowne coates of cloth	One spinnet
Ten pairs of shoes	One little galloway
Twelve day shifts	One whipp
Eleven night shifts	One sidesaddle
One velvet hood and scarf	Two pearl necklaces and crosses
Four sets of night clothes	Ten fans
Seven sets of head clothes	Three pairs clogs
Ten muslin aprons	Six petticoats and hoops
Eight pairs wool socks	Four paires of stays
	24 coloured handkerchiefs
Eleven undercaps	23 books
Eight stomachers	Two pen sets
18 cloth aprons	Black aprons and hoods
One riding habit trimmed with silver	One red satton gown
One cloth riding coat with hood	

The only surviving daughter, Katharine was married in 1703 to Sir James Clavering of Axwell Park, Co. Durham,[30] who settled a handsome sum upon her and proved a kind and loving husband.

As time went on, the burgage properties in Richmond were gradually bought up and became concentrated in the hands of a few families, the Wyvills of Constable Burton, the Whartons of Aske, and the Darcys and Yorkes of Richmond. Out of a population of about 1,500 only 273 burgesses remained enfranchised after 1696. In 1695 Thomas Yorke was returned to Parliament again, and he retained his seat over the next twenty years, consistently voting with the court Whigs. He was twice given leave to go into the country, and his only committee was to hear a petition from a Yorkshire village against its Catholic landlord.[31]

The sessions in the houses of Parliament had by then become more regular, and usually ran from November to May. This period was divided into three, with adjournments for four to five weeks at Christmas and about ten days at Easter. The amount of time an M.P. spent in the House varied greatly. Some negligent members of burgage boroughs scarecely went near them, but those representing counties and large towns were more conscientious. In the smaller boroughs local political life centred round the electioneering itself more than round the ends such electioneering was supposed to serve.

However, as Thomas Yorke gives the impression of a responsible man, we may assume his attendance was somewhere between that of the best and the worst of his contemporaries. It is reasonable to believe that he spent at least three months of each year in London, and, after his daughter's marriage, his wife sometimes accompanied him.

Queen Mary had died of the smallpox in 1694, making Princess Anne heiress presumptive. Anne had been reconciled with William, and by 1696 the war with France reached an inconclusive end.

The political story of William III's reign, in which Thomas was closely involved, was a continuous see saw. The Whigs managed two or three years of war, then the Tories were returned to power as the people wearied of it. The landed gentry were suspicious of the Whig creation of the Bank of England. They feared the rise of political influence in the merchant classes enhanced by a credit institution, but the labels Whig and Tory were not as clearly defined as are the political parties of today, and men accounted one or the other did not always vote accordingly. The Whigs on the whole were well organised and stood for religious toleration, the Protestant succession and the defeat of France. The high Tories believed in the old order, Crown and Church allied. They were cool on war and disliked the political power of dissent. There was also a Country party of about one hundred and fifty, mainly country gentlemen, a majority of whom would usually support the government.

The London that Thomas spent his time in as an M.P. had changed considerably from the days when his ancestor, Sir John, had lived in Wallbrook.

The Great Fire had destroyed the medieval timbered houses with storeys projecting out one beyond the other across the narrow filthy streets. Much ground had been given up to leave room to enlarge the streets, and trim rows of neat brick houses had replaced the wooden ones. Squares like Bloomsbury Square were planned around large mansions, and fashionable people moved into them to be near the nobility. The latter had moved out from the City and the Strand into the regions of of Covent Garden, Piccadilly, Westminster and Bloomsbury, and Thomas may have taken a house in that area. The merchant princes and shopkeepers still lived and slept with their families above their places of business in the City. Defoe noted that 'several villages formerly standing, as it were in the country, are now joined to the streets by continued buildings. Westminster is in a fair way to shake hands with Chelsea, and

St Giles with Marylebone. . . whither will this monstrous city then extend? The extent of the circumference of the buildings of the cities of London and Westminster and the borough of Southwark. . . is now over 36 miles.'

He descibes the City as running from Temple Bar to the Tower, which was hardly ever used as a state prison any longer but contained the Mint, an arsenal, a zoo and a museum. (The old mint in Southwark had become a refuge for debtors.) The great edifices of the City were the Royal Exchange, the Bethlehem or Bedlam Hospital, the Bank and the Custom house. Above all the other buildings and churches, St Paul's Cathedral was, he says, the most exceeding beautiful and magnificent. In amongst these were the offices of the South Sea Company, the East India Company and the Hudson's Bay Company whose stocks supported 'that prodigious paper commerce called stock jobbing', a trade in which 'many thousands of families are deeply concerned'.

One reason that the order in the city was better than previously was that 'it was best supplied with water of any city in the world, the water brought in large leaden pipes from distant springs to several beautiful conduits'. Other improvements were the provision of the two great hospitals, St Thomas's and St Bartholomew's, eighty three charity schools, eight public schools and twenty seven gaols. Mr Guy's Hospital for incurables was just being built.

The busy river traffic reflected the bad state of the roads. Along the Thames came an infinite variety of provisions to the London markets, corn, leather, fish, broadcloth, meal, hay, lead and coal. These were sold at Bear Quay and Billingsgate, Stocks Market and Covent Garden, Leadenhall and Smithfield and the Haymarket.[32] In 1720 Defoe counted over 2,000 sail in the Pool of London, 'not reckoning barges, lighters or pleasure boats, but vessels that really go to sea'. He also states there were twenty two dry docks, three wet docks for laying up and thirty three ship building yards.

When Thomas Yorke decided to cross to Southwark, he hired a boatman to row him over, for there was only London Bridge then, athrong with horses and carts. As the boat slipped along, he saw the river sides 'full of villages and charming gardens, and a hundred fine houses.' Near Hampton Court the river was pleasantly rapid, clear and clean, the bottom in view and fish playing in sight. Green fields soon came into his view.

When Parliament was sitting, Thomas would have put on his fashionable long skirted coat which buttoned all the way down, and added a low crowned, wide brimmed hat over his carefully curled locks. He adjusted his jabot, took up his cane and walked to the House of Commons to take his seat about 9 a.m. If the day was wet he rode in his sedan chair.

The chamber in which he sat was St Stephen's Hall, the long narrow chamber which now leads to the Central Lobby. Westminster Hall, 'though noble in size, had no doors, so resembled a great barn, three hundred feet long', and the other old buildings of the king's old palace were in a sorry state. Westminster Abbey was almost a ruin. The Courts of Justice and the Exchequer were near Parliament but the approach to them was along King Street, 'a long dark dirty and inconvenient passage', and past 'little offices for clerks, rooms for coffee houses, auction rooms and toyshops'. Men with barrows, selling hot spiced gingerbread or walnuts cried their wares, and the sign boards over the shops swung to and fro in the wind.

The centre of social life in London then was the coffee house and Whigs like Thomas, frequented the one in St James's. It was one long room divided up by wooden partitions into small areas, each with a table. This served not only as a club, but was also the place where the latest news could most easily be heard. The spoken word then did many things that print does today, and no Member of Parliament could keep up to date without a daily visit to his favourite coffee house, just as no merchant could afford to miss a visit to Edward Lloyds' coffee house to hear the latest shipping news. No alcohol was allowed on the premises, but coffee, tea or 'Hot Chocolate at 12d the quart' was on sale.

It was there that Thomas and his cronies would have heard the news of the death of Princess Anne's only surviving son, aged nine, from smallpox in 1700. By an Act of Settlement Parliament declared the grandson of James I next in line. (His mother had been Queen of Bohemia.)

The following year however, when James II died, Louis XIV announced that he recognised James II's son as rightful King of England. The British were furious at the interference of a foreign despot, and again prepared for war.

Only a few months later, on a cold February day in 1702, the air inside Thomas's coffee house was blue with pipe smoke, and the usual cross section of his friends, M.P.s, merchants, 'blue ribbons' and private gentlemen sat, talking freely as Englishmen were proud to be able to do. Suddenly there was a commotion in the street outside. Mine host went to the door and heard shouts of 'The King! An accident!' He caught hold of a passing fellow and questioned him, then came back indoors, grave faced. He told the company that the King's favourite horse Sorrel, had stumbled badly on a molehill earlier in the day at Hampton Court and the King had been thrown and was badly injured. He had in fact only broken his collarbone, but complications set in, and, although he remained able to

THOMAS YORKE OF RICHMOND, GOUTHWAITE, BEWERLEY 1658–1716

22. Thomas Yorke of Richmond, when older

speak clearly, he went downhill fast. Within a fortnight he was dead. In his last hours he commended Marlborough as the fittest man in the realm to guide the country.

Queen Anne ascended the throne amidst considerable rejoicing for William had never captured the affection of the people. She had led the life of a semi-invalid, bearing seventeen children (only one of which reached childhood), but she was no weak willed woman. Her three certainties were that the Anglican church must be protected at all costs, the war against France won, and that the Whigs were enemies of the monarchy. A period of Tory prosperity seemed to open. The Tory view was that England should only intervene in the Continental struggle by sea power, but the Whigs, though out of office, advocated great military efforts. At any event Marlborough's masterly military manoeuvre at the battle of Blenheim in 1704 saved the allied cause, and raised England to the rank of a first rate power.

Whig support for the Government was essential, both for the war effort and also for Godolphin's great Act of Union with Scotland in 1707. For hundreds of years the Scots had hated the English as overbearing neighbours, while the English had regarded the Scots as little better than barbarians, so it must be accounted one of the great achievements of the eighteenth century.

By 1708 the Whigs were back in power, with Wharton, Walpole and Somers in high office, but in the bitterly contested election of 1710 they were routed. It was however to be the last four years of power for the old Tory party. The Queen died in 1714, and a middle aged German, who spoke little English, and understood the country's institutions even less, became George I.

The Whigs triumphed in 1715 and acted with vigour over the Jacobite uprising in Scotland, which was soon crushed. In the following year the Government passed the Septennial Act, which by extending the period between elections, gave M.P.s more time in which to gain experience and assurance. It also enabled the Whigs to rule Britain for the next forty years, through two more reigns, and to give the country moderate, peaceful and tolerant government under Walpole. He was the King's choice and always considered his office to be dependent on the King's will. These then were the events in the last years of Thomas Yorke's life.

One of Katherine's nephews, Thomas Lister, had joined him as an M.P., and his eldest son John, who oversaw affairs at home after he left Cambridge, had evidently followed his father's interest in politics too. The younger son, Thomas, is described as a merchant and lived in Hatton Gardens in Kensington. The only daughter, Katherine, lived in County Durham.

There is no record of the cause of Thomas's death but it occurred in his fifty eighth year. To have a swift end to an illness was everyone's hope when medicine was so rudimentary. Contemporary descriptions of weeks of acute suffering, and the groans and cries of the dying in agonies of pain, make heart-rending reading. One hopes Katherine was spared the feelings of helpless anguish common to those close to the patient.

Thomas was laid to rest with due ceremony in Richmond parish church. The mourners wore black silk hatbands and gloves, the servants new black coats and waistcoats, and the pallbearers black gloves. Before the service hot chocolate, cake and wine was served to those assembling at The Green. Then the hearse set off drawn by two horses, followed by six chaises which carried Katherine and John, and other members of the family. Crowds of townspeople lined the steep cobbled road leading to the church, and the stewards and tenants from the various estates walked behind the carriages in the procession. They returned to the house in the same order, where again wine, cake, toast and chocolate were handed round. The tenants and servants were given beer and a good meal before they set off home.

John was the heir but Thomas left a legacy of £2,000 to his wife together with £450 a year for her lifetime. John also gave her annuities which increased to £32 a year by 1730.[33]

Katherine lived on at The Green at first, but later spent much time with her daughter at Axwell. She died fifteen years after her husband, in 1731, so did not live to see John marry.

In the will that Katherine made when her husband died, she made over all her estate and money to her eldest son John,[34] including £90 in the Queen's lottery, and excluding only some personal chattels, linen and the silver dressing set. This will was witnessed by her son Thomas.

Eight years later, it seems that she felt John had not done his duty by her during her widowhood. She had also grown to dislike her son in law, with whom she was living. In a fresh will made in 1725, which must have caused an upheaval in the family, she wrote,

'I give, devise and bequeath all my lands. . . unto my son Thomas Yorke and his heirs. . . for ever. I give unto my eldest son John Yorke ten pounds and no more by reason of his undutiful and unnatural behaviour towards me and his hard usage of me. I give unto my son in law James Clavering the sum of five pounds and no more by reason of his disrespectfull and unhandsome behaviour towards me and his causeless Contention with me, which hath occasioned a change of my Intention to do for him and his family.'

CHAPTER X

JOHN YORKE   1685 – 1757
OF
RICHMOND, GOUTHWAITE AND BEWERLEY

JOHN WAS BORN IN 1685, the same year as Bach and Handel. He was thirty-one when he succeeded his father and was brought up at The Green knowing all his Yorke, Blackett, Norton, Assheton and Lister cousins well. He would often have visited Bewerley and Nidderdale with his parents as he grew older, and, early in his life, come to his responsibilities as the heir. At thirteen he was sent to school at Eton, which, after being tutored at home, may have been a formidable experience. His father paid about £25 a year for his board, instruction, clothes and all charges. Although the flogging in many schools was cruel, a contemporary of John's wrote, 'I think Eaton is a very easy scholl. I am shure one cannot offend without they be meare rakes indeed.' The school year was divided into two halves, so John only made the long journey home in July and December. In the latter month the roads were little better than muddy farm tracks and travellers met with many hazards. Droves of sheep and cattle on their way to market, troops of horses and colts, strings of pack ponies, and heavy wagons drawn by six or eight horses crowded the way. Rivers overflowed their banks and swamped the road. Axles stuck fast in the mud, and wheels broke in the potholes. Long waits at cold dirty inns had to be endured while repairs were made. 'Was terribly bit by the Buggs last night,' wrote one traveller, 'and my face and hands swelled terribly'.

After Eton he went to the family college of Peterhouse, Cambridge in 1703.[1] There he joined in the dicing, gambling, horse racing and cock fighting of the day. The discipline had declined and no examinations were needed to gain a degree. He no doubt enjoyed the celebrations which were made for his sister's wedding that year.

The area around Ripon was still noted for the finest galloping horses. . . 'swift horses, bred for the light saddle, that is to say for the race, the chase, for running or hunting'. The country was full of dealers and breeders of horses, and the names of the stallions and the breeds were well known by all.

Defoe wrote, 'Match two horses and the barb (Barbary or Arab) may beat Yorkshire for a mile but the Yorkshire shall distance him at the end of four miles; the barb shall beat Yorkshire on a dry soft carpet ground, but

Yorkshire for a deep country'. There were constant contests and races, both private and public, and the spectators often galloped up the course behind the racers, yelling encouragement. We can be sure John, with his father's fine stable, wagered a good deal of money on such trials of speed and endurance. He was accustomed to 'fine fleet horses, strong enough for charging, fleet enough for hunting and tempered enough for travelling'.

He took an early interest in politics[2] for he is listed as a member for Richmond from 1710–1713 when his father was still sitting for the borough, and he continued to hold the seat there for the next forty years.

By 1718 the Yorkes owned about twenty burgage properties. Lord Wharton had bought up as many as he could, so for a time Wharton and John Yorke held sway, though not, it is said, without some dubious practices. Marmaduke Wyvill claimed that 'notorious bribery' had been used in 1714 to secure Thomas's election. His complaint was referred to the Committee of Privileges of the House of Commons but no report was ever submitted. The fifth Lord Wharton, for long the party's great organiser, was succeeded by his son in 1715. He became a Duke, soon ran into debt, and turned from Whig to Tory. It was during that period, when Walpole rose to be first Chancellor, then leader of the party, that John Yorke entered into an arrangement with Lord Holderness and Sir Conyers d'Arcy. They 'entered into a strict league and union to support each others interests', and agreed that every burgage house of the d'Arcys should, for ever, give one vote for the Yorkes, and vice versa. They also agreed that before the next election Sir Conyers should lay out £2,000 and Yorke £1,000 to be made use of for ever in their joint family interest. By 1721 Lord Holderness was writing to John to say he was 'glad our affairs go on prosperously'.[3] The union of the two families, coupled with Philip Wharton's erratic career, overthrew the Whartons.

The death of George I in 1727 caused an election earlier than this alliance wanted. d'Arcy wrote to John on June 20th,

'Dear Jn., The hurry and bustle of the sudden and unexpected news of the king's death has occasioned among us in this part of the world, prevented me answering the favour of your letter as soon as I designed, and must I fear lay us under the necessity of troubling our friends at Richmond with an earlier application than than either they or we would have wished. . . .'

John feared that some rival might buy up Wharton's estate and burgage houses, but in the end d'Arcy managed to do so. But other difficulties arose. Wyvill, Bathurst of Arkengarthdale and Davile, the mayor of

Richmond, banded together against Yorke and d'Arcy. The mayor, as returning officer allowed all the freemen of the trade guilds to be named 'burgesses', and admitted them to vote. It was also claimed that he created new burgages and disqualified old ones. Wyvill and Bathurst campaigned busily. The description of the visits and meetings made by the agents in such an election make lively reading. The expense accounts reveal the entertainment of freeholders at various inns, the hire of transport and horses to the polls, and even the free accomodation provided. Each candidate gave out coloured cockades for their supporters to wear in their hats. Yorke and d'Arcy paraded the town on horseback with their followers bearing flags, but Wyvill and Bathurst hired a band and were chaired around by their supporters, making a great commotion.

The treating and entertainment went on for weeks but in the end the numbers of the 'new burgesses' won the day, and Wyvill and Bathurst were declared elected by 823 votes. An uproar broke out at the declaration. No one could gainsay the numbers, but there were plenty to join in noisy protest against the means used to gain them. Inflamed by the free liquor the rival supporters brawled round the town, punching and fighting most of the night.

Yorke and d'Arcy rode off to London and petitioned Parliament to seek support for their protest. Sir Conyers anticipated that 'our worthy friend Matt Wyvill and his mayor may meet with a warm reception at the Bar of the House. . .'. The Commissioner of Stamps told Conyers that nearly thirty Richmond people had been admitted without the necessary legal stamp papers. d'Arcy warned Yorke to see that their agent, Ralph Close, made sure none of their voters could be so disqualified. He ends this letter, 'Parliament will not meet till Jan. 20th so I hope you will have sufficient time to entertain yourself with your Rural recreations, which I wish may afford you every imaginable satisfaction'.[4]

During February 1728, Bathurst and Wyvill collected about 150 signatures for a petition in their favour, but to no avail. Their case was defeated in the House of Lords. They were then unseated and Yorke and d'Arcy declared elected. Parliament declared that the only burgesses with the right of election were those with the ancient 'right of pasture in a common field called Whitcliffe Pasture'. So, by this, even the mayor and aldermen, who had been specifically enfranchised in 1668, were now without a vote unless they owned burgage houses.[5]

It is not difficult to imagine the intensity of local feeling after this result, but perhaps support for the mayor may have dwindled when he turned out to be on the losing side.

For the next thirty years d'Arcys and Yorkes represented the borough in peace and tranquillity and remained close friends. In 1730 d'Arcy wrote to John '. . . I hope to be very well enabled to encounter you at a game of bowls on Hornby Green, in the mean time I desire you will accept my thanks and believe me with great truth, Your most faithfull and humble servant. . .'.

23. Anne, wife of John Yorke

In 1732, at the age of forty seven, John Yorke completed his negotiations to marry the Hon. Anne Darcy, daughter of James Darcy M.P., 1st

Baron Darcy of Navan. She was a cousin of Lord Holderness, and it was clearly an ideal match between the two families.[6] From her portrait it can be seen that Anne was a lively girl with a fresh complexion and cheerful aspect. She appears a good deal younger than her husband, in his corresponding portrait.

They no doubt entertained a good deal both at The Green and in London, and attended many masquerade balls, routs and assemblies. Anne's costume in the portrait may well have been one specially made for a masquerade, for guests often dressed as shepherdesses or characters from plays.

On these special occasions the guests were provided with 'a very genteel dinner' about four o'clock. A typical menu might include first some soles with lobster sauce, spring chickens and tongue, a fillet of veal roasted with truffles, and pigeon pie. Then cheesecakes, apricot pie, stewed mushrooms and trifle. Tea and coffee were served about six o'clock, then a band played for dancing, violins, a bass viol, hautboy, French horn, tabor and pipe. Minuets were followed by country dances. Card tables were set out and many people enjoyed a game or two of quadrille, faro or loo. Some gambled heavily.

About ten o'clock, supper was brought in which often included a fine large ham, veal cutlets, oysters, some tarts and a syllabub, melons, apples pears and nuts. This was accompanied by quantities of punch, red and white wine, beer and cider.

During the forty years John was in Parliament he became close friends with the leading figures in both parties. Some of these kept splendid houses built in the classical style and containing beautiful furnishings. Their long dinner tables were decorated with artificial gardens designed round miniature temples and pillars wreathed in flowers, with urns and figures. The rich silk dresses of the ladies with their stiffened skirts, and their carefully dressed ringlets and glowing jewellery were complemented by the elegance of the gentlemens' coloured silk coats, powdered wigs and silver buckled shoes. Conversation was an art, and leisure allowed it to flourish. Wit and gossip, politics and scandal, discourse and religious topics ran through the evenings, but in the day time the men were quite ready to enjoy a cockfight, a bear baiting or even a public hanging.

Drunkeness was common amongst men of all classes, and both sexes gambled freely at cards and dice. Tobacco was smoked in long churchwarden pipes, but not usually in the ladies' presence. As swords were worn by all fashionable gentlemen in London, and as many of them grew well drunk by the evening, quarrels and duels were frequent and dangerous. In the country however, greater opportunities for exercise and sport reduced the drunkeness, and swords were seldom worn.

Life was lived to the full in the country houses. Zeal for the chase, and for agricultural improvement took the master out on his horse at all hours, and the mistress was kept equally busy indoors and in her garden.

Breakfast was no more than a cup of ale or chocolate, and a country gentleman might ride to hounds all day, go coursing for hares, or walk up partridges, plovers and landrail behind dogs, carrying his muzzle loading gun. He would think nothing of a twenty mile journey on horseback, so he would be ready to tackle what sounds to us a huge meal by evening.

When John and Anne entertained their friends and relatives in Richmond the guests would drive up in their carriages about three o'clock and assemble for dinner. The table was decorated with some of the beautiful collection of family silver. Tankards, sugar castors, salvers and dishes were all engraved with the Yorke, Lister or Darcy arms. The first course could be a dish of freshly caught trout from the Swale, three boiled fowls, a couple of roasted duck, a neck of pork and a plum pudding. Puffs, apricot dumplings, custards and a lemon cream followed, and both red and white wine was drunk. After dinner the ladies withdrew to have tea and coffee in the new withdrawing room.

The walls of this room were no longer panelled but hung with silk. The chairs, carved by Chippendale, had seats of the same silk and the woodwork was gilded.

A large and handsome looking glass in a carved and gilded frame hung on one wall, and the room was lighted by an imposing chandelier holding expensive wax candles.

When the gentlemen rejoined the party, the card tables came out, and the backgammon sets, and there was usually some music during the evening. Around a light supper of roasted pheasant, (shot at Bewerley), a tongue, a currant pudding, a blamange and some nuts, the conversation and merriment continued till midnight or after. Then the sleepy grooms harnessed up the horses and drove the guests home in the moonlight.

As Anne had no children she was able to go about with John in London, visit the playhouse to watch Voltaire's clever ironic pieces, and Garrick's plays, and attend any important events to which he was invited. They saw Gainsborough's new portraits and heard the latest of Handel's Oratorios. They also attended the races at Richmond, for which John had a special gold pass.

They may have gone to take the waters at Bath which was then such a fashionable haunt, and met Beau Nash at the height of his powers. (Lord Holderness wrote to John from there to say, 'For my part I have been so slashed and butchered (by the surgeons) since I came hither that it will be yet two months before my sores will be tolerably healed'.)[7]

24. John Yorke M.P. for Richmond

Anne must have spent a good deal of time on her clothes and on sending and answering invitations. Her own family also had numerous connections with whom to keep in touch, both in London and Yorkshire, but we know from her letters that she was also a practical, capable housewife. Her finger remained firmly on the pulse even during her many absences from home.

Two years after her marriage she wrote to their steward, Francis Lodge, in Richmond,

'Frank, We are glad to hear by your letter to me last post that all our affairs goes forward for prosperity at Richmond, and pleased with your assurances of dilligence in keeping our family orderly in our absence.' After some detailed instructions about Hangings for the Bedchamber, she goes on, 'If the weather be as calm and sunshine as is here with us, I would have you tell Tom Leaming not to neglect fireing air into my greenhouse in the middle of the days. I want to know how all our quick (live) goods does of every species, and if either of my cows are calved yet. Our hamper came safe. . . I wish you all your healths, I am your faithfull mistress, A. Yorke.'[8]

Two years later she wrote to Frank,

'. . . I hope all my servants moves about their business in a Regular manner in our absence. I shall depend upon you to let me know if any of them dont as I dont know how much longer I may stay here (Helperby). Would be glad not to lose the present opportunity as tis fair good weather for filling the remainder of our empty Hogsheads with Ale. Would you sett Betty to brewing as I hope she and you can manage it to be good. You must make what room you can to sett what more is to be brewed in ye Ale and Strong beer cellars, as none more must be put in ye Arch'd cellar. I hope ye seeds I sent to Tom Leaming come safe; if he can spare us a little baskitt of apples to keep some for your Master's eating when he returns, send me some by next week's carryer hither. . . . The pens you made me last prove all very bad ones, so try and make me a few more and send with the apples. I would have ye green window curtains which are in ye Garret where you lay, put up in my dressing room, and I hope blue ones are there to put into the green ones place, but it may be done at leisure. Pray take care of fire and all affairs. I am your friend, A. Yorke.'

Naturally many of the orders and letters concern travelling arrangements, and marketing.

'Remember my Pillion seat be sent along with the mare and ye Chariot. Tell ye cook to kill a couple of hens on Saturday night next. As I meet with plenty of chickens here, would have you make inquiries for some for me. Bespeak them but dont buy any except you meet with them only in ye publick markitt. Tell Alice to make ready ye green bed for Lady Darcy, next to my room. Tell Anabel to put my hens into ye hut and feed them with oatmeal and meat, and to clean them out every day.'

One April she writes,

'Make a better markitting against I come besides Beef and Mutton, a quarter of lamb, a calf's head and feet, and a little fish if their (sic) be any good. . . I hope fat geese and chickens are not wanting. If the gardener can cutt a large dish of asparagus against ye carryer coming here next Tuesday, you can send some, and a Dish of Trouts and Eels hither by him.'

John's letters are more formal. They begin 'Francis Lodge', and end, 'Do not fail observing these orders punctually, I am your faithful master, John Yorke'.

In one he says,

'. . .I find now you have so many doubts and want advice and think the miners are not to be depended upon, (which I understood by you before there were some you could trust), I think this project so hazardous to your circumstances had much better be laid aside, at least till I come down. . . in the mean time I desire you'll mind affairs at home and do not build castles in the air to give yourself or me any more uneasiness. I recommend steadiness in your conduct, a contrary behaviour will always displease me. See my dogs and horses are well taken care of without and within doors, without any waste, that the hay is well fodder'd and the mould well shaken out.'

The daily hazards of travel, horses foundering or taking fright, carriages overturning or harness breaking, provided a constant topic too. Far more long journeys were regularly undertaken than we imagine today, in all weathers. In one letter John describes a journey in February,[9]

'We had a favourable journey, only had the misfortune to break the hind axle tree, by indiscreet management of the coachman, betwixt Newark and Grantham after we had cleared the bad roads, which lost us seven hours repairing so we proceeded no further than Colesworth that day.'

For all the high standard of living that John enjoyed, he was as likely as the next man to face conditions such as Defoe described in 1720,

'. . .when we were come up near the top of the mountain, the wind blew exceeding hard and blew the snow directly in our faces, and that so thick the cold pierced our very eyes and made it impossible to keep them open to see our way. We could see no track except when we were showed it by a frightful precipice on one hand and a uneven ground on the other, even our horses discovered their uneasiness at it, and a poor spaniel dog that was my fellow traveller, turned tail to it and cried. Just then one of our men called out and said he was on top of the hill and could see into Yorkshire.'

In another passage he describes

'the continued waste of black, ill looking desolate moors, over which travellers are guided by posts set up for fear of bogs and holes, to a town called Ripley, that stands upon. . . the Nydd, smaller than the Wharfe but furiously rapid and very dangerous to pass in places especially upon sudden rains. No other part of England can show such lofty high built bridges as this part, nor so many of them.' (Some of these were the packhorse bridges. Packhorse transport was not only the most economical but often the only form possible for long distance carriers. Loads of 240lbs were carried regularly.)

John of course would not consider the moors desolate or ill looking, for he had known their secrets and their beauty all his life, riding shooting and hunting over them regularly. The moors remained, but the pattern of farming in Nidderdale and Swaledale was beginning to change, albeit extremely slowly. Turnips were coming in as a field crop which allowed more stock to be carried through the winter. Better drainage and the ploughing in of lime and manure enabled better crops to be grown. Enclosures of the common arable land were on the increase. Miles and miles of dry stone walls began to be built up the fellsides, and great stone out-barns for the stock to winter in. The Acts for Nidderdale and Appletreewick were not passed before 1804,[10] but between 1718–1748 a growing number of closes (enclosed fields) were named in leases, New Close, Calfe Close, Farside Close, Eight Acre Close, Jackson's Close, Wood Close etc.[11] Scotch cattle and sheep began to be imported from the middle of this century onwards, indeed Thomas Yorke had bought in a hundred as early as 1706, which had cost him £19.1.1.[12] The horned sheep with their black-speckled faces and legs were well adapted to the bleak conditions of the moors and had good coarse fleeces. The Craven Longhorn cattle crossed with Durham shorthorn was the main breed by 1800. These were colourful, (red, grey, blue roan, brown and black), as well as useful for both milk and beef.

The farms were mostly still worked by tenants and their families who almost always had another occupation as well.

When John first took over the estate, being occupied with Parliamentary business, he did not keep a close enough watch over his steward,

Christopher Clarke, at Bewerley. Clarke turned out to be a great defaulter, and after his death various relatives contested his will.[13] This involved John in a costly Chancery suit. The detailed questions we read in John's letters to his Richmond steward are a result of that. By 1730 he was keeping his rent book and current expenses book in his own hand.

He wrote from London,

'I hope the weather continued and favoured manuring the low close without any damage to the walk. When the season offers you must take care to have my ground well dressed and scaled (limed) att a reasonable charge and I hope you will take care that Michael doe well to my horses and my dogs, the two coach horses must be reduced in their allowance of corn and I depend my hay is not lavished away. My ground must be cleared at Lady Day and the dung left upon it to be cleared and spread in all necessary places. Be sure not to forget turning the oats that they do not suffer for want of due and proper care, and in every thing I depend upon your true regard to all my affairs during my absence, wherein, if you are circumspect and take time by the foretop I please myself by such regularity I shall find everything to my mind. In the meantime I am your assured master, J. Yorke.'

The comments of the servants when the steward passed on these instructions must have been worth hearing.

"Ey oop, Joe, we've another letter from't Maister. Tha'd best be stirrin' thi'sel and get them oats turned. Bill, tek yon 'oss an' cart to 't lower ground and get agate wi' muck spreeadin'. And think on John, when tha' fothers them nags, tha' don't give 'em so bloody mich. Ah don't want 'im on at me at back end.'

In the six months of 1729, (from Mayday to Martinmas), what John classified as his household expenses came to £67.2.0. These included the following wages,

Thomas Kaye, gardener, £18 per year
John Buckle, groom, £4 per year
Francis Lodge, steward, £4 per year
Thomas Lowe,   ?   £15 per year
Housekeeper, £6 per year
Anne Bradley, chambermaid, £2 per year
Eliza Carter, cookmaid, £2 per year

Kaye and Lowe probably received more money because they lived out, whereas the others had board, lodging and some clothing.

In his garden John paid wages to two regular men, three part time men, and two part time women. From April to August this came to £7.7.10. Other items were,

Mowing and leading his hay and finishing the stack, (for which he paid eleven men, two women and some boys £2.18.2.)

Loads of lime	£2.3.0
Four bushells of barley	£0.12.4
Shooing	£1.12.10
Liverys	£5.7.8
For painting my room	£1.11.6
72 yards of orange camblett	£4.0.2
15 gallons of red port	£4.7.6
1 gallon white	
A hogshead of portwine	£0.13.10
For candles	£2.11.6

For Mr Close for my share of gratification for his journey up to London upon the petitions of the Richmond election £26.5.0
[This last expense was considerable in proportion.]

The total rent roll in 1730 amounted to £1,172.7.2, from 205 separate tenants in Richmond, Bewerley, the Manor and Forest of Netherdale, Appletreewick, Newton, Barton, Skeeby and Theakstone. (His father's rents amounted to £479 less in 1706.)[14]

Out of this John had to pay land tax at 2/- in the £, repairs to all his buildings, and, as landlord, in each separate parish he was assessed for tithes, poor relief, church upkeep, the constable's fund and maintenance of the highways. He built a family vault in Richmond Church, and erected a gallery bearing a shield with the Yorke, Darcy and Lister arms on it.[15]

As well as his farming concerns, John's mineral rights gave him the title of Lord of the Manor of the Underworld. After 1700 many manorial lords began to invest directly in their mines instead of simply providing a mill and drawing royalties. By applying capital to new drainage techniques, they were able to exploit more promising veins at deeper levels than the small partnerships could manage. Although leadmining was still a highly speculative activity both for the investors and the miners, it did, in John's time, become more profitable.

The development of a mine could be achieved either by shafts or a network of levels. Some ore lay in vertical veins, some in horizontal. If a shaft was dug, both haulage and drainage depended on a windlass and ropes, and leather or wooden buckets. A horse drawn engine, or water wheel was needed to draw up the buckets, and few shafts were sunk to more than 100ft. Each miner had to climb down a series of slippery wooden ladders, interspersed with resting platforms, into the cold damp inky darkness, his candle lantern tied to his jacket, 'Nivver let go o'one stepper till tha 'as 'od o't next' was the only advice a novice was given.

Crouched in the narrow tunnel, hacking at the rockface they developed an alertness to impending danger by flood or rock fall, and an amazing memory of every twist and turn underground. Terrifying tales of being caught like a rat in a trap were equalled by tales of the rescuers unsparing efforts, and the joy of reunion, or the tragedy of failure.

A horse level, i.e. one large enough to take a pony pulling a train of wagons, could be driven out from a spot like Troller's Gill on the Appletreewick side of Greenhow. This opened up a large area of mining grounds and provided free drainage and cheap haulage. Some other levels were only shallow and led into the hillside. Some had to start a long way down the valley in order to reach rich mineral areas. Yorke Level may have started as a small drainage level before 1757, but grew in importance as the Ashfold Gill and Cockhill–Sunside area was developed. A rich vein could be struck which might peter out a few yards further on.

A steward or bar master was employed to manage the mines, let the contracts and bargains, and see that the shafts and levels were properly constructed and supported by timber or stone. Formerly picks and wedges had been used on the hard rock, but after 1700 the introduction of gunpowder made matters easier. The smelting mill at Heathfield was fully engaged.[16]

Small partnerships were made up of very varied people, weavers, maltsters, merchants, saddlers, doctors and experienced lead miners. In 1755, between March and October, £1,200 worth of lead was sold from the Yorke mines.

John's letters show a minute interest,

'Mr Sykes advises the sale of thirty and forty lbs of my lead att £13 per Fodder, and says there is no demand and expects it to decline, but I do not encourage a less price. I have no advice yet of my lead being at Milby a considerable time, yet arrived at York crane. If detained much longer there I shall lose all the ships going their spring voyages.'

In April he wrote,

'Mr Sykes has sold both my marks at £13 per Fodder, but I hear nothing of yours.'

25. Richard Moor hews out fluospar ore in Dry Gill which is loaded onto a barrow by Ian Menzies. Photo by Paul Berriff

Then in May,

'I have heard nothing yet from Mr Sykes relating you that if the bills and accounts do not come in, they will not find me in town.'

Even when a sale was made the payment took months to come through. One of the best returns on the Yorke lead mines on record occurred in 1735 when the sales for one year amounted to £8,000. This was never equalled again.

By 1750 the population was only five and a half million, though it rose to nearly double that by 1800. Eighty percent of the people still lived in the country. Each district kept its own traditions, interests and dialect, for no city printed newspapers had yet stamped a uniform mentality on the nation. Local affrays, scandals, accidents, thefts or poaching made up the news.

Over the next fifty years the growth of knowledge in John's lifetime developed into the agricultural revolution as well as the industrial revolution. Each helped on the other.

The forty years that John sat at Westminster earned him the affectionate title of Father of the House of Commons. He was an independent Whig and all his recorded votes up to 1741 were against the Government, excepting Walpole's unpopular measures, (the excise bill and the Spanish convention), for both of which he voted. He was described as one of the 'capricious. . . or neutrals in the party'.[18] In the electoral survey made by the 2nd Lord Egremont John is described as 'a whimsical fellow but in the main will be with the Government'. He watched the rise of the once imprisoned Walpole, (whose native passion for hunting in Norfolk gradually reduced the working week at Westminster from six days to five). He experienced the thrill and the deflation of the South Sea Bubble. He backed Walpole's excise reform aimed against smugglers, but saw it defeated. Due to the 'War of Jenkin's Ear', Walpole's power slipped from him, and in 1742, the man mockingly known as the 'Prime Minister' fell. He had kept the peace for twenty years.

Like all the northern landowners, John was horrified by the Jacobite rising in 1744, especially when the Highland troops crossed the Border and marched south as far as Derby and Preston. (The ancient fear of the Scots remained in people's minds.) By 1746 Cumberland had driven them back and butchered the last of the Stuarts at Culloden. John's brother Thomas, for one, was so relieved at the outcome that he built a tower on the hill above The Green to mark the battle.[19] This cost him £403 and still stands today, a curious remnant now that the house itself is no more.

William Pitt by then was working his political way upwards, and John must often have listened to his oratory. His speeches were said to have had the strength of thunder and the splendour of lightning. By 1756 he had become Secretary of State.

Like so many of his contemporaries in Parliament, John had inherited his land and money from the careful gathering and husbanding of his forebears, and had obtained his seat by buying property.[20] He lived in an elegant and secure age, and enjoyed life to the full, yet never lost touch with the reality of the land.

John had very many concerns and many temptations to lure him from undue application or responsibility, and could simply have been an extravagant playboy. It would be fascinating to have more light shed on his character, but we can only try to discern that from the few letters that remain. He writes of his dearly beloved wife Anne, but was held by his mother to be unkind and ungenerous to her in her own widowhood.

When he died, childless, in 1757, he left The Green to his brother Thomas, but added that all the beautiful furniture in it must be bought in at an appraised price. This must have annoyed Thomas who was his rightful heir. One is tempted to wonder whether the younger brother had rather envied John's luxurious lifestyle and ease. Thomas and Anne were good friends, however, for she frequently stayed with him at Helperby and must have been a great support to Thomas when his wife's early death left him to bring up four children alone.

John's funeral at Richmond was a huge affair, attracting as large a crowd in the market place as on an Election Day. Most of the townspeople turned out, and Anne saw to it that all were entertained well afterwards. In his will John left his land to his brother,[21]

. . . 'all my personal estate to my Dearly beloved wife Anne and the sum of £2,000, and also all the Diamonds, jewels and apparell she at any time wears, and together with my Coach, Chariot, Chair, Coach horses and all appurtenances.' He left £20 to each of his godchildren and one year's wages to each of his servants, to the poor of Richmond £30, and of Stonebeck Up and Down, and Bewerley £30. He was laid in the vault he had made.

It was during John's lifetime that the Hardwicke family rose to eminence. They were descended from Simon Yorke of Dover, a man of good property and of an old Wiltshire family, who died in 1682 leaving two sons. The eldest, Philip, became the 1st Earl of Hardwicke and Lord High Chancellor. Applying to the College of Heralds for a full coat of arms, they found bearings belonging to the Yorke family and asked John for permission to adopt them. He consented on condition that some distinction should be made. A ball or shell was therefore inserted in the centre of their shield. Simon, the second son, married the sister and heiress of John Meller and was the ancestor of the Yorkes of Erdigg, county Denbigh.[22]

CHAPTER XI

THOMAS YORKE   1688 – 1768
OF
HALTON WEST AND GOUTHWAITE

THE SECOND SON OF THOMAS AND KATHERINE YORKE was three years younger than his brother John whom he succeeded. Born at The Green in 1688, he and John were close companions in their early days, and enjoyed the freedom of the dales and moors together. What school he went to is unknown but, as the younger son, from an early age he was made aware of the need to make his own way in life. After leaving university he was probably put under the tutelage of a merchant friend of his father's, and worked hard to establish himself in London. His carefully kept ledgers show that he was given £1,053 by his father and mother, and thereafter his fortunes increased rapidly. He lent money on mortgages and had extensive mercantile transactions.

He was thirty-six before he found a wife. She was Abigail, daughter and co-heiress of William Andrews of Barneshall, Worcestershire. They were married in 1724. In their settlement, land in Ovenden, Denholme, Warley, Thornton, Allerton cum Wilsden, Hipperholme cum Brighouse and Northowram was put in trust both for Thomas and to pay Abigail an annuity.[1] Some of this land lay between Bradford and Halifax, and contained several coal mines so was valuable property.

On his marriage he was given £2,000 by his mother, and £1,500 by Abigail's father.[2] As 'King's waiter' (gentleman in waiting?) he received £70.19.0 annually.

A rather badly painted portrait of Abigail gives the impression of a practical, brown haired, neat featured woman of some determination but no great beauty.

The portrait of her husband bears a resemblance to his brother, but his face is sharper, and he has a more decisive and business like air.

They had seven children of whom five survived - Katharine, born 1730, John 1733, Mary, Thomas 1738 and Anne 1740. They lived at Hatton Gardens in London for some time when the first children were small, but later acquired a house in Helperby near Boroughbridge where Thomas and Anne were born. This lay about thirty miles from Richmond and fourteen from Gowthwaite.[3] Thomas paid £890.10.0 for it. In 1731 he had inherited some money from his mother's will, and her land at Worston and Cleasby, so by 1737 he was prospering. His detailed ledgers and records of many of his business transactions are preserved.

26. Abigail, wife of Thomas Yorke

It is from these that we know that a coach journey from Helperby to London with six horses changing every fifty miles cost £14.14.0 plus £17 expenses en route. The hire of a coach to take his children to London was £25.14.6, and a long trip from Richmond to London and back from London to Helperby cost £54.

Mutton and beef cost 2d per lb., a couple of rabbits 10d, a couple of chickens 7d, and six ducks 3/6,

His household consisted of

A housekeeper, paid £6 per annum plus £2 gratuity
A butler, paid £3 per annum plus £5 gratuity
A gardener, paid £5 per annum
A groom, paid £4 per annum plus 10/6 gratuity
A housemaid, paid £2 per annum plus 10/- gratuity
A cook, paid £2 per annum plus 10/6 gratuity[4]

When at Helperby he visited Gouthwaite and Bewerley, and from there would sometimes ride over to see his Worston property. Crossing over the moors to Grassington and on to Malham was rough going, but then he dropped down through Airton into the Ribble valley at Hellifield. He followed the curve of the river past the Nappa stepping stones, through Newsholme and Gisburn on to Worston. He put up his horse with his Assheton cousins at Downham for the night, or with his Lister uncle at Gisburn. It was perhaps from them that he learned that the land beside the Ribble around Halton West was for sale.

He rode back to Paythorne and crossing the river there picked his way carefully over boggy Paythorne Moor, following the winding sheep tracks, to Nappa Flatts. He passed one or two stone farmhouses with outbuildings and barns where dogs ran out barking furiously at his horse. A few sheep grazed on the sour peaty ground but most of it was covered with rushes, or bents. Some young cattle fared better on the pastures around the farms.

When he reached the tiny village of Halton West he found three farms and a handful of cottages. [Even with the nine outlying farms the population of the township was only slightly larger than that recorded in the Poll Tax returns in 1349, about fifty taxable men, so a total of perhaps one hundred.]

Thomas realised that the recent emphasis on enclosure had enabled poor land to be drained, manured and limed to produce better yields, and better stock. If he bought this land he could work to have it enclosed and improve it. He noticed too, as he looked back from the old stone bridge where he recrossed the river, that there was an agreeable site for a house up on the hill, overlooking the bend of the Ribble.

Thomas was thoughtful as he rode the rest of his journey. He considered his prospective purchase carefully, and sent a steward over to make a thorough survey. Finally he agreed with Mr E. Mundy of Allestry in Derbyshire, (the most recent owner), on a price of £9,756 for the 2,123 acres.[5] This was a large sum, but Thomas knew that this area of Craven had a reputation for its good grazing land, and the short, hardy men who

27. Thomas Yorke M.P. for Richmond

farmed it were first class judges of stock. The Scottish drovers who walked their herds down England to Smithfield Market knew the value of the grass for their beasts, and made regular visits, leaving valuable manure in payment.

Two years after the purchase of Halton, a second son, Thomas, was born at Helperby. This was a great joy after the loss of two other babies. Poor Abigail watched over him with the greatest care, glad he could grow up in the clear Yorkshire air instead of in London. Alas for the little boy, his mother died soon after the birth of his sister Anne, when he was only two. His father was desolate. He wrote in his journal,

'My dearest wife was snatched suddenly from me Nov. 26th 1741, in her confinement at Helperby, not having the strength to bring forth, she fell into a slumber and expired with the same tranquillity she had always lived in, and left a truly affectionate husband and five children to lament her loss. Such was her uncommon goodness to all that had any intercourse with her, that few are so much regretted as this virtuous woman. If considered in the situation in which she stood to her great Creator, she was most exemplary in her practice, or to her husband, to him she had endeared herself by every action that could make her sex amiable to man, to her Parents she was most dutiful and affectionate, to her children most indulgent and loving. To her servants, she showed great kindness and forbearance, to her superiors, great civility and respect, to her inferiors, great condescension and good manners, and such readiness to assist the needy and distressed as is not often met with. As to friendship, she esteemed it the bond of society, and thought that, without it, life was not desirable. She contracted most intimate and sincere friendships with a few well chosen persons.'

Left with five young children under seven, Thomas would rather have stayed at Helperby, but was obliged to live in London to carry on his business. He moved to Kensington, and took great pains to bring up his family and to keep kind and suitable people in his household to that end. Anne, his sister in law, was a great support to him, and was never happier than when she was with them.

Abigal's funeral cost £50, with 'other disbursements to my dearest Wife', doctor's fees etc. £510.14.6; mournung rings as gifts, 19/11, and mourning clothes for their daughter, £7.10

King George II's young family were growing up at Kensington Palace at the time, and the two parties used to meet and enjoy games together in the Gardens.[6] The little Yorkes often joked about the Royal Salutes they received from the Prince of Wales and the Duke of York.

Over the next fifteen years Thomas combined the roles of father and mother, as well as maintaining his business and land efficiently and profitably. He sent John to school at Kingston on Thames, and later entered him for Clare Hall, Cambridge. He paid £34.7.8 for his entry fee. Young Thomas joined him there in due course. Their father evidently earned the approbation of their tutor, William Talbot, who wrote in January 1757,

'Dear Sir, . . . Your elder son came to me yesterday to ask for a room, larger and more commodious than his present, which is just become vacant. I am very willing to accomodate him with it and fancy from your known indulgent compliance with the reasonable desires of your children that I may presume upon your consent.

Give me leave to add, dear Sir. . . that I honour your character, as on other accounts, so particularly for that unwearied Vigilance and Sollicitude you manifest for the true welfare of your children, which has led you for many years alone to sustain in so exemplary a manner the duties of both Parents. I wish you heartily many happy years of health that you may enjoy in seeing the prosperity and success of your family the full fruit of your. . . attention to so important an obligation.'[7]

Indeed it can be seen from the letter he wrote to his younger son that Thomas was close to the boy, and took a real interest in his doings.

1758, to Clare Hall Cambridge

'. . . it bespeaks an approbation on both sides of what the one expects from the others, and I truste this may always be the case between me and all my children.

College bills are like the unerring laws of the Medes and Persians not to be contraverted. I have had your a/c to Xmas from your tutor and immediately discharged it, and as you desired to know, particulars are as follows,

Matriculation 3/1, Cash £3.3.0, Chamber £1, Laundry 18/-, Bedmaking 12/6, porter 2d, cutlery £1.15.7, Cook £1.19.5, Millinery 15/10, Apothecary 2/6, Bookseller £1.3.3, joyner 13/4, grocer 17/5, bricklayer 4/10, Coals £1.5.6, tuition £1.10.0.

I met lately your quondam schoolfellow Mr Meadow – he is grown into a lusty man, his Father told me he had left Eaton – was going to serve on board his majesty's ship of Torbay; he seemed to look very grave, if he could not bring himself to be subject to discipline of a school, he will find it much harder on a Man of War.

I have not met with Mr Voltaire's book you mention and when we next meete you'll tell me about it. I suppose you have had lectures on mathematicks this winter as it is quite a new study for you, how do you like it? I have often heard ye difficulty lessens the more one enters into it, and becomes a very pleasant entertainment at last.

I fell in with a young Gentleman lately, yt is at ye Bar. I believe is Conscious to himself of not having got all ye advantages he might have done at College, he said if he was to go through it again, he would never miss attending all ye Wrangling disputes in school he possibly could, which he thought might have corrected a bashfulness natural to him and laid a foundation of handling an argument by hearing such as excel or were defective in their method of reasoning.

Vertue is not only a preservation against pain but also misfortune. Epicureans, which sect is mightily increased of late years seem to be most dismayed because, I suppose, they do not care to parte with their dear pleasures, . . . tell your brother from me to look at the date of my last letter to him. My blessings to you both with your sisters love, and am yr. mt. aff. Father,

T. Yorke.'

Since Abigail's death, Thomas had followed his own concerns and raised his family while his brother John had lived his full cosmopolitan and country life. When John had died, Thomas was sixty nine. He was able to enjoy his inheritance for another eleven years, and one thing which must have given him great pleasure was taking on John's seat in Parliament.

At the start of the five year period that he sat at Westminster, the brilliant, dictatorial Pitt had just become Secretary of State.[8] Gradually he gathered power into his hands, tolerating no interference. The year 1759 brought fame to the British Forces, from India to America, and in another year Canada was won. In 1760 George II died and Pitt's greatest period was over. A profound change came over the political scene. In the elections of 1761, many Tory members of the Country Party supported George III who wanted to break the Whig monopoly of power, and turn out 'the old gang'.

At the same moment, and quite contrary to the long standing agreement between the Darcy and Yorke families, the Darcys had bought up an additional number of burgage houses in Richmond. Thomas contested this in vain, over two years. Writing to Lord Holderness in 1759 he said,

'My Lord, I have not the honour to be personally known to your Lordship and therefore. . . excuse me. . . applying to a matter which concerns us both.[9] The interest of the borough of Richmond was formerly in Lord Wharton's family and mine, and the late Lord Holderness, your father, being desirous of (obtaining) a footing there, purchased several borough houses, but ye. . . Wharton family being most powerfull, your Lordship's father, ye late Conyers d'Arcy and my late brother entered into a strict league and union to support each other's interests. For ye purpose, articles and agreements entered into between them and signed by them, all dated 6th June 1721. By these articles ye firmest union is established between your Lordship's family and mine. . . that ye two families and all their descendants should unite in interest and in all future times mutually support each other, and every burgage house belonging to your Lordship's family was for ever to give one vote for my family and mine vice versa your Lordship's.'

Thomas goes on to detail the monies laid out in each case and adds,

'. . . how far the articles are binding. . . in point of law, I am not lawyer enough to determine. . . but I think they are clearly binding in honour, and as I am ready to perform every article on my parte, I cannot doubt your Lordship will do the same on yours. . . .from 1721. . . they have been religiously observed. . . . As a General Election is not far off. . . and I am not sure yr Lordship may have seen these articles. . . I will send you a copy of mine and show ye original. . . I hope I may rely nothing at ye nexte, or any further election, will be done to violate ye union. . . .. so long established.'

When, in spite of this letter, the other side defaulted, Thomas could have bought back his half share for £2,000, but was unwilling to diminish the fortunes of his younger children. It was in this way that the borough was lost to the Yorke family, who had represented it almost continuously from 1688 to 1763.

The year that Thomas lost his seat, he wrote to the Mayor of Richmond, revealing some of his feelings,[10]

'Since I came up I find publick business in greate forwardness which looks as though ye session would not be long continued, so. . . I'll not neglect ye opportunity of congratulating you on ye honourable office the corporation has conferred upon you, and ye great trust I doubt not will be well executed by you. My trust is drawing near an end and (as) I am not thought worthy by those into whose hands ye power is now fallen, to hold it any longer.

I can the more contentedly acquiesce to live amongst you as a private man, having inherited ye same self denying principles of my family who have faithfully and disinterestedly served you since I was born, now upwards of 70 years ago, of not profiting myself by a seate in parliament.

To my best compliments, I beg leave to add my ack.ts and best wishes to the corporation in general, and every member of it for their prosperity, that they may enjoy their liberty and franchise in as ample a manner as ever they did.'

The following year the corporation elected Thomas, Mayor, which must have made him both proud and honoured.

His son John had been attracted to a young lady called Sophia Glynne, daughter of Sir John Glynne of Hawarden Castle, whilst still at Cambridge, and we can share in some of his father's anxieties from letters received from his solicitor, (clearly a friend and adviser), in September 1758.

Goose Green Lodge

'Dear Sir,
When I came in from shooting on Friday I found your son here, which I was glad of. He went to town yesterday, I could not prevail upon him to stay longer, however we had time to say all I had to say on the Subject. I find he has never seen either Sir John or Lady Glynne, and has never made any proposal at all to the young lady.

There is a certain shyness about young men in these affairs so that a man cannot tell what they will do, nor do they well know themselves. I told him the wisest thing was to think no more of this. That he should pursue his studies and get into good company, attend the house of commons, marry 5 or 6 years hence, or if he must marry now, seek a good fortune and good alliance, do it upon such a footing as he might live like a Gentleman, in such manner as was proper for him who would succeed to a good Estate. That he would certainly be mistaken in point of fortune, that it was not probable that a Country Gent. of about £2,000 a year would give seven younger children £4,000 apiece, but if he did, if this was not wholly with your approbation, you (would) give an equivalent only , he must live in a very cheap County, in a little way, in a very private manner; there would be an end to his Studies and Improvements, and his amusements would be confined to a Garden.

He subscribed to the soundness of this but he said(?) that if she had but £2,000 a year he should marry her.

I endeavoured to convince him that his going into Wales before he went to Richmond on all accounts was Improper, but as he was unacquainted with Sir John, he would go on no other footing than that of a lover. That Sir John would certainly desire an explanation of his visit, that if he did not, it would be incumbent upon your son to declare his intention, and how ridiculous this would be before he knows whether the lady has £1,000, before he has a personal conference with you, so he knew what you would. . . . That it was his interest to oblige you; that you had much in your power; and that during your life, he had nothing at his Command. This he seemed to approve entirely and I believe will not go to Wales till he has seen you, but there is nothing certain in the determination of a young man in love.

I dwelt largely on the folly of his suffering himself to bank(?) at all on the. . . of the. . . which ought to be left to you. I said much on this head, gave him many instances how unequall he was to the subject and how he might be imposed upon to his future disquiet, and how prudent it was to keep his. . . in his own power instead of exhausting it. In the . . . of this he sounded fully convinced.

Though I am inclined to think he will see you before he goes to Wales, yet I found he did not seem inclinable to go to Richmond immediately. He had. . . and not on account of the girl, but I found because it was disagreeable, he said he wished he had never left Cambridge, that his lodging the next door to you was a wrong step, that he never had had any quarrel with you but there were many little annoyances which made talking together disagreeable.

If he comes to Richmond make it as agreeable to him as you can. Let him visit about and go to Sir John etc., etc., etc.

And now let me give you a piece of advice, I mean with regard to . . . either refuse your consent to his match, let him continue at his allowance, augment it if necessary; or, if you do consent, offer, don't confirm your settlement to the proportion of her fortune, but make it such as is proper for him to have. Nor if he is determined to have her . . . benefit . . . and the consequence will be that he will . . . £1,000 in debt before he comes to the Estate, or if he is more prudent, he will contract such a little way of life as will not become him hereafter.

My wife joins me desiring her compliments to you and your family, your obliged and faithfull servant,[11]

Henry Wilmot'

It seems that Thomas needed even more advice and did not succeed in having an easy talk with John. In another letter, his friend Wilmot tells him,

'. . . the absolute dependence of the son, when the father has everything in his power, is not always sufficient to prevent young things of his kind. But where the son has a certainty at his father's death, these things always happen. You should see it in this light,' he goes on, 'Your son is not a sot nor extravagant nor a gamester. The woman he has taken a fancy to is a Gentlewoman, and your estate is not in debt so as to want a fortune. If you look round you will see few fathers who would not be glad to compound for such a step as this. . . . make the best out and look at the most agreeable side. . . .'

In spite of Thomas's forbodings, John obviously continued his courtship. He was fascinated by the close and loving Glynne family, who were both intelligent and eccentric. They were long established in their large and comfortable house with its well kept gardens, and John enjoyed his visits there. The lawn sloped up to the old ruined castle and made a pleasant walk under the fine trees.[12] The ladies of Hawarden were on friendly terms with their tenants, and interested themselves in the lives and needs of their neighbours in the village.

Four more years went by before John and Sophia were able to think of marriage, and even then a remarkable exchange of letters took place between the two fathers.

In April 1763 Sir John Glynne replied to Thomas,

'I am favoured with your letter. . . and I had the satisfaction to here (sic) they are all well and that my daughter is vastly pleased with the situation of Richmond Green.

I had the pleasure of great fimiliarity with yr. Brother and I am sorry our acquaintance will commence so late, seeing the great satisfaction I expect to enjoy thereby. . . . in respect of Equity, Justice and Impartiality I hope I never have been (deficient) in Publick Life, and I am sure, so far as it regards my own children, there cannot at present be the least inducement to depart from it. My respects. . . etc., yr. most affect.

J. Glynne.'

A rather sharp answer was sent back by Thomas, on April 23rd,

'. . . ye lament our acquaintance began so late, permit me to say this was not my fault, ye saw me frequently in ye house of commons and ye coffee house in Grosvenor St in 1759 after ye treaty had begun, but ye declined speaking to me on the subject.

My son, when he had opened it to me, said he was given to understand ye fortune would be £4,000 and as I did not intend to take any part of it, I made no objection, but was surprised when ye summe was dwindled away at last, yet I acquiesced; but if I had been with you at Mr Wilmot's Chambers, I should have insisted yr daughter might be put on an equal footing with your other daughters. I do now (ask) on behalf of your daughter and mine, she may be placed so at last for the sake of our grandchildren, and, I flatter myself, from yr natural affection to her. Yr known justice will not deny me this satisfaction under your hand, and is all I now require, it being my intention to cultivate such a harmony as ought to subsist between us.'

Sir John then did his best to clear up any misunderstandings,

'The subject of your letter of the 23rd instant will furnish me with an opportunity of explaining to you some things at present understood to my disadvantage, and heretofor to your dissatisfaction, which is that (as I suppose), you were given to understand that I had promised £4,000 with my daughter, and that I afterwards receded from such promise. The fact is this, upon the very first intimation of this affair to me, it was from a friend at a great distance, intimating that there was a Gentleman in the world who was looking for a Lady whereon to fix his affections, and that, as much as he knew of both the Gent. and my daughter, he thought they were formed for each other and all that was desired was the sum above mentioned.

As at this time, I knew not so much as the name of the Gent., his merrits or his family, it is rather unnatural to think I should answer this letter in the affirmative under those circumstances, and I am sure at no other time did I ever give reason whereon to found that expectation. This I hope will clear that matter up, and lead me to observe upon another part of your letter, which seems to make me the chief cause of our not being on a better footing much sooner, as the opportunities you mention did certainly happen, but please Sir to recollect, they happened at so critical a time when I had from some circumstances about that time not the least reason to think that there remained even a probability of such an event happening, as has since taken place.'

He then adds rather disarmingly,

'Upon the whole I dont think that you or I have had any considerable share in the whole Proceeding. But upon the whole, altho' it will with great truth be said, that your son hath made no considerable acquisition to his Family in point of Fortune, yet I hope I have sent into it one, who in every other respect must be unexceptional.'

He concludes,

'. . . whatever you would please that I should do to testify to you my sincerity of my Daughter being assured of her equality in fortune with the rest of her sisters, I am ready to do and by every act assure your Family I hold the alliance with it in the greatest esteem, and remain, Dear Sir, yr. very affect. Friend and obedient Servt.

J. Glynne'

This frank and charming letter did the trick, and Thomas came round. He replied on May 3rd,

'The latter part of your letter . . . has given me great satisfaction so I'll not endeavour to make an answer to yr note but accept yr honourable offer of making our daughter ye equal in point of fortune wth any of yr other daughters and to secure it by your act and deed, as I shall desire for ye benefit of our said daughter and their issue.[13] As ye are to be so soon in town if ye please to let Mr Wilmot draw such an instrument for you to execute here. You show yourself a man of probity and you cannot think me unreasonable hereon, of which our Son knows nothing of my pleading thus for him. . . .

By all accounts of my daughter she is very deserving of all I have and you can do for them, and doubt not of her prudence in making a good Wife and its being a happy marriage.'

Thomas was by then seventy five and must have been thankful to have that all important matter completed at last. He wrote in his ledger,

'1763 Paid my son John on his marriage to Miss Glynne the appraised value (£750) of the plate, furniture and goods in the house at Richmond, to be laid out in land for the uses therein, which I have obliged myself to do by the deed of his marriage settlement, having allowed him £176 for the use of the said goods since 1757, whilst I lived there, and have now delivered them up to my son John, with the house.'

Despite his age he had lost none of his fire or business acumen. In 1767 a Commission was appointed to erect boundary posts for the Knaresborough Forest mining areas. Thomas did not agree with their position and ordered the erring stones to be broken down.

He had a lucky escape once when he was travelling to London from Bewerley. His servant rode behind him, carrying a portmanteau containing £2,000 in cash.[14] They reached the London house and had just dismounted when a constable came up to the servant. He charged him with a robbery committed some months earlier, and arrested him. Thomas must have been thankful the precious saddle bag was safe.

At the great age of eighty, he died, presumably in London, for he was buried at St George's, Hanover Square, and not in the family vault in

Richmond. His sister in law, Anne, may have made her home with Thomas after her husband's death, for she was also buried there, near Thomas.

His son John was left the bulk of his estate, including 'the furniture in my house at Richmond, which I took at an appraised price'. He mentioned some of his capital which included 1,300 East India Co. annuities £3,500, and some South Sea annuities from brother John's estate of £8,600.

To his son Thomas, he gave his 'estates at West Halton . . . and Worston . . . worth £450 a year'.[15]

CHAPTER XII

JOHN YORKE 1733 – 1813
OF
RICHMOND AND BEWERLEY

JOHN WAS THIRTY-FIVE WHEN HE SUCCEEDED to his father's property, but had already been living at The Green since his marriage to Sophia, daughter of Sir John Glynne Bt., of Hawarden Castle, Flintshire.

He was brought up at Helperby and in London, where he went to school at Kingston on Thames. He went on to Clare College, Cambridge. Although he left Cambridge before his father wished,[1] parental power prevented him from marrying until he was thirty. With hindsight we can see the tragedy of that long wait.

John and Sophia's only daughter was born in 1764, but died in her infancy. A year later her parents made a long journey to Spain and Portugal, 'whither she went, but alas without success, by advice of Physicians for the recovery of her health'.

It was on the return voyage from Lisbon 'that the severe illness under which she had lingered for months, put an end to her life, on board the Hamden Packet'.

John's dearly loved Sophia was buried at Falmouth when they landed, in 1766, only three years after their marriage.

It was a heart breaking home coming for John, back to the house they had arranged together with such hopes and happiness. His household was assembled to greet the lonely figure, holding his wife's jewel box forlornly in his hand. The maid servants shed tears as they unpacked her exquisite dresses from the trunks. Only her beautiful portrait remained.

John's devoted sisters, Katharine, Mary and Anne did their best to comfort him, as did his elderly father, but in only two years time, Thomas too was dead.

John was described by his nephew as having 'a highly cultivated, practical and talented mind'.[2] He wrote poetry as well as plays, but he was also devoted to his estates, country pursuits, his horses and his dogs, and local affairs.

One of five letters from the Rev. Christopher Wyvill of Constable Burton to John in 1777 asks him to join with 'several of your friends (who) have agreed to form a Society for the Encouragement of Agriculture in Richmondshire. The subscriptions are now 32.' This was one of the many societies of that time, when the breeding of stock was being rapidly improved all over the country.

28. Sophia, first wife of John Yorke

A new breed of sheep, Teeswater crossed with Scotch Blackface, had been introduced into the Dales. Known locally as 'mugs' they proved successful both for wool and mutton. The new breed of cattle then, noted by Arthur Young, was the Shorthorn, good for beef and milk.

John's great enjoyment was shooting, and he was skilful with the heavy flint and steel muzzle loader of the day. As well as being encumbered with a powder flask, shot pouch and charges, wads and a ramrod, he had to reload laboriously after every shot, and keep everything dry in bad weather. It was a sport for individuals, not parties, and the excitement lay in the unexpected bird or animal springing up after a long search. A good brace of pointers with him, a bag of a couple of teal, two hares, a woodcock and a brace of partridge, and his day was made.

John was an extremely good natured man, and charitable to all. His own portrait reveals his dislike of pomp and show, for he chose to be painted sitting on the ground beside his spaniel, wearing a plain brown suit. His friend, Colonel Coore, beside him is decked out in a tricorn hat, scarlet uniform and white breeches, and the composition of the painting makes John look like the gamekeeper, which no doubt pleased him.

After three years as a widower he met and married Elizabeth Woodstock, daughter of Peter Campbell of Kilmory, Argyllshire, and of Fish River, Hanover, Jamaica.[3] There were no children of the marriage, but John's sisters and Elizabeth's nieces spent much of their time with them, and accompanied them on their many travels on the Continent.

The Yorkes entertained a good deal at The Green, and at Bewerley. Their house parties must have resembled the ones described by the American Ambassador, Willis, on a visit to England,

29. Colonel Coore and John Yorke of Richmond and Bewerley

'Dinner is announced by a dignified butler and the gentlemen lead the ladies into the dining room. After the dessert is set, all the servants leave the room. The ladies sit a little longer, then rise from the table. About eleven, the gentlemen move to the drawing room, where cards, tea and music fill the time till twelve, then the ladies take their departure and the men sit down to supper until two.

The next morning at breakfast all the splendour of the scene of the night before was gone. The host in rough shooting coat, read a newspaper, and the hostess was in a a plain simple morning dress and cap. Between breakfast and lunch the gentlemen rode or shot or played billiards. At two o'clock, a dish or two of hot game or cold meats were set on a small table, and a sort of lounging half meal took up an hour. Outside, carriages and riding horses were drawing up, and parties were made up for riding or driving, with footmen and grooms in attendance.'

In 1772 John's sister Katharine was married to her first cousin, a widower named Sir John Clavering. He was the youngest son of Sir James Clavering, (who had married the previous Katharine Yorke in 1702), and he already had two sons and three daughters. Sir John was evidently very attached to Katharine's brother Thomas, for he wrote to him on his engagement, 'I can have no further wish than to deserve the esteem of a person like yourself'.

When in December of the following year Thomas announced his own engagement, Clavering wrote, 'I assure you that both Katharine and I take the greatest share that is possible in the happy prospect that is opening to you, in establishing yourself with an amiable woman'.[4] A month later he enthuses, 'Every account I receive of Miss Reay confirms the report already related of her. . . you have certainly laid the best foundation of happiness that we are capable of. . . .'

By April 1774 Clavering had been appointed to command some of His Majesty's forces in India. The close Yorke family dreaded what their sister might have to endure in the way of climate and danger, but she set sail cheerfully with her husband and his children.

On board the 'Ashburnam' on April 12th the General wrote to his well loved cousin and brother-in-law, Thomas,

'The wind which has detained us since the first of the month, has become fair this a.m. and we are now at the back of the Isle of Wight. I cannot look back on the shore we are quitting without the greatest sensibility, and with this impression on me I have taken my pen to assure you that I leave nobody behind whom I esteem and love more than yourself.

Yr sister accomodates herself exceedingly well to this new strange life, and I hope she has got her seasoning over as she is now recovered of the sea sickness she felt on first coming on board, indeed in common with us all . . . . Inform us how you are at least once a year.'

In fact they were never to see each other again. At this moment troops in America were arming and drilling, ready for their war of Independence. In the India for which the Claverings were bound, Warren Hastings was Governor General in Calcutta, but the power, (on paper at least) was divided between the Nawab of Bengal, the Board of Directors of the East India Company, the Governor General, and a Council appointed by Parliament to veto and control him. Hastings had a hard struggle to keep his patience in his shackled situation, for intrigue and corruption were rife. Clavering's comments to Thomas Yorke on the difficulties that faced the British are most revealing.

He wrote on January 10th 1777,

'The total engrossment of my time in publick business will, I hope, excuse me to my friends for not writing. . . . The Military Department of the three residencies, the situation of opposition which I have stood in to the measures of the former administration of this Country having rendered it necessary for me to take an active part in every measure as well political as civil in this Government, the accumulated weight of the whole has been rather more than I could bear. I should not grudge my labour. . . but I am sorry to say that every evil that existed in the Government previously at the passing of the Act of Parliament, now exists and flourishes with more vigour than before.

The combination of Interests subsisting between all ranks of men both in India and in Europe, waiting in a common cause, have proved too powerfull for us, and I am afraid even the legislature itself find they cannot break it, much less overcome it. Unfortunately the Judges, whose duty it was to have supported our authority, betrayed us. They might indeed have broken the Phalanx but, seduced by their passions and their desire to extend their jurisdiction, they . . . threw the weight of their authority into the other scale.

. . . Whilst I could do good I was ready to sacrifice my health and my time to the service, but when I am only to remain to be a spectator of villany of every kind, without being able to prevent it, it would be highly unreasonable . . . more particularly when those who sent me are not able to support me . . . .

The rest of my family look forward to the happy moment of their return which I hope will not be later than 1778.'

In March the same year, Katharine Clavering wrote happily of her

'very pleasant Garden House close upon the banks of the river Ganges'. 'No prospect', says she, 'is equal to that of a navigable river. . . we see ships at a great distance and vessels of all sizes passing and repassing . . ., even your Richmond can not outdo it.'[5]

But within a year Sir John's health had broken under the strain and he was dead.

His widow wrote,

'This sad year has been a cruel one to me. I have felt more than it is possible I can again. Human creatures never loved one another more than I did Sir John. I always prayed to go first, yet I am left . . . . I am engaged in my duties to my large family, the only manner I can prove my affection to my beloved Husband.'

She made the long arduous return journey and settled her family in a small furnished house in London. Clearly she gave all her time and energy to the stepchildren, and especially to their marriage prospects. In 1780 she wrote to brother John in Florence,

'Sir John Warren is a very pleasing young Baronet, not seven and twenty, a large estate and M.P. for Marlow. . . . Caroline wishes you to be informed of the secret.'

This letter was followed soon after by a frantic scrawl about preventing Caroline's threatened elopement. Her efforts were apparently successful for the girl soon became Lady Warren and lived happily as such. The other two daughters married the 8th Lord Napier and Sir Thomas Brooke Pechell, all three 'of a distinguished appearance'.

Thomas Yorke's journal says, 'Lady Warren was 6ft in height and most dignified in manner. Her hair, often fastened only by a single pin, has been seen at a Ball touching the floor.'

The same year that General Clavering died, John Yorke had taken his wife, with Mary, Anne, a Campbell niece and the Rev. John Wheeler abroad and spent a year in Nice, for the sake of Anne's health. Poor invalid Anne died there however, and was buried in the Protestant cemetery. Grief stricken letters passed between the family, and her sister Mary felt it particularly deeply.

The rest of the party stayed on and travelled about for another year. The Rev. John Wheeler was evidently an amusing and worldly parson who paid a curate to care for his parish at home. This was quite a common practice then. Several journals remain of their travels describing the Italian scenery and schools of art.

While John was abroad he gave his brother Thomas power to oversee all his mines and their working, so Thomas had a thorough knowledge of his affairs.

John and Elizabeth returned home in 1780, bringing back a carved lion in marble, purchased by Anne, which they had set into the mantelpiece in the morning room at Bewerley.[6] Mary went to live at The Friary in Richmond, where she 'was highly valued by all her family'. Anne had left Mary her money so she was reasonably well off, unlike most unmarried ladies of that time.

John applied himself to his Nidderdale property and spent much of his time at Bewerley. When he moved his household from Richmond it made quite a procession. A coach and six horses led the party, which held the upper servants, with a coachman, two postilions and three outriders. The latter paid the tolls, saw the gates were open, and kept off any lurking highwaymen. A chariot or post chaise followed drawn by two horses, carrying Mr and Mrs Yorke. Then came the heavy chaise marine with four horses, in which was the butler and all the family plate.

The hunters ridden by the stud groom and huntsman came next, with a small pack of hounds, a whipper in and the grooms on riding nags brought up the rear. The journey took all day, and the unpacking almost another day.

John built the two east towers on to the old rectangular house, and added the morning room and the room above it. He laid out beautiful walks in Ravensgill and Fishpond wood, and built the arched ruin called The Folly on the top of the hill near Guisecliffe. These outdoor works were largely done to provide employment at this time of great need.

John was known locally as The Poor Man's Friend and was noted for his generous nature. After his death his nephew wrote, 'My uncle was a most benevolent man, charitable even to a fault, but often imposed upon to a great extent.'

He educated several poor boys, giving them college educations, and one, Peter Fraser, became a clergyman in Leicestershire.

He built and equipped the new school and school house at Bridgehouse Gate for the children in Pateley Bridge, for old Abbot Huby's chapel had become far too small. He also bought more property including the old Tudor house, or Gardener's house.

He erected a gallery in Middlesmoor church in 1774, and on Easter Sunday presented two large silver flagons and a patten.

He was one of the Commissioners in 1767, (with Sir John Ingilby), who managed the Navigation when the river Ure was made navigable from Milby to Ripon. Five locks and three cuts were made and fixed tolls were charged,[7] 3/- a ton for general merchandise, 2/- for lead, 1/6 for bricks and stone, etc. This waterway was a vital link in the journey from the mines to the river port of Boroughbridge.

From this period too, the narrow and sometimes impassable roads were improved by the Turnpike Trusts, set up by an Act of Parliament. The Trustees appointed were leading spirits like the Ingilbys and Yorkes, and under their care, for the first time, specialist contractors were employed to make properly surfaced roads. Local labour was also used and tolls were fixed to pay for the maintenance. The toll collectors, known as pikemen, were housed at each toll bar, but of course the lesser used roads did not gather enough income for their upkeep. Although bridges were widened and there was considerable improvement, one could travel a sound turnpike road for a few miles, then be back for fifty miles of poorly maintained parish road.

Several of the Yorke tenants in Nidderdale were spinning flax and weaving linen by this time, and cotton spinning was also a growing industry. Kay's flying shuttle was in general use by 1770, and Hargreaves spinning jenny was hailed as a great improvement. Stocking knitting was declining. Lead mining remained a highly speculative occupation, but as the miners were usually only underground for five or six hours of the day, they had time to attend to their 2 or 3 acres, and to produce at least the food for their own families. John Yorke leased some ground in Appletreewick to William Wood[8] for one seventh of the output of smelted lead. (Owners of larger mines often took 1/5th which indicated that the mine was, or was expected to be rich.) If Wood left the mine unworked for more than thirty working days, he had to pay a fine of £1 a day. Wood had a successful strike in the Craven Cross mine, which was said to have yielded nearly 300 tons a year, but the only lucky venture on the Appletreewick ground was achieved by two former stewards of the Yorke family from Richmond, Leonard Raw and George Kearton. John's neighbours Sir John Ingilby and Sir Thomas White leased the minerals under their land in the same way, and plans for joint working of Yorke and White mines led to the formation of several interlocking partnerships. Yorke in 1795 paid £2,100 towards the joint cost of carrying

Cockdale Level into Craven Moor but trouble soon started between him and White, which recurred over many years.

It was said of John that when he came to collect his rents from Bewerley, he had often given them away again before he left. This sounds altogether too generous, but the poverty and distress amongst the poorer people at this time was very great. Few could earn enough money to live and there was absolutely no margin for sickness or accident. One only has to read Parson Woodforde's diary to know of the many cases of hardship in his Norfolk parish in the 1790s, and it was the same all over the country. There was no shortage of opportunities for relief.

Their friend John Wheeler, in London, missed the Yorkes' company, and felt that they were too immersed in their local interests, for he wrote to John, 'I fear I shall have to come and set fire to your house for I know that no other way will I rummage you out of your Dale'.

In 1780 John was appointed High Sheriff of Yorkshire. This ancient office carries with it the duty of guarding the King's Justices at the Assize. John, wearing black velvet Court Dress with a cocked hat and a sword, was accompanied by his own 24 javelin men, two trumpeters and a private chaplain, as well as a large number of his tenantry. They must have thoroughly enjoyed the ceremonies, and the feasting.

Due to the mental incapacity of George III,[9] John was obliged to continue in office and bear the not inconsiderable cost of a second Assize. Not only did he have to provide food and lodging for his entourage and stabling for his and their horses but he was also expected to lavish quarts of sack and beer, a hogshead of port wine, 18lbs of candles, 6lb tobacco and 15 pipes on his guests. Whilst they feasted they were entertained with musick. On the way home he distributed shillings to 'poor people about ye doore'.

By 1783 an Armistice with France had been made at last, and Pitt the Younger, aged only twenty four, was asked to form a Government. Parliamentary reform was in the air. The shock of the American Revolution, John Wesley's revival, and the huge increase in population all added to the general dissolution of the world of the eighteenth century. Steam engines, the canal network, the newly surfaced roads, new smelting methods, improved agriculture and stock breeding, and the growth of an urban working class – all these changes and problems confronted Pitt. Wilberforce, his friend and confidant, shared his strong anti-slavery views, which led them both towards the low church movement.[10] Adam Smith's 'The Wealth of Nations' advocated free trade, and aroused new aspirations. By 1789 when the world shaking upheavals were shattering Paris, Pitt held to an even course of neutrality. Appalled though a man such as John Yorke must have been, with a close knowledge of the French people and their country, many of the English seem to have managed to take little notice of the French Revolution at the start. The execution of the French King and the massacre of political prisoners in 1793 was followed by France declaring war on Britain. This brought matters nearer home.

Whilst these weighty affairs were in train, John Yorke was reaping the result of what his nephew described as 'the one flaw in his character'.

At some time John had fathered a natural daughter. Her mother's name and the date of her birth are not known, but when the child grew up she was known and introduced as Miss Yorke, so was evidently accepted by the family. She met Richard Moseley Atkinson, who had been educated at Westminster School, and Clare, Cambridge. He took Holy Orders and became a curate in 1787. He was ordained a priest at York the following year, and married Mary in Richmond in 1792.[11]

'This event', wrote John's heir and nephew, 'led to the many evils which arose to the family and which caused much of the property to be alienated'.

The Rev. Moseley Atkinson ingratiated himself with the kind hearted and generous John, who was clearly very fond of his daughter. He gave her a marriage portion of £3,000 and made them both welcome in his house. Once Atkinson, as an ordained and educated man, had gained John's complete trust, he appears to have pretended to behave as the son John never had. He gradually took over more and more of the management of the estate, but either through incompetence or dishonesty, he neglected the proper care of the agricultural improvements, the mining enterprises and the real interests of the property and the tenants. Naturally Thomas Yorke was worried by all this.

Over the last twenty years of John's life, when his health and eyesight were worsening steadily, the corpulent Atkinson, (said to have weighed over thirty stone at his death), gained more and more influence over him. He kept him away from Bewerley on various false pretexts, and cut down nearly all the valuable timber without John's knowledge. He also kept him from his brother and nephew as well.

Elizabeth, John's wife, connived at this, for John and Thomas had always had the closest family ties, together with their sisters. Somehow a wedge was driven between them, to the exclusion of young John the heir, at a time when he should have been learning about family affairs. He said afterwards that he was never left an instant alone with his uncle.

Although he seldom saw him, John was writing affectionate and intimate letters to his brother in 1805, about the troublesome business of the dispute with Sir Thomas White his neighbour, about his mines at

Merryfield and about his health, 'though much altered, I have no cause to complain of my infirmities'.

His wife however wrote,

'Dear Brother, You'll pardon I trust the liberty I am now taking to address you on a subject which it may appear impertinent for me to interfere,[12] but in justice to Mr Atkinson, I take up my pen lest you suppose him negligent in not paying due attention to the two or three letters you have lately written to him about the new Levels which you purpose beginning – that it has been at my request that he has delayed communicating their contents to Mr Yorke – my motive in so doing proceeds from my tender regard towards my Husband. We fear that in his debilitated state of health the consequence might be serious as he is always particularly agitated when he speaks on the subject of Lead and Mining. He has been scarcely a whole day tolerably well since he returned. . . indeed Dr Pannell. . . was much shocked at the alteration in his looks for the worse, grown thin, the humour gone from his face, his pulse not good, complaining continuously of his Head, and hardly able to hold it up. . . his Physician wishes him to be kept free from business or anything that can vex or harry him, that I may use every means in my power to comply with these directions, from my affection for one whose life is of so much consequence to my happiness. These considerations if I have acted wrong will plead my excuse.

I heard him say the other day. . . that he heartily wished you success (with the new Level) but for his part he was so far advanced in years and his infirm state. . . not to enter into the expense of so great an undertaking. I am sure he has always had yours and the family's interests at heart, but a man who is in debt and only a life income to pay it off cannot be as generous as his inclination to be – his Mines he has had so considerable losses by, I often lament he had any mining concerns for they are a continual plague and expense.

Distribute my love to the family, and believe me, Dear Brother your sincere friend and affect. Elizabeth Woodstock Yorke'

Soon after this, Atkinson wrote to Thomas telling him some history of the Appletreewick mines and adding, 'Your brother is charmingly. . . they hope to set out for Devonshire soon. Mrs Atkinson and my little girl send their affectionate greetings.'

However one construes these contrasting letters, the following one from old John to his nephew and heir shows his real intentions in 1811.

'I hope that the account of your Father's health as given by you. . . will prove that he is in a mending state after having suffered so much. Were he in . . . a condition to treat with Sir Thomas White about his offer of his whole property in Nidderdale for 100,000 guineas, I should certainly consult with him on so eligible and truly desirable an object. . . the purchase of farms intermixed with my own and mines interfering also with mine, and also. . . to be rid of a contentious neighbour whose agents are continuously raising disturbances.

I think this will be in your power and that the time cannot be far off . . . therefore the whole property of ye family will enable you to compass the acquisition of so very desirable an object. I would live almost on bread and cheese were I young again, could I become Master of these Grounds.'[13]

However John had made his will in a curious manner, influenced by Atkinson. He left all his land in Richmond and Bewerley in the hands of his Trustees, (who were Atkinson and William Chaytor). They were to value the properties and give an option to Thomas, his heirs and assigns, to purchase seven eighths of them at valuation price, as his own father had had to do. The land around The Green was to be handled in the same manner, for Thomas and his heirs to buy in at £400, and in the same way all the plate, furniture, books, cattle, horses, sheep, carriages and carts to be bought in at £1,000. If Thomas did not take up the options, the goods were to be sold and the money used to pay off debts.

One reason for this odd wording was that John owed the enormous sum of over £21,000 to various people. Most of these debts had been incurred for philanthropic reasons. He appears to have had a warm heart but a poor head for business, as some of his codicils show. (One annuity to be paid to Mary Haynes of Cheshunt for life may have been to the mother of his daughter Mary.)

He left £20 to the poor in each township of Bewerley and of Richmond, a year's wages and 'mourning cloaths' to each servant in his employ, £70 to his servant Henry Bennison, £30 to his servant Wm. Dawson, who, 'tho' not dismissed is incapable of attending me through ill health'. He left money for four rings to go to Mr Martin and his partners for allowing him credit in Italy when 'disappointment in the expected profits from my mines had kept me bare of money'. He remitted to each tenant 'all arrears of money owing at my death', and '£100 towards the subscription already set on foot for building a school for the poor and ignorant children on Greenhow Hill'.

When John died in 1813, the heir and his family felt bound to contest the will, for they knew the main part could not have been John's real intention. Taking the case to court united Elizabeth and the Atkinsons even more, and they sought counsel's opinion from Sir James Scarlett, a noted K.C. [who had married Louise Campbell, Elizabeth's niece.][14]

Scarlett gave his opinion that the options given to Thomas had lapsed on his death in 1811, so the Trustees were not bound to offer them to the heir at law. Moreover, 'the options of purchase had been entirely confined to Mr Thomas Yorke and were at an end by his decease'.

This was patently untrue as the form of words used in each case was 'Mr Thomas Yorke, his heirs and assigns'. The Scarlett family stood to benefit considerably from the outcome, and young John lost a large part of his birth right.

'By his powerful ability and talent, but not by his honesty', wrote the deprived heir, 'the case was given against me. Had my beloved Father not been taken from us in 1811, three years before my uncle, much would have been spared.' (Thomas, his father, had been a barrister.)

The Merryfield and Craven Moor Mines were left in trust for William Chaytor to work them and divide the profits between Elizabeth and the Atkinsons.

John, whose last desire would have been to cause injustice, was buried at his own request, not in the family vault in Richmond, (for which he had an aversion) but 'in the most private manner and without the least appearance of parade in Hudswell churchyard, or where ever I may chance to die, whether at home or on the road'. He asked only for a plain stone to bear no more than his name, the date, his father's name 'and nothing more added thereon'. He had always preferred to worship in the little church at Hudswell, to the larger parish church in Richmond, and now his grave lies surrounded by the fields he loved, in peace.

He was the last member of the family to live at Richmond.

His wife Elizabeth died in August of the same year and was buried in the vault at Richmond. She left all her estate 'of what nature or kind so ever' to her three nieces, Deborah and Elizabeth Campbell and Louise Scarlett to be shared equally. This included all the Yorke family jewels. Her sole legacy to the Yorke family was an enamel and diamond brooch, left to Margaret Anne, John's unmarried niece.

Another great sorrow to nephew John was that Elizabeth and Atkinson swept away and destroyed a valuable accumulation of family papers and documents of the greatest interest, which had been kept at Richmond. These included his grandfather's ledgers.

John's devoted sister Mary, who died three years after him,[15] left £200 to her sister in law Jane Yorke, but also £10 each to Mrs Moseley Atkinson, her daughter Mary, and the three nieces of Elizabeth, 'as a token of her regard'. Mary remembered happier days and could not make a breach of friendship there.

Chapter XIII

THOMAS YORKE   1738 – 1811
OF
HALTON PLACE

THE SECOND SON OF THOMAS AND ABIGAIL YORKE, was born in 1738 at Helperby. His mother died when he was only two years old, but his father succeeded in creating a happy family and keeping his children attached to him and to each other. The family moved to Kensington, and young Thomas went to school at Kingston on Thames, then on to Clare, Cambridge. He read for the bar at the Middle Temple and practised as a barrister in London.

The London he lived in was still so small that many country pleasures were easily in reach. Wapping was the furthest point east, Knightsbridge still had a country inn, ('The Halfway House'), Kensington and Fulham were almost wholly market gardens. Brompton was a village with leafy lanes, and in the fields between Paddington and Bayswater, hay was made.

The Old Berkeley hounds hunted right up to Kensington Gardens, and a popular pack of stag hounds hunted the country round Hounslow and Twickenham. It seems that the market gardens were a hindrance, for Lord Alvanley complained, 'Melon and asparagus beds are devilish heavy. We were up to our hocks in glass all day.'

Thomas, as a bachelor, travelled north sometimes on the speedy new mail coaches. If no mail was being carried, and the coachman felt kindly disposed, whenever game was sighted along the road side the coach would halt, so that the young men could take a shot. 'When it became too dark to shoot', wrote Peter Hawker in his diary, 'we all sang choruses on top of the coach. I got four partridge.'

It was a beautiful sight to see four well matched horses step out together, and the skilful coachman hold them in hand. The wheels hummed cheerfully, the greys skimmed along, the bugle was in high spirits and the coachman's voice chimed in too . . . clinking, jingling, rattling smoothly on, the whole concern . . . was one great instrument of music.[1]

Some of the inns were damp and dirty with poor food, but at the 'Spread Eagle' in Settle, Thomas could eat beef steaks, lambchops, pickled salmon and tart for the sum of 9d.

Realising that his brother John would inherit the bulk of the Yorke property, he took a special interest in the Halton West estate from the start.

He succeeded to the property when his father died in 1768 and he was determined to develop and improve it. He obtained an Enclosure Act from Parliament, (for which he had to pay heavily), and began to drain the land, improve the soil and repair and build farm buildings.

He made enquiries in London for a good architect, for he wanted to build himself a house over looking the river. John Crunden was recommended to him, who also built Belfield House in Weymouth, and Boodles Club in London.[2]

The two men got on well and drew up plans for a delightful Georgian house, in brick, faced with stone, with sash windows, facing west. A woodyard, a walled kitchen garden, stables and a farmyard were laid out in front across a lawn, and a carriage drive led up to the house from the old stone bridge across the river. From the east windows a superb view of the purple moors and blue hills of Ingleboro' and Pen y ghent stretched to the north, and the curving banks of the Ribble to the south. Peel Hill and

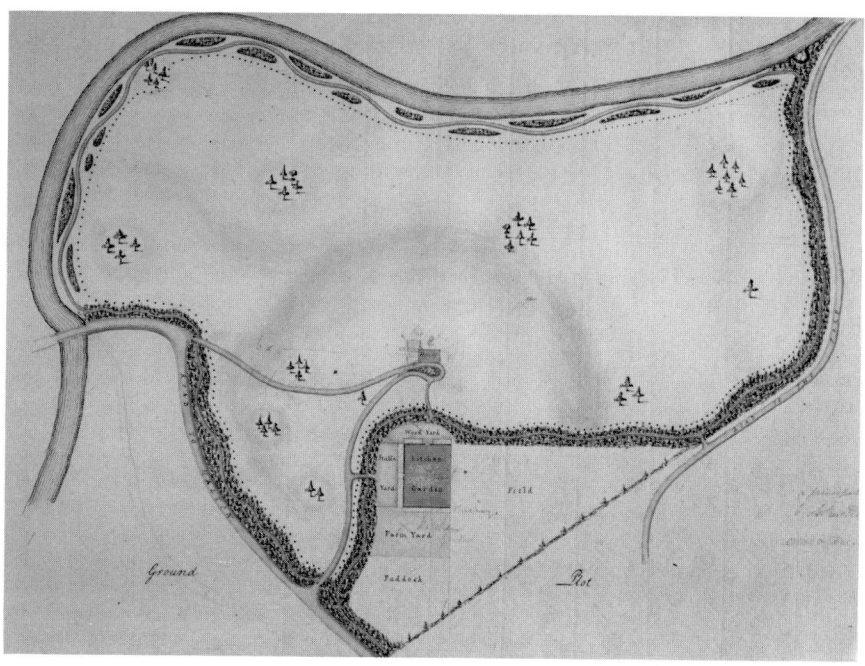

30. Field Book of Halton Place Estate 1813 Made by Sam'l Swire, Land Surveyor
(6 chains to one Inch) Plan of lands in hand

Goosemere Heights formed the eastern horizon, and the dark crouching shape of Pendle Hill could be seen to the south west. The call of the curlew and the 'pee wit' of the plover mingled with the bleating of the sheep.

By November 1773 Thomas had made the acquaintance of Jane, daughter of Joseph Reay, of Killingworth, Northumberland. Thomas had declared himself to her, but the charming letter which he then wrote to her shows that he was far from certain of her acceptance, but could scarecely wait for her answer

Nov. 7th 1773[3]

'Dear Madam,

I cannot prevail upon myself to defer any longer making use of the Permission you gave me of writing to you, though the time prescribed is not expired, not that I wish to precipitate your Judgement in an affair so important to our mutual happiness; though after a full examination of your Heart the speediness of your Determination in my favour, would add, if possible to my Obligation.

As we are apt to entertain Hopes of succeeding in that which we wish, I acknowledge I have been making some Enquiry what additional accomodation I should be able to make immediately; and though the account is not quite so favourable as I could wish yet I hope my little mantion may be made comfortable till further accomodation can be provided.

I called at Richmond on my way home and communicated to my Brother and Sister my wishes; to which they both heartily joined in wishing me success. As to my journey, I tired one of my horses, and one of the bags was thoroughly drenched by the rain. The country between Richmond and Halton is mountainous which breaks the clouds, tho' for the most part the Road winds amongst the Vallies.

I beg my respects . . . and remain, dear Madam, with the greatest regard, yr. obedient and most humble servant,

Thomas Yorke.'

Whatever she replied, it encouraged him to write again and express his feelings even more warmly, by the standards and etiquette of the day.

'My dear Madam,

In answer to your very obliging letter . . . it shall be my Study to cultivate your esteem, permit me to say, your regard, which I own I cannot but entertain hope of obtaining by assiduity. Fortunate indeed I shall think myself, if I should succeed. I wish you to follow the dictates of your own heart,. . . and I refer myself entirely to your . . . generous nature.

I think of setting out soon, after next Sunday, if I should receive nothing from yourself to stop me, and that I hope to be in Newcastle by the middle of the week. A line from you signifying whether a visit would be agreeable would give me great pleasure.'

They were married the following year and the reports circulated round the family clearly commended his choice, as one extract shows, '. . . every account I receive of Miss Reay confirms . . . her accomplishments, her understanding, and what gives a lustre to them all, her sweet nature.'

A miniature of Jane shows a slim, dark haired girl with fine features and a long neck. No portrait of Thomas remains but he is warmly commended by his cousin and his son, as 'a man of talent and sound judgement, a kind master and landlord, beloved by all around him, and an affectionate husband and father.'

They moved into Halton Place, and Thomas gave up his legal practice and settled down to his family concerns. It would be interesting to know how much of the house furnishings had been completed before Jane came on the scene, but the young couple certainly had the chance to plan their new home together.

Compared to The Green or Bewerley, the whole lay out was on a far more modest scale, but it contained the same areas necessary for a self reliant household. The garden had to provide fruit, vegetables and flowers throughout the season, including potatoes, now in regular use. Apple and plum trees were espaliered on the brick walls, which backed the stables, and there may have been a hothouse too.

The stables contained eight or ten stalls and loose boxes for the riding and carriage horses. Three coach houses held the carriage, chariot and shandry, with living quarters for the grooms above, and round the cobbled yard were the hay lofts and tack rooms.

The home farm had to supply milk, butter, cream, eggs, mutton, beef and poultry for the house, as well as pasture, hay and straw for the stock. The estate provided venison, hares, rabbits, waterfowl, and game birds. The river was a constant source of both food and sport, with trout, grayling and salmon each in their season.

The timber needed for fencing and building was cut locally and sawn in the wood yard. Metalwork needed was worked in the blacksmith's forge. Estate men and local craftsmen built and plastered, glazed and roofed the new houses and farm buildings as they were improved. New stone walls and hedges enclosed the land near the village, but it was to be a long time

31. Halton Place 1800. Print taken from Dr Whitaker's Craven

before the acres of wet rushy moor land were tilled. Lime and manure was used on the enclosed land to increase the grass growth, so the stock fattened faster, and the extra hay grown kept more animals alive through the long cold winters.

All these alterations came about very very slowly, and I have no doubt Thomas's new ideas met with a good deal of opposition from the tenants. The ten families who farmed the main farms had lived in the Craven area for generations and had battled to make a living out of stock rearing. They knew the endless round of tending animals day in, day out, in all weathers. Their work was laborious and unremitting, and each member of the family put all their energy and strength into the farm. Short cuts, labour saving devices and holidays were totally unknown. The margin between just making a living and failure was pitifully small, and the loss of a beast or the sickness of a man could be catastrophic.

Because of this, the people had developed a tough endurance to hardship and toil, and a private philosophy with a dry humour to overcome the rough patches. Their understatement was, and still is, masterly, and their kindness, though done without display, unfailing. They were however deeply conservative in outlook, and although one or two had heard of improvements succeeding elsewhere, they did not care to run risks by innovations.

The population in 1801 was 180, so approximately the same number would have become Thomas's tenants, cottagers and work people.[4]

Halton, mentioned in the Domesday Book when Roger de Poitou owned about 180 taxable cultivated acres, had passed into the hands of Bolton Priory about 1102. The Prior had a grange there and men were sent to gather and store the corn at harvest time, and take back a tithe to the Priory. A water mill, beside the river, was mentioned in 1268.

The Scots raided the area frequently, but particularly so from 1316–19, as entries in the Prior's Compotus show,

'1317 Recd from Halton 63 qtrs of oats and not more owing to the adventurous Scots removing our servants at Halton away.'
'1318 For rebuilding the grange at Halton destroyed by the Scots, £7.16.9'
'1318 Owing to the ravages of the Scots the cornlands at Halton went almost untilled.'

The de Halton family held the land under the Prior until the last heiress married into the Talbot family in 1485. The Talbots held the thirteen messuages and the water mill for the next two hundred years, but it seems that, after them, the township changed hands several times before Thomas Yorke bought it from Edward Mundy in 1737.

In 1689 the house of John Wilkinson was licensed for worship as a non conformist chapel.[5] The Old Hall is of that date, and could have been that one, for it appears to have been the main house of the village. There were four thatched cottages of the same date nearby. The parish church was in Long Preston, which was a three mile walk past Scale Farm and over Cow Bridge.

In 1770 there was much to be done on the estate, and Thomas, with his good head for business inherited from his father, and his well trained legal mind, set about it.

The eleven farms and their tenants then were
The Home Farm,
Old Hall, William Frankland,
Town End, Charles Batty,
Low Field, John Elsworth,
Cow Hill, Ellis Kay,
Scale Farm (High and Low), Richard Franklin,
Long Bank, Thos. Parker?
New House, John Carr,

Low Thornber, William Banks,
North Thornber, Thos. Smith,
West Thornber, Jas. Parker
Pye Cross, Wm. Taylor?

Scale Farm was the largest at 359 acres, and the Old Hall the smallest at 80. Many of the houses and buildings were in a poor and dilapidated state and needed improving, and the total rents came to just £500 a year.

In Thomas's day the droving of cattle down from Scotland to the English markets was at its height.[6] Immense herds followed the green trackways and drove roads through Yorkshire, and many used Malham as an important resting place, where they fattened up on the succulent pasture of Great Close. John Birtwistle, the famous Craven grazier, rented the 700 acre Close, on which more than 5,000 cattle might graze at any one time, and through which 20,000 would pass in a summer.

Other herds came down from Horton in Ribblesdale through Settle, Long Preston and Hellifield and on towards Lancashire. So Thomas and Jane frequently saw the stalwart, bare kneed, bare headed drovers in their kilts and plaids striding along behind their black cattle, with their trusty 'Coallie' or cur dogs beside them. Each man carried a small bag of oatmeal and a few onions, which they cut up and mixed with milk or blood. They usually slept out with their beasts in all weathers, and carried a large cudgel and often a small dirk with them for protection. They had sole responsibility for driving and selling their beasts, and for collecting and delivering the very large sums of money involved.

At the cattle fairs in Skipton, Hellifield or Malham the black Galloways mingled with the Highland kyloes, the local shorthorns and the Craven Longhorns. The Yorkes attended these fairs along with their neighbours, the Hamertons from Hellifield Peel, Thomas Clarke from Swinden Hall and Thomas Metcalfe of Nappa, as well as many of their tenants. Horses and sheep were also sold and through all the fields around was 'a brisk stream hurrying across the way, hundreds of healthy people in their best apparel, Farmers and their families, Esquires and their daughters, hastening up from the dales and down from the fells on every side, pressing forward to join the throng.'[7]

Thomas and Jane lived on close terms with the people around and were deeply involved in their farm and estate. Every calf born, every horse sold, sheep sheared, crop grown, fruit gathered and barrel of beer brewed was under their eye, and carefully accounted for by Thomas . His shoulders ached and his hands grew blistered when he helped to fork the hay on to the cart and then into the barn. When Thomas needed a tooth drawing, he went to the farrier and suffered horribly like everyone else. When a wheel came off his chariot, he stood in the driving wind and rain and helped to put it on again. The only remedies available were rhubarb, poultices or a little quinine, for whatever ill.

Like his brother John, Thomas was one of the 'resident native gentry' described by Cobbett, 'attached to the soil, known to every farmer and labourer from their childhood, frequently mixing with them in those pursuits where all artificial distinction is lost. . .'.

He walked miles with his spaniels after game, and rode miles to hunt or course with his neighbours, by whom he was held in respect for his knowledge of the law.

He gave help to the poor and needy but was prepared to see rough justice done when it was considered necessary. One entry in a constable's book was, 'Robert Biggen for stealing potatoes was whipped through the parish and back'.

Jane, with her sweet nature and happy family upbringing, settled into Halton and took up the reins of her new life. Her first son Thomas was born a year later, to her joy, and her second son John a year after that, in 1776. Little Thomas died while still very young, as so many infants did then, and sad Jane and Thomas had to accompany his tiny coffin to Long Preston churchyard.

The following year brother John took his wife and sisters to France, hoping that Anne's health would improve in a better climate. Thomas wrote to him,[8]

'I was glad to hear by yours dated Calais that you had all got safe on shore. . . I hope Miss Nanny bore her journey well. . . we are both so particularly anxious for her welfare and hope speedily to hear a good account of her.

Instead of going to church this morning I staid at Home to write this letter, having got a slight cold. . . and a few minutes before I began to write I was surprised with a very sensible shake of the whole room and of my chair under me. Upon going into the Kitchen to inquire I found the Kitchin and the furniture had been sensibly shaken, which I have not the least doubt proceeded from an earthquake. . . today has been very fine and warm. Another such week will get in most of our Wheat and Barley. which is mostly ripe or cut. Our Harvest is unusually late this year (Sept 14th).

My wife and little boy are both well. My Wife desires to finish my letter and I know her fingers are much nimbler than mine, for fear I should not leave her room enough I will conclude. . .' (then follows Jane's exquisitely neat hand)

'With Mr Yorke's leave I beg to add a few words to my Dear Sisters but despair of filling up so large a share of paper as my husband has left me. . .

I hope Miss Anne may have found some benefit from her sickness, tho' far be it from me to rejoice that you are at such a distance from us.

My brother went to see ye Coalworks at Manchester and had a very narrow escape, his Horse and self falling into a canal – it luckily was not deeper than his shoulders and he did not even catch cold.'

The next summer they heard the sad news of two deaths, first Sir John Clavering, sister Katharine's husband.

An affectionate letter from John's wife says,

'We have been much affected by the late melancoly but . . . with hearing the agreeable news of Mrs Yorke and a little stranger soon we all unite and send kind regards and best wishes.'

In July Thomas wrote,

'My wife is as well as a Woman can be who expects to be confined any day. We have part of our Attendants in the house and expect Mrs Reay in day or two. A few nights ago we were alarmed with the apprehension that the attendance of a Midwife was necessary . . . but it proved a false alarm . . . . we had Company in the house and a Lady with child too, whom we were afraid of frightening into the same situation.

The wet weather has prevented the beginning of the Hay harvest and rendered the Halton bridge well nigh impassable, and the temporary bridge was only finished the day before yesterday. Our footman Thomas has engaged himself to our maid Sarah, who turns out to be a lady of some fortune, but we begin to be apprehensive from her very forward appearance lest she should be brought to bed before her regular time after marriage,'

A few days later came the joyful news,

'I have the satisfaction to inform you that my Wife was brought to bed yesterday . . . of a very fine little girl. She is rather a large and very strong child, and, if she should prove a scold, will make herself heard.

Our love to our dear Anne and to assure her how much we participate with her in her sufferings, and how ready we should have been to have contributed to her comfort, if it had been in our power. We think you all have the greatest merit in discharging so kind an office.'

Only a short time after the birth they grieved to hear the news of Anne's death. Little Margaret Anne was a consolation to them all, as well as a welcome playmate for young John. Jane was clearly an excellent wife and mother, and made Halton the happiest of homes. She took a keen interest in all Thomas's plans and improvements, and ran her household with care and kindness.

In 1782 her much loved unmarried uncle, John Cuthbert, of Witton Castle in Durham, died, leaving a legacy to Jane of £1,000. She was determined her husband should use the money on the Halton estate, and it came at a much needed moment. There were taxes on horses, on servants and on windows. (There are three false windows at Halton which balance the design but saved the tax.)

Sir Thomas Clavering M.P. wrote to Thomas from Axwell Park,[9]

'Your letter found me as usual at this season . . . enjoying my social amusements. . . Here my dear Sir I was obliged to break off. The Coach came to the door and I was waited for . . . I was called to pay my last respects to the remains of poor Cuthbert . . . .

The expected Peace becomes every day more uncertain . . . neither can any Treaty with America . . . unless a universal Peace takes place. It is impossible to leave that contry at liberty to assist France, and to have our own power tied up. . . . It was inconsistent in Mr Foxe's motion to produce Treaties to the wild ideas of the House of Commons, unsigned and unsettled, and France will not permit her ally America to make peace with us in which she is not included.

Our Naval force is most certainly at this moment equal, if not superior to, all the Maritime Forces of all the other Belligerent powers but yet I hope . . . this would not induce us to stretch the cord too far. Our finances are exhausted, and let who will be Minister, the difficulty will be great to raise taxes for another year's war.

We are in this neighbourhood using every means to guard against the high price of corn, with a failure in some degree of both Turnips and Potatoes. Rewards are offered for the latter and most of the coal owners have agreed to make up the difference in the price of corn to their workmen.'

During this period between the French Revolution and the onset of war, Thomas kept in close touch with his sister Mary in Richmond, and his widowed sister Katharine in London. Young John was growing up and was now able to ride out with his father.

For seven years after Margaret Anne's birth there were no more babies at Halton, but then came Thomas Henry in 1785 and lastly Edmund. It is not hard for me to picture their daily life at Halton where I myself was brought up. 'The small mansion' kept the family as one unit. There could be little or no exclusion of the children, as happened in larger houses, and the servants, too, lived close to the family.

There was far less formality than at The Green or Bewerley, and the four little Yorkes ran in and out, into the garden, out to their ponies in the stables, down to the river to play or paddle or fish. Although both their parents had been brought up in larger establishments, I have the feeling they enjoyed the intimacy of this life and surroundings. Thomas may of course have had to shut himself away in his library to get some peace. This room lay to the right of the front door, across the stone flagged hall with its pattern of polished black slate squares. It was small, but the shelves were well stocked, as we know from a list of Thomas's books. There were many volumes on Divinity and Law, and also the works of Pope, Swift, Milton, Prior and Clarendon. Donville's maps and the Spectator kept him up to date. Jane also owned '40 or 50 small books' and two volumes of Bowdler's Sermons.

Jane papered and arranged her own drawing room to suit her taste, and entertained her company there. The windows of the dining room looked east across to the old mill by the river, where the estate corn was still ground.

The servants' hall lay to the left of the front door, with the kitchen behind it. The view from the slopstone kitchen sink was across to the river and the hills. The cooking was done in a cast iron oven and side boiler, with a bakstone beside it for baking the oatcakes. Hams, sides of bacon and salted beef and strings of dried herbs hung from hooks in the ceiling, over the well scrubbed wooden table. Damp circles of oatcake were hung up to dry on the airing rack, alongside the clean clothes.

The laundry had its wash boiler, dolly tubs, and heavy iron mangle. The dairy had great wooden bowls of milk set on stone shelves for the cream to rise. A plug in a hole in the base of each bowl allowed the skim milk to be run off. The butter was made in a stand churn or a barrel churn, and shaped into pats. Cheeses wrapped in muslin lay in one corner. Hares, rabbits and game birds were hung on hooks in the game larder. All these out buildings were at the back, and the privy, (or 'necessary') stood a little way away.

Upstairs, Jane and Thomas slept in a large curtained bed, with a coal fire in the grate and a dressing room next door. Three other bedrooms and the housekeeper's room led off the landing, and there was also that most up to date of inventions, a water closet.

The second floor had four smaller bedrooms, in one of which the younger children slept with their nurse, and in others, the maidservants. The footman slept in the main attic.

32. Section through centre of Halton Place from East to West, 1770

Highlights of the week were driving to church at Long Preston, visiting the neighbours, or the arrival of the packman. The latter brought more than just muslins, holland, laces and ribbons – he brought excitement, for he carried news from the outside world, patent medicines for ague or rheumatism, political comment, the latest fashion tips and the newest song. As yet there were no shops outside the towns. Commissions for staple goods like sugar, tea and cloth, (as well as letters), were delivered by carrier cart from Skipton. One of the many articles that we take for granted had to be made at home, and that was ink.

This is a family recipe for it.

To make excellent black ink
6oz blue Galls. pounded of Aleppo
$\frac{1}{2}$oz green Coperas, clean and rocky
1oz Gum Arabic, clean, bright and clear
1oz Roach Allum
1 quart of rain water unboiled

To stand near the Fire about three weeks and frequently stirred during that time and then poured off the Dreggs.

The local gentry who called on Thomas and Jane, and were entertained at Halton, lived within a radius of about fifteen miles around. They included the Hamertons of Hellifield Peel, the Coulthursts of Gargrave, the Roundells of Gledstone, the Tempests of Broughton, the Listers of Gisburn, the Littledales of Bolton Hall, the Garforths of Coniston, the Ingilbys of Lawkland and the Asshetons of Downham. Further afield, too far for just a call, were the Starkies of Huntroyde, the Peels of Knowlmere and the Parkers of Browsholme.

Thomas certainly joined in the sport with the local pack of harriers. The Craven country then consisted of fine open pasture land and miles of rougher ground, crossed by many becks and small banks. Drystone walls and a few hedges were the only obstacles.

One pack was kennelled at Broughton at this period, and Stephen Tempest hunted them himself. Another was kept by Mr Dyneley at Halton East.[10]

Thomas would often ride the ten miles over to Broughton, across the stepping stones at Nappa, via Gledstone to East Marton, on a strong dock-tailed horse, with his groom alongside. There he met up with six or eight other neighbours and had a stirrup cup. Hounds drew off towards Gargrave, and if a hare was put up, she would run in a wide circle, perhaps back to Nappa. If a deer was raised, hounds might run for miles, even over to Elslack. The groom, in his low crowned hat, followed quietly, carrying a spare stirrup leather, ready to change horses with his master if his mount grew weary.

Riding home together in the dusk, the two men talked over the day, until, stiff and weary, they reached home. Together they cleaned, strapped and rugged up the horses and fed them, before they went in to change.

The story is told that some wags in Skipton got hold of a donkey and fastened a pair of antlers to its head. They sent word to Mr Tempest that a fine deer had been seen near the moor. Out went the huntsman with his pack until the 'deer' was sighted,

> Clap on the hounds, the quarry's here!
> And chase, oh chase the flying deer!
> But sooth to tell no deer would fly,
> The donkey cried 'Hic ho! hic hi!'

Thomas and his friends must have retold this tale many times over their dinner tables.

When in 1792, brother John's natural daughter, Mary, was married at Richmond to the Reverend Moseley Atkinson the family made them both welcome.[11]

Thomas's letters reveal his gentle humour as well as his devotion to all his family. He remained very close to his brother who frequently sought his advice on many matters, particularly on his mining affairs. As John aged, however, and Atkinson gained more influence over him, John only communicated by letter. Meetings between them were constantly postponed on grounds of health, but their letters remained intimate, open and affectionate.

By this time young John had left St John's Cambridge and had joined the Militia. He was quartered in many different places all over the country. Margaret Anne was still living at home and her two younger brothers were at school, aged twelve and fourteen.

Peace was made between France and Britain, and Sir John Borlase Warren was appointed Ambassador in St Petersburgh. He wrote to young John inviting him to accompany him to Russia as attaché. Thomas and Jane were highly delighted, as indeed was John. He left in September 1802, and, anxious though they were over such a journey, John kept them well informed of all his adventures. His descriptions of Russian court life are fascinating.

By 1811 brother John's health was in a poor state. His handwriting became a shaky scrawl but his mind and ideas were perfectly sound. He longed to be fit enough to undertake the proposal Sir Thomas White had made, to buy up his land and mines. He wrote to young John, home again from Russia, explaining his wishes and making it clear to him that he was to inherit.

Just at this time however Thomas was struck by a severe paralysis – perhaps caused by a stroke. He recovered partially but only for a few months. Jane nursed him in an agony of anxiety, but he finally died in the place he had loved and for which he had worked so hard. He had quadrupled the value of the estate by his care.

It was as well for him that he died before the family breakup over John's will, although he was the only person who could have prevented the disaster.

As it was, fully expecting his son to inherit all the family property,[12] he made his will in terms which laid an added burden on John, the very last thing he would have wished.

After asking John to see that his two younger brothers should be fairly treated, he went on,

'I am not unmindful that my wife voluntarily presented me with the legacy left her by her uncle Cuthbert, or of her uniformity, amiable and correct conduct in every respect, but more particularly as a Wife and as a Mother, but as I am not able in my present situation to bequeath her anything that will essentially add to her comforts, (over and above her due), I hope she will accept the following bequests as tokens of affection and as memorials of me; viz. I give to her all her Jewels, apparel and the effects which she has in her bureau, my Gold Watch, my chaise and chaise horses, my silver urn, my silver teapot, my silver dish. . . the furniture, books and prints left her by her Mother and any other articles which she may wish to choose, (excepting the dressing set to my son John).'

The events following both Thomas' and John's deaths bore most heavily on the heir, but almost as heavily on Jane, his most loving widowed mother. She had to watch her dearly loved son being swindled out of his birthright by cunning and dishonesty, and was powerless to help. She, whose one main wish always was to preserve family unity and affection had to see it wrenched apart.

It was as well that Elizabeth died only six months after her husband John, so family wounds could heal. For young John however, many difficulties lay ahead.

Chapter XIV

JOHN YORKE   1776 – 1857
OF
BEWERLEY AND HALTON PLACE

JOHN WAS THE SECOND BUT ELDEST SURVIVING SON of Thomas and Jane Yorke, born and brought up at Halton. He and his sister Margaret Anne were two years apart, while their brothers were younger by more than seven and nine years. John had a happy carefree childhood with his particularly loving parents, in the open expanses of Ribblesdale in Craven. He grew up alongside the children of his father's tenants, and rode all over the area, on visiting terms at every farmhouse he passed. From his earliest days he was aware of his father's meticulous care for the upkeep and improvement of the land, the buildings, fences, walls and crops.

After he left school he went to St John's College, Cambridge. By this time his sister was growing up and entering local society, and his brothers were at school. His elderly uncle at Richmond was in poor health, and his aunt made every possible excuse to keep John and his father away from him. John therefore had little opportunity to learn about family affairs, or to get to know the properties or the tenants at Bewerley. Moseley Atkinson also conspired to keep John ignorant of what was going on.

As John's parents were wholly desirous of preserving family harmony, they accepted the joint excuses offered, but could not help feeling uneasy. The reasons given were always most plausible, but suspicions had begun to form.

The war with France was declared, and John decided to join the North Yorkshire Militia. He was quartered in many different areas around the country, north and south. When a brief period of peace occurred, the Militia was disbanded. To John's great delight he received an invitation from Sir John Borlase Warren to accompany him to Russia. [Sir John had recently been appointed Ambassador in St Petersburgh.]

This was a brilliant opportunity for him, and he gladly accepted. He kept an excellent journal of his whole tour which makes enthralling reading.

'I had the honour of being requested to accompany Sir John Warren, appointed as Ambassador to the Court of St Petersburgh, along with two friends Captains Bisschopp and Bouverie of the Guards, and Captain Hawes who went as Private Secretary.'

The journey on board the Clyde Frigate[1] took from September 17th to October 12th. They were met at Oranienbaum by coaches with four horses driven abreast, by long bearded coachmen in loose cloaks tied with a sash, 'extremely dirty in appearance'.

The country was very flat, wet and swampy, with many woods; the peasants cottages miserable, and made of wood. After a twenty-four mile journey they reached the outskirts of St Petersburgh. It was extremely dirty, with narrow, ill lighted, ill paved streets, but good houses. When they had settled in, John and his friends decided to hire a coach, for the streets were so dirty. They could have travelled by droshkey – 'like a saddle on wheels without springs, drawn by one horse – you ride side or across'.

They attended the Ball and Supper given for the Marriage of Prince and Princess Volkonski, which was magnificent.

'When we entered they were dancing the Polonaise, which is the rage here, then English country dances and afterwards the waltz, which is difficult at first. . . and must make anyone giddy who is not used to it. The ladies are, in general, fat, many pretty but with bad figures; they certainly have not the native modesty of an English woman, nor that delicacy of manner. . . they wear a great deal of rouge and a quantity of Tinsel and silver ornaments in their dress and very long trains. . . . The gentlemen wore uniform with a profusion of stars, ribbons etc., the ladies wore flowers in wreaths round the head, but no feathers. Their dresses were of Gauze. . .'.

He was presented to the twenty six year old, handsome but shy Emperor, and his pretty, elegantly dressed, much rouged Empress, and attended several Court Balls and Masquerades. The men's dark green Court Dress, much embroidered with gold, was only worn on special days. John danced two polonaises in the Emperor's set, but Sir John Warren had to sit and play Boston, (a kind of whist), with the Empress Dowager. It was the first time he had played, and she was expert. They had a fine supper at the Hermitage, caviare, sterlet, beef and hams. 'The Russians eat and drink all day', wrote John.

By the end of October a sharp frost and some snow warned people to prepare their Furs. John ordered a bear skin pelisse, to be covered in cloth, gloves lined with swansdown, fur boots and a cap. His ears became frozen one day later in the season, but Bouverie rubbed them quickly with snow, and thereafter John wore a silk handkerchief.

He described the Ice Hills, which were specially constructed ice covered scaffolds, down which he was swept on a little sledge, and up the next one. 'Our Ambassador went down in his gold laced Hat, he liked it much and said the sensation was like being thrown out of a window. Some skait down it on one leg.'

Two novelties which struck John do not seem strange to us now. One was the frozen meat market where all kinds of meat, game and poultry was preserved quite cheaply – and not spoilt by salting like the English meat. The other was a sauna, which he called a Vapour Bath. These were used weekly by the Russians, and were a completely new experience for John.

In March there was talk of war between Russia and Sweden, as well as between England and France, and the two Guards Captains left to rejoin their respective corps. John attended the Easter celebration of the Resurrection in the Emperor's Chapel, a highly colourful and magnificent ceremony with superb singing.

On May 20th he heard that war had been declared between England and France, after many rumours. John felt he could not desert Sir John, for he was acting Private Secretary in place of Captain Hawes, and Lady Warren had also left to attend her daughter's confinement.

He went to one more brilliant Fete at Peterhof, at which the whole Court was present.

'The Gardens were most beautifully illuminated . . . the numerous and very fine Fountains played . . . Lamps were so contrived that the water appeared to pass over them ; the Palace. . . was a complete blaze of Fire, a Balloon was sent up with fireworks by Mr Gornerin in front of the gardens, the Emperor's Yachts were also fully illuminated – for my part I may truly say I never was present at anything equal to it.'

By August 15th he had made up his mind to rejoin the Militia, as an Invasion was daily expected in England. After a five week voyage via Sweden, he 'had the satisfaction of finding myself on English ground' although feeling considerable regret at leaving St Petersburgh.

Poor Lady Warren had waited three weeks for a convoy, been delayed by contrary winds, and finally heard her grandchild had arrived and her efforts were in vain. She travelled back to St Petersburgh only to pack up and make the same journey again.

John did rejoin the Militia on his return and continued his service in Portsmouth, Weymouth, Hull and Ipswich, (reaching the rank of Major), until the death of his father in 1811.

The paralysis which struck his father left him severely ill for some time before he died and John returned to support his mother. He was a tower

33. John Yorke, 1802, taken at St. Petersburg

of strength to her. Together they saw to all the necessary formalities and arranged the funeral at Long Preston Church.

John left the army and lived at Halton with his mother and sister for the next eight years. This must have seemed rather a quiet life after his Russian adventures, but he took over the estate and did his best to carry out his father's wishes in every way.

The death of his uncle three years later, brought much heartache and many problems for him. When the will was read, he and his mother were appalled. They had had no idea of the conditions laid upon his inheritance, and he felt quite certain that he had properly understood his uncle's real intentions.

His decision to contest the will, (which went entirely against the grain), was a hard one to make, but he felt confident of success. However, the opinion of James Scarlett, obtained by Elizabeth Yorke, tipped the balance. A brilliant K.C. (later Lord Abinger), Scarlett ensured that the case went against John, and in favour of his own wife's family.

Poor John. As well as very many financial problems, he was filled with feelings of resentment and disappointment.[2] His Father's property at Worston was sold (by his wish) to William Assheton, for the sum of £3,470 for 1020 acres and 10 sheep gates, to the advantage of Jane and the younger children. Only £3,000 was left to each of these children, but John had promised his father to make up their portions to £8,000. He raised his mother's income from £300 to £700 a year. He wrote,

'My Father having done so much for the Halton estate and given his three sons college education, on his death had left it to me to fulfill his wishes. I deeply lamented that he did not live to settle all his affairs himself, but I anxiously endeavoured to fulfill the duties he left me to perform. At the time he expected that I should have inherited all my uncle's property, instead of which I had to purchase from the Exors. for £32,000 the lands around Bewerley, without which I could not have made it my residence; also all the Family plate and books, (the Family jewels my Aunt kept). This made me a poor instead of a rich man. My uncle's intentions were clearly shown in his letter to me in which he said,

'I am now exceedingly infirm, therefore the whole property of the family will enable you to encompass the acquisition of this (extra land).'

Six months later, his aunt died. Her will proved yet another loss to the family as all she had been left by her husband went to her nieces. As a result of this combination of lost expectations, and to meet the heavy costs, John was obliged to sell The Green and all the Richmond property. His deep regret at this can be imagined, particularly as the family had had a two hundred year connection with the town, and a hundred years of Parliamentary representation.

He wrote,

'After many debates I decided on making Bewerley my residence, although strongly attached to the house of my birth, Halton Place. The beauty and extent of Bewerley made it desirable though I found the property in a most dilapidated state, not a house or barn or fence in order.'

34. Bewerley Hall 1815 before alterations. Watercolour by Mary Wright

To put all this into perspective, John was not of course reduced to being a poor man (as he felt), but his pride in his family and lands, so carefully inculcated by his parents, was severely bruised. His mother however was a strong and constant support to him, and continued in her loving way to soothe the wounded feelings and to heal every possible breach. Fortunately John was no boy, but a mature, travelled man of thirty-seven, and so better able to handle the problems, though they were many.

Waterloo had been a triumph for the British people but by the end of the Napoleonic wars, to a huge National Debt, excessive taxation, and an enormous poor rate, was added great unemployment. The price of wheat fell from 110s a quarter in 1813 to 66s a quarter in 1815. The rent roll at Halton was £1,580 in 1811, but only £232 of rent was collected in 1816,[3] and the income from the Bewerley rents fell correspondingly. There was a very wet and poor harvest in 1816, the potato crop failed and sheep died in their hundreds. Sheepdogs were taxed at 8s a dog, which laid a terrible burden on sheep farmers. 8s was a week's wage and the dalesmen needed at least two good dogs each, with more to train on.

John did his best to alleviate the local distress caused by this post war depression, and worked hard to sort out his duties and do necessary repairs.[4] New applications for land enclosure were made and John safeguarded his ancient mining rights. He had plans drawn up for enlarging Halton Place to a handsome design, but these could not be carried out. Nancy Bullock and Betty Geldard were the mainstays of the Halton household then, and Thomas Shorrock worked in the house or in the garden. John Kidd acted as steward.

John Yorke was appointed High Sheriff of Yorkshire in 1818, and followed his uncle's example in asking his tenants to attend some of the ceremonies. He wore his military uniform, and his mother particularly rejoiced to see him recognised in the county, and enjoyed playing her part in the entertaining.

The next year he spent some time travelling in Italy, where he bought several marble statues and a round marble table. He also bought two seascapes by Bakhuysen in Rome for £120.

In 1815 John had made the acquaintance of the Wright family from Mapperley Park, Nottingham. Ichabod Wright had married Harriet Day and had had three sons and ten daughters, of whom the elder of twin girls was Mary. John visited them frequently and paid Mary particular attention. They must have laughed together over his stories of the fat Russian ladies. One day he gave her a little leather bound private diary as his first gift. In it she wrote all the events she felt most deeply during her life.

John was forty-four years old when he proposed to Mary who was then twenty-five. He wrote delightful letters to her before their marriage,[5]

Bewerley, 1821

'Dear Mary,

I think I have given you a little employment in writing letters, but if you do not object to writing them, and I think you do not, I have no objection to receiving them; indeed I feel a real pleasure in receiving them, and it is a great comfort and satisfaction to me, and *in some degree* makes up for your absence.

I have now to thank you for your charming long letter today. . . . I am truly happy that mine give you any pleasure my sweetest Mary, but I only express half what I feel, and of which I hope ere long to convince you, and believe me I speak from the heart, ... I wish I could thank you enough for all they contain.'

He goes on to describe the rooms at Bewerley, and his sister's ideas for wallpapers.

'I hope you will choose a pretty one for your own Boudoir, which I wish to be fitted up according to your own Taste. My sister has chose a Room which has the prettiest view outside, therefore I wish it to be elegant within. . . but in my opinion the principal ornament of it will be a *certain* person who is to inhabit it. You wish for a description of the Rooms – first one bow Window Room with two dressing rooms, one of which is a Turret, this the bedroom, three single rooms, one of which is to be your Boudoir – they are all *sun* rooms. . . . The morning Room has been painted once all over with. . . not quite a lavender, which will go well with the furniture. . . . I am now only thinking of the day when I shall have the happiness of embracing my dearest Mary. . . accept yourself my most sincere love and tender regards and believe me to be, ever your most faithful and attached

John Yorke'

One can picture Mary reading out the description of the rooms to her mother and sisters, and endlessly imagining the house she is to make her home. What discussions of materials, colours and papers they must have had. Each letter was a fresh excitement.

Halton Place 1821[6]

'My dearest Mary,

. . . I left my Mother well at Bewerley. The day though showery was favourable for crossing the mountains which will put you in mind of Derbyshire, though you may not think the Roads quite so good, being

35. Bewerley Hall 1821 by Mary Yorke (drawing)

rather rough and shaking – I must not however prejudice you against our high hills and the roads before you come into Yorkshire. . . the truth is, however, the road I travelled today is a very bad one, and uneasy for Carriages, which you will find as you will probably have to pass over it on your way to the Lakes.

I now think only of the joyful meeting which I am vain enough to fancy some others of my acquaintance entertain the same thoughts – am I right in my conjecture? but you need not allow it my sweetest Mary, unless you chuse.

I hope that nothing will prevent me leaving here on Monday . . . you may be sure I shall make a long day of it, and I may be able to reach Mapperley early the next day.

I have not forgot your beautiful drawings . . . my sister was so enchanted with your lovely Madonna . . . that she quite longed to steal it, and I had some difficulty getting it back into the Carriage.

What delight it will be for me to accompany you in the Garden and Shrubbery to talk over our future arrangements – I assure you my Gardener has used double diligence lately in mowing and dressing the Shrubbery at Bewerley that it may be neat for the arrival of a certain Stranger, who, though she may not think it as gay as her own, I flatter myself will admire it a little.'

The next letter is the last he wrote before their marriage. (Years later, as an old lady, Mary put these letters into a folder. She wrote a note inside – 'These letters from my Dear Husband have never been read by anyone but myself. I cannot burn them, we were seldom separated. They may be of interest to Children and Grandchildren, Mary Yorke 1867.')

'My dearest Mary,   Halton July 29th 1821

You ask me what I have been doing at Bewerley – the answer is very easy, working in your service – making preparations to receive a certain personage, I could not be better employed. Whilst giving orders about the Boudoir you are to inhabit, I fancied I saw you seated in the easy arm chair by the fireside, or reclining on the sofa. I need not tell you with what pleasure I look forward to that time. The Curtains are ordered for the Dining room and Morning room . . . I have not forgotten the Cake which my sister has ordered from York.

I have ordered horses for *tomorrow* – the last time I trust I shall travel *alone* – I shall probably sleep at Ferrybridge near Doncaster and endeavour to reach Mapperley in good time the following day.

I need not, I think, say with what joy I shall return to you. I will now only beg you to be assured of my most affectionate love and Regard, and that I remain your ever faithful and truly attached

John Yorke'

In 1817 a beautiful portrait of Mary had been painted. Her short dark hair curls round her intelligent and graceful face, with its well defined nose and mobile mouth. Her low cut muslin dress is high waisted and tied with a pink sash.

She and John were married on August 9th 1821 at Basford Church, in Nottinghamshire. John wrote in his Journal,

'I had the happiness of being united to my wife . . . a union which has been blessed to us both.'

[That same year George IV was crowned, after many years as Prince Regent. The huge public scandal over Queen Caroline ended only with her death, a month later. The penal code was reformed by Peel and the first London police force created. The old political parties were breaking up and a new interpretation of government was needed.]

John Yorke's mother and sister had been back and forth from Halton to Bewerley, over the 'uneasy roads' helping him to prepare the house and grounds. The decision was made that they should go to live in York, and John bought them a house at 49 Micklegate. It was a great wrench for them both to leave Halton, which they loved so dearly, but Jane faced it with courage. Her splendid personality and good sense shine out of her affectionate letters. It is from these that one gains an intimate view on the new occupants of Bewerley, and all their doings.

August 10th 1821

I trust I may now address you my *dear daughter* at *Bewerley*,[7] and shall be very happy to hear you had a tolerable journey, tho' the weather is far from being what we wished for your entrance into the Vale of Nid, which I was of course most sincerely anxious should appear to you in an advantageous light. I cannot have a doubt but that you and your *husband* will make the *happiness of each other*, and of course when the Person is dear the Place of residence is only of secondary consideration.

I earnestly pray that in all places you may both enjoy the truest felicity that this world can bestow. . . . Pray tell dear John we hope he won't quite forget to write to us . . . and I am of the opinion you will have the goodness to give him leave, even if I was not confident the subject would be your praise. . . my warmest love, Jane Yorke'

Two years later John was at Halton, seeing to matters over there, and wrote to Mary,

'My dearest and ever beloved Mary's letter I have just read: our guests cannot come so if you have not already ordered the Haunch of Venison for Friday, you should put it off till Saturday.

I fear I cannot bring you much game, the weather is against our getting near the Partridges, which I found extremely wild yesterday afternoon. I only killed a brace of hares of which there are plenty around the house – we are going out this Morn to try our luck.

We dined at Mr Hamerton's, where we met a male party, Mr Lister of Gargrave, Mr Garforth (of Coniston), and Mrs H. very blooming and agreeable as ever.[8] Edmund goes to the Tempests tomorrow. A note just arrived from Mr Tempest saying they hope to visit us at Bewerley about the second week in November. Accept everything kind and tender yourself, and believe me your ever affect. and attached   John Yorke.'

Jane too was writing with family news,

'I am anxious you should be good friends with your new sister, (Thomas Henry had just married Maria Napier), which I trust will conduce to the comfort of both – I think I told you not to expect beauty, but . . . you will think her sensible and judicious, with a high sense of Henry's goodness. . .' (Maria was indeed very plain, but made Henry an excellent clergyman's wife. He became Vicar of Bishop Middleham where they lived for over fifty years.)

John and Mary had a long wait of six years before the birth of their first child, and both were longing for the event. Mary in particular, who had helped to bring up so many little brothers and sisters, had grown anxious as the years went by.

In 1826, Jane wrote, 'You will readily believe, my dearest John, how much I was pleased with your joyful communication'. Then at the end of March, 1827, she is able to rejoice at the safe arrival of a son,

49 Micklegate, York
'You will believe with what joy I received yours my dearest John at breakfast, I could scarcely read it for tears and thanks, and ran to announce it to Margaret Anne. You have our warmest congratulations and prayers that all may go on as prosperously as they have begun, but I beg dear Mary will think more about *herself* than anything, and keep *quiet*. The dear Baby will grow fatter daily – I can see it in my mind's eye and would like a kiss of its little hands.

Whisper my love to dearest Mary, and that I rejoice with her on getting it over so cleverly – I have thought of her every night lately, but glad I did not know the moment she was suffering.'

A week or so later,

'I was surprised at the sight of your most welcome letter today, my dearest Mary, and delighted on reading the contents. I picture the happy Group to myself you may imagine *very frequently*, and see Dear Baby giving joy to Papa, Mama and Grandmama, with Peace, Innocence and Health, tho' yet unconscious of the Happiness he imparts.'

Clearly Jane spent that summer at Bewerley with the family for she wrote,

'Thank you. . . dearest Mary. . . and your dear Husband for *so many months* of happiness enjoyed with you – where there is comfort in meeting, equal pain must of course attend the parting. Every day we picture Baby sitting on the sofa with his smile.

If when you come here, you incline to the higher room which would save your going up and down stairs, I would have the bedding of this lower one removed. . . and when the camp bed is set across the Dressing room, the cot would stand next to it. Cameron may sleep with Hall.'

The silhouette of Jane in a neat dress and lace cap shows her brisk affectionate efficiency in a delightful profile.

After the initially long wait, Mary's next three babies followed at two yearly intervals, each greeted fondly by their grandmother.

York, December 22nd 1829

'. . . I give you both joy on the addition of this sweet baby, (Frances Mary), with heartfelt wishes that you may long enjoy every happiness from these dear Treasures. Tell Johnny we desire him to kiss his sister for us.'

Caroline was born in August 1830, the year William IV was crowned, and the Catholic Emancipation Act was passed. At long last the English Catholics could take their part in the life of their country.

All this time John had been improving the neglected Bewerley estate, the houses, woods and mines.[9] The extent of it then was 12,103 acres with a rent roll of £5,208, and ninety tenants. This included thirty or so farms of varying sizes, four or five larger houses, an inn, shops and cottages.

36. Silhouette of Jane, wife of Thomas Yorke of Halton Place

The people of Nidderdale included the blacksmiths, the saddlers, joiners, cloggers, weavers and tailors, as well as the hedgers, the thatchers, wallers, ropemakers and shepherds, many of whom had small holdings too. Their wives did the milking, made the oatcakes, the butter, the cheeses, plucked and dressed the geese and poultry, knitted and spun the wool. Men, women and children joined forces to rake, turn and lead the hay, and to work, wash and dress the lead ore.

Of the 12,000 Bewerley acres, 10,000 were moorland, Ramsgill, Stean, Heathfield, Gouthwaite and Fountain's Earth. On each of these so many sheep gates were let, allotted to each farm. The mineral workings and smelt mills were scattered across the moors. Greenhow Hill was one of the centres for the mining community, and between 1780 to 1829, when there was a rapid expansion in mining, many new families moved into the area, and new cottages were built. Almost every miner's household still had a hound, with which they hunted foxes and hares, following on foot. [Over eighty foxes were killed around Middlesmoor in 1825, and the churchwardens paid a shilling a mask.] The depression in 1829–33 when the price of lead fell from £23 a ton to £13.10 caused many families to move away again.

A lease given by John in 1838 to a lead mine adventurer, William Watson, was for 21 years at £40 annual rent, plus 1/8th of lead got for five years, and 1/7th thereafter. He asked Watson to ensure that the miners were paid at least once in 6 months, but by 1841 Watson had gone bankrupt.[10] Several leases were given for mining coal in the moors and waste ground of the manor of Ramsgill, but tho' these brought in some money, the return was only small.[11] The lessees had various occupations, grocer, spinning machine maker, carpenter, farmer, collier and so on. These leases ran from twelve to twenty four years and from £10 to £20 annually.

Boundary disputes continued to take up much time and energy. The contentious Sir Thomas White whose royalty had 4 small mills, Cockhill, Sunside, Providence and Prosperous, was a continuing thorn in John's flesh. In 1826 Samuel Swire was settling a boundary quarrel between them concerning Prosperous and Merryfield Mines. A note on the award in 1826 says, 'It has been ascertained that Mr Swire was detained at the Public House at Greenhow Hill,[12] where *parties* made him drunk and he gave his Award under their influence without even having seen the Spot'.

The turnpike records of this period show that roads were improved with money borrowed on the security of tolls collected. However the creditors received a poor return – their debt was over £7,000 and the toll income only £326 a year. John Yorke who had lent £2,000, and his fellow creditors had to cease repair work until they were repaid.

The Game Laws were very severe at this time and the local paper ran a headline on March 23rd 1833 saying,
 '*Capture of a desperate character at Ripon.*'
This was Jack Sinclair, whose daring feats and hairbreadth escapes from the police over eleven years were widely known. He had several

serious affrays with the police and carried loaded pistols with him at all times.

John Yorke's gamekeeper, Robinson, had arrested Jack's brother, Elijah, six weeks earlier, and then succeeded in capturing Jack too. For this Robinson was given a reward of £100 and the poacher's gun. The brothers were sentenced at York Assizes, (in the cruel manner of the age,)to transportation for life to Australia. After serving fifteen years Jack had such a good conduct record he was made a warder. Later the brothers farmed in Tasmania and America, but returned to live in Nidderdale about 1870.[13]

In 1832 John further altered Bewerley Hall, enlarging the bow windows and refronting the south side. He built on the tower and east wing, and erected the lodge. The architect was Mr Salain who was 'assisted by the taste of Lord Ribblesdale of Gisburn Park', a close friend of John's.

By then the house, roofed in green Westmoreland slate, with two turrets, consisted of an entrance hall leading to a study, drawing room and dining room. Through a side hall lay the garden entrance, near the ballroom, morning room and library, of which the latter was panelled in cedar wood.

In the back regions, the kitchen, scullery, larder, still room and butler's pantry were next each other, while the housekeeper's room, servants' hall, and housemaids' pantry made up the other two sides of the ground plan.

Eighteen bedrooms, three of which had dressing rooms adjoining, one bathroom and one lavatory made up the first floor, together with the linen room. On the second floor were seven more bedrooms and one bathroom for the maids.

Around the backyard stood the game larder, gun room, laundry, drying room, and plumber's shop. The stable yard contained seven loose boxes in one block with two harness rooms, a granary, ten more stalls and a coach house. The lower stable yard held the carthorse stables, the potato house and the joiner's shop. Still self-supplying and self-reliant the estate was a small world of its own.

Mary laid out the flower garden, 'an occupation in which she took great delight.'

Together they added a second kitchen garden, hot houses and new stables. John continued the walks his uncle had started in Fishpond Wood, and to the waterfall in Ravensgill, and made a new entrance to the wood walk. Mary, who had considerable artistic talent, spent many hours drawing and painting views all around Bewerley, which are a delightful record of her time.

It seems that John inherited the tendency to cataract from his uncle, for, by 1832 Mary was writing, 'His failing sight prevented him from continuing his journal in his own hand. He was operated on . . . for cataract by Alexander with wonderful success – not a murmur escaped him, much might be said of his Patience, Kindness, uprightness and truly Christian character, but I must forbear.'

His mother wrote, York 1832[14]

'You were indeed kind, dearest Mary, in giving us another letter last night to continue the relief given by your former one to our anxious hearts. Most truly, (I trust) are we thankful to the Almighty for the mercy so far attending this wonderful operation, for the great blessing of returning sight, and that He may reward dearest John for his long suffering and composed bearing of it.

It is very natural John should wish to hear the voices of his sweet Pets but he is. . . much better alone, as by their lively actions and wonder at his bandages, they might have done him no small mischief. I have written this with callers sitting next me so it may be an odd mixture.'

After this intense anxiety, the family spirits were restored by the birth, in August that year of another son, Thomas Edward. He was especially loved by his Grandmother, and mention was made of him in all her letters.

York 1833

'We were greatly pleased with your good letter last night my dearest Mary, and very happy to find. . . our trifles had given pleasure to the dear Pets, whose screams of joy I should like to have heard – a happy age when such matters draw them forth.

I have got a new cook housekeeper who I hope will suit us, but strangers are unpleasant at first, and one does not feel confidence. . . I have to thank you for a good Pig and Hare last week, which she dressed well. I must look out a crib for Edward, who I shall like much to see.'

A very attractive portrait of Mary holding little John in her arms was painted about this time. Her girlish face had matured and softened, and her dark hair contrasts with the baby's very fair skin and blonde curls.

That same year Jane invited John and Mary to stay for York Assizes, saying 'go in and out as you please'. She thanked for delightful locks of the children's hair – much prized, and a variety of roses. She adds, 'Dear little Edward I have not seen since he was two months old, and should be

37. Mary, wife of John Yorke of Bewerley

happy to be introduced to him, tho' I won't expect him to take much notice of his old Grandmama'.

Inevitably the next four years were filled with childish ailments and parental worries. First young John developed scarlet fever, which was very dangerous then. The other children all caught it too. A year later they all had whooping cough. Worse was to come, for Caroline had typhoid fever and was desperately poorly for a time. The frightening statistics of the day show that there was very good reason to fear these infections. Mary had experience and sense, and spent much time in the sickrooms herself. Measles followed the next year, but mercifully the family survived, and grew up strong and healthy.

The young Queen Victoria had ascended the throne and, with her husband, began the new standard of conduct for the monarchy which has been so well continued.

The Poor Law Amendment Act caused great hardship, and parish relief was much reduced. In keeping with the spirit of the times scores of schools were built and churches restored at this period and John and Mary took a great interest in education and in church life in the Dale.

They gave 'the schoolhouse at Bridgehousegate with garden, in the occupation of William Swires, together with two cottages', in 1818. This took the place of the old school in Bewerley chapel, given by Dame Mary Yorke in 1678. The Yorkes also provided free coal for both the school and the master's house, as well as books and other incidental expenses.[15] They gave £5 and tried to get other subscribers to raise the teacher's salary, so a better teacher could be obtained.

In 1852 they added a new back kitchen, new windows and made other improvements. The old kitchen was turned into a girls' school. Mary

38. Bewerley school, Pateley Bridge, photo by Muriel Swires

took her responsibilities to the children very seriously. She attended a regular examination of the work at school, approved the code of rules made out by the master, and kept a close eye on all that went on.[16] There was no other form of oversight for such a school for the School Boards were not set up until 1870. On the annual half holiday, the whole school, numbering about 130, walked in procession to the Hall for their tea and treat. Dressed in their very best, white dresses and black stockings for the girls, stiff collars, suits and boots for the boys, they played around on the big lawns and finished up with a 'scramble' for sweets. Mary set up a Clothing Club, and by purchasing bed linen, blankets, shirting material etc. at wholesale prices, their workpeople and families were able to pay by weekly instalments for the articles they needed, as and when they could.

John also repaired the school at Heathfield in 1849, and 'rescued the Lofthouse school from the hands of John Moor and secured it to the Minister and churchwardens'. Moor was almost certainly a Dissenter, but presumably John felt he was not running the school well. John contributed to the parsonage at Lofthouse too.

When the new church was built at Pateley Bridge, John made a donation of £850 towards the cost, and gave ten pews and two blinds. Mary and Jane gave the font and service books. The church was dedicated to St Cuthbert and consecrated by Archbishop Harcourt. The first ceremony performed in it was the baptism of John and Mary's eldest son, on November 29th, 1827.

A carriage house and stables were built on a site given by John, at the entrance to the church in 1830.

John gave £1,100 to build a church at Ramsgill, and provided the land for it and the parsonage in 1842. He also rebuilt 'The Yorke Arms' there, which is now a delightful residential hotel. He endowed Ramsgill school with £7.4.0 for the free education of seven children. The remaining 25 children paid some fees.[17] He contributed handsomely to the building of Dacre church, consecrated by the Bishop of Ripon, and to the upkeep of the ancient church at Middlesmoor. Greenhow church also had a substantial donation, and Greenhow school, the site of which had been given by John's uncle, was endowed by John with £5 a year and 'was removed from the influence of the Dissenters'. Thomas Blackah, a leading miner, resented John's action and there was a long religious dispute over many years. Wesley's influence was strong amongst the mining community. His fiery teaching appealed to their fervent spirits, and his rousing hymns to their great love of singing.[18]

In 1836 Jane Yorke wrote to say how sad it was they could not visit Bewerley, 'the enjoyment of the gardens is, I am afraid, quite beyond my powers. Aunt M.A. is most mortified . . . by the Ripon carrier on his way y'day when she understood him to be coming today, or she would have had a letter ready for dear Johnny whose courageous exploits up Greenhow Hill amused us greatly. We however got a parcel sent, but. . . no time to seal it. . . as the carrier had to be run after beyond the (Micklegate) Bar. . . . I would like so much to have dear Edward if you think he would be happy with us alone. Kissings and blessings to all the Pets. . .'.

A year later young John was sent to school in Southwell, Nottinghamshire. Jane knew what a wrench that would be for Mary and wrote,

'I trust you will tell us of dear little John's Journey to Southwell, when you hear from him. You may believe it brings back old Times to my Remembrance when Parents and their dear boys are obliged to part, but it is perhaps for the benefit of both.'

Jane knew the interest Mary took in the Bewerley school,

'You are now not a little busy, I dare say, about your new school, and anxious respecting your new master and his family. . . we hope to hear of your approval. . . many thanks for the partridges. . . so glad dear John's frisky hunt was performed with safety and pleasure.'

In January 1838, after a long illness, her letter said,

'Though my Pen and Fingers have long been at variance and my Eyes are not yet very princely, I am very desirous to make some trial of them. Thank you dear Mary for all your kind attention and affectionate anxieties about us, and pray tell the dear little Group how gratified I am by their Thoughts and Prayers for me. . . . Best thanks dearest Mary for the beautiful basket. . . the Strawberries were a most wonderful treat and the asparagus so nicely packed.'

Jane's mind remained perfectly clear to the end, but she became increasingly infirm. Her last note was added to a letter from her daughter, sending her love and saying, 'my hand not very steady this morn but I hope you can make it out'. She died early in March, 1840, well into her eighties. To John especially, and to the rest of the family, she had been a constant source of encouragement and wisdom.

In the previous fifty years she had seen the population almost double, and by 1851 there were more people in England living in urban surroundings than in the country. The 'railway mania' of the 1840s had opened up the country in a remarkable way, bringing new opportunities for many,

More and cheaper newspapers were available and the invention of the telegraph brought international events closer to home. Lord Shaftesbury's efforts had at last made it illegal to employ women or children under nine, in the coal mines, but appalling factory conditions were still prevalent. The potato famine in Ireland was reducing the population there to pitiful starving scarecrows.

When young John Yorke went to St. John's Cambridge in 1846, his father, who accompanied him by train, wrote,

'Last night John slept in his rooms in college – very good ones . . . and tolerably well furnished, but perhaps in a day or two. . . he may have some of the chairs new covered.

I haven't yet seen the Master . . . I like Dr Highen. . . plain and particularly kind in his manner, and I have no doubt. . . he will give John good advice. John got his Cap and Gown in time to dine in Hall at 1 o'clock, and I dined there also.

I was most fortunate in meeting with an agreeable companion in the train – Mr Worsley, the Head of Downing College, with his wife – brother to Sir William – they came that morning from Hovingham Hall. The moment I saw him and heard him speak I was sure he was a Worsley. He is a very clever man and plenty of conversation – she a nice but delicate person. They both promised to patronise John. . . .

I hope you will receive this tomorrow as it goes by a Mail (coach) direct to Leeds, not by London.'

The great event in Bewerley two years later was the Fete held for John's coming of age. His mother records the arrangements,

'Commencing with a Ball on August 2nd at which 130 people were present, the Fete lasted three days. The Tenants, their wives and children and the neighbouring Gentry were entertained.' That was a topic of conversation for many a long day in the Dale.

John continued to add to his property, buying in Harefield Farm, and Low Wood, cottages in Ramsgill, and others in Bewerley. His agent, Armstrong, took advantage of his master's poor sight, and began a series of deceptions and frauds which were not discovered until John's death. 'How unworthy he was', wrote Mary in her Journal, 'of the trust reposed in him for seventeen years'.

Lead mining prospered and John invested in a new smelt mill, condenser and under ground chimney, 'at great cost' in 1856. The long one storey building held two roasting furnaces and four smelting hearths.[19] The ore was calcined in the first, then smelted and run into 'pigs' of 112lbs each. The new water powered fan drove the noxious smoke and fumes into an underground flue to the condenser, where they passed through water sixteen times. The remaining vapours were then carried underground and upwards for a mile and a quarter, until they escaped up a chimney emerging from the hillside. Before this system was introduced, not a blade of grass grew, nor was there a green tree to be seen within reach. Afterwards the vegetation returned and cattle could graze nearby again. This was an early example of pollution treatment and a great improvement, and most of the estimated 6,000 tons of lead mined by the new Appletreewick Lead Mining Company was smelted there, over the next twenty-five years.

John also continued to enclose large areas of land, and so convert moorland to better pasture. (As a result of his care he was able to invest in 'some diamonds and emeralds' in 1852 which cost him £781.)

Mary had gone to Scarborough for some medical treatment, and John wrote,

Bewerley 1856

'My dearest Mary,

Many thanks for your kind and affectionate letter – may it please God you may both receive benefit from Dr Dale's advice. I am sorry for Caroline's disappointment at not being able to go to the Ball at York.

We get on very well here notwithstanding we sometimes wish you were with us. Fanny reads the Prayers very nicely morning and evening. John has gone shooting today

May Heaven's blessings attend you. . . John Yorke.'

Mary's own journal tells the rest of his story,

'1856, we spent some weeks in London, paid a visit to my brother-in-law Mr Barclay Bary, there my dear Husband fell from his chair – (a loose cushion,) and broke three ribs on 15th June. Though we lavished every care and kindness, and great energy, he was unable to return home till July 3rd. We had long felt his strength was declining, and tho' we felt he required great care we knew not how near his valuable life was to its close. We received our friends . . . in August and on 22nd the Bishop and Mrs Longley for a confirmation. Nov. 3rd we went to Sir William ?. . ., and my dear Husband walked to his own Lodge gate, all in happy spirits. We all proceeded to Scarborough to the Cliff Bridge Terrace.

On 19th my dear Husband seemed unwell. On 24th Mr Teal, an eminent surgeon from Leeds saw him, but gave no hope. He bore all with perfect resignation. On 30th he forbid me to hope he could ever return to his dear Home, still, encouraged by good Dr Murray, we prepared, having sent for his own family coach, and on January 1st, 1857, in an agony of hope and fear we were permitted to take him, in his own carriage, at 9 a.m. by rail to York, and on by an express train to Ripley, and were at Bewerley by 4 p.m., thankful and deeply grateful to be there, but SO CHANGED.

We all attended him with love and tenderness till 5th Feby. No suffering till the last day tried him, after his return home, but then it was an agony to hear the struggling breath. In his last moments of peaceful change, joy, ineffable joy lighted up his beloved countenance. We all watched in awful suspense till we saw his spirit had returned to God who gave it. He was on the eve of completing his 82nd year and was deeply mourned by all who knew him, and by me from my inmost heart. On 10th his still unaltered countenance was hid from my sight.

On 12th we all followed him to the Tomb, which he had himself caused to be made under the Porch of the Pateley church. A memorial window was put up to his memory in the Pateley Church, designed by Waites of Newcastle, cost £63. Also a Tablet by his own desire at Long Preston recording his father's death as well as his own.'

Mary was only sixty six years old when her husband died. In a miniature done about this time, she is shown as a striking and impressive woman, her raven hair dressed in ringlets, wearing a red velvet gown. She was to live a widow for another twenty years, but she maintained all her interests, and occupied much of her time researching and writing up the history of the family.[20]

39. St. Cuthbert's, Pateley Bridge, photo by Muriel Swires

CHAPTER XV

JOHN YORKE   1827 – 1883
OF
BEWERLEY AND HALTON

JOHN SUCCEEDED HIS FATHER IN 1857, at the age of thirty. He had been helping his father to run the estate for a long time and he continued to live on at Bewerley. His mother remained with him for two more years, but also spent time at Halton with Edward and at Mapperley with her father.

'To provide the fortunes of his brother and two sisters, and to pay the debt on the estate,'[1] wrote his mother, 'he was obliged to take out a mortgage, and, the property being strictly entailed, I grieved to see the burden he had to contend with'.

He gave his brother £1,000, his two sisters, £8,000 each, legacies of £300, and had a mortgage interest of £666 each year.

The long awaited and dearly loved eldest son, he was brought up with his brother and sisters in the happiest of homes, with the whole of Nidderdale as his playground. His father taught him to ride, shoot and know the moors. With his mother he explored the beauty of the woods and gardens, and watched her concern for the people around.

After first boarding at Mr Fletcher's school at Southwell in Nottinghamshire, he went on to Eton. He spent a year in Brussels with a tutor, then went on to take a degree in law at St John's, Cambridge. His coming of age was celebrated by a Fete which lasted three days, at which all the tenants and their families, and the friends around were entertained. By all accounts he grew up into a intelligent, capable man.

Although he had every opportunity to travel, and meet a variety of people, he chose to remain at home, and devote himself to improving the property. He served as a J.P. for the West Riding, and for the Liberty of Ripon. He was Chairman of the Board of Guardians for many years, and became Deputy Lieutenant for the West Riding. He supported the Nidderdale Agricultural Society, which had been a great interest of his father's, and continued to keep up the local churches and schools.

He greatly enjoyed hunting, and regularly rode long distances to the York and Ainsty, the Bedale and the Bramham.

Up the valley behind Bewerley lay Westcliffe Farm, rented by James Simpson, through which John very often rode. Simpson had five daughters, and the youngest was an attractive girl. John and she began to meet

40. Mary Yorke, seated, in black. Her four children behind her, Edward in the window, Fanny, Caroline and John against the wall. Other guests include the Bishop of Ripon and Mrs. Bickersteth, Lady E. Stanhope, Mr. G. and Mr. J. Howard

by chance, then not only by chance. Whether John's father ever knew of this attachment I doubt. The only mention of it at all are the anguished notes in Mary's journal,
'Sep. 7th 1859, Fanny and I returned – *John gone* – married that day to *Alice Simpson* – what grief!'
'8th a letter from him – what grief, no words can describe so sad a union.
'12th Edward and Caroline came to us in an agony of grief.
'19th Edward left us to prepare to receive us!

It sounds as if John was well aware what a terrible shock this marriage would be and so made it a fait accompli. A dreadful month followed while the rest of the family made plans for the future. Again it is Mary's diary which tells us,

'Oct. 12th we left this long loved home – fled after packing up and taking leave of all midst tears and grief of rich and poor. We were received by dear Edward with tender affection. A heartfelt life sorrow, this false step of my unhappy son.'

The bitter disappointment she felt, and the up rooting from Bewerley after thirty-eight years, were undoubtedly made worse by her strong belief that this marriage could not be a happy one for her dear son.[2] In this, sadly, she was proved right. The couple drifted apart, and, after twelve increasingly sad years, they obtained a separation, and finally a divorce.

During those twelve years, however John and Alice lived at Bewerley and tried to carry out their duties. He managed to secure 'the great acquisition' of the property which had been Sir Thomas White's, and saw the rise and fall of several mining companies between 1850–1870. He also built a new steading at the Home Farm.

Two months after their wedding, on the advice of many friends, Mary made an immense effort and went to stay with John and Alice. She held her Clothing Club in the village, and stayed a week. She wrote, 'It was a *great and trying affair* to see this daughter-in-law.' At the end of 1859 she wrote, 'A year of very great trial and grief.'

Over the next years the diary tells us that John and Alice visited Mary about once a year, (usually for the Hunt Ball), and she went to Bewerley once a year, but always with Fanny or other members of the family. The brevity of the entries give a hint of the strain felt. When John visited his mother on his own however, her old affection for him came flooding back.

There were of course many occupations to interest John, particularly the making of the Nidd railway line. This was begun by the North Eastern Railway Co. and completed in 1862 at a cost of £8,000 per mile. John was one of the eight members of the management committee, representing the economic interests of the area. It was an immense undertaking, and the $11^1/_2$ miles of track and six stations opened up the Dale, bringing new horizons to its people.

Between 1865–1869 the Appletreewick Mining Co., under a lease from John, averaged nearly 400 tons of lead a year, but the partners drew too heavily on the profits, and John gave them notice. By the following year the Greenhow field was almost at a standstill. New companies which formed faced a market depression. With only the occasional lucky strike, the lead mining enterprises dwindled away through until 1910, though there was still a market for barytes.

Soon after the Stump Cross Caverns had been discovered by the Newbould brothers in 1860, with their fantastic stalagmites and rock formations, William Grainge wrote his descriptive book on Nidderdale to explain the local beauty spots and history to visitors now able to reach it.

John kept in touch with Edward, for he was his agent at Halton and, I feel sure, did his best to help him in every way. For some years John suffered from a very painful internal complaint, which made him lead a quiet and secluded life latterly. Edward visited him often with his elder children.

In 1871 Mary wrote,

'March 6th John came, in trouble.
'March 31 Alice left Bewerley for ever!!!

After this Mary spent many weeks a year with John and the breach was healed. Together they enjoyed articles in the new Yorkshire Post about the Yorkshire Agricultural Society,[3] and the Archeological Society. People had begun to record old customs and to take an interest in local dialects.

The final entry in Edward's journal reads,

'Sept. 3 1883, Drove from Skipton to Bewerley: poor John died. Sept. 6 Funeral at Pateley Church. I returned home.'

John was liked and respected by his tenants, many of whom attended his funeral, but it was a sad ending to a life which had begun with such promise.

CHAPTER XVI

THOMAS EDWARD YORKE   1832 – 1923
OF
BEWERLEY AND HALTON PLACE

EDWARD SUCCEEDED HIS BROTHER at the age of fifty-one, and lived through the Victorian period which was deeply influenced by self discipline of character and seriousness of thought.

Born in 1832, (two months after the Reform Bill), his childhood was a particularly happy and fortunate one.[1] The youngest of four, his devoted and understanding parents lavished every care upon him. (Had he been born to another family, a few miles away, he could have spent each day standing as a 'doffer' by a spinning frame in a cotton mill, for fourteen hours at a stretch, with one hour off for dinner.)

However, his opportunities to explore the big house, the extensive gardens, stables and yards were endless when he was small. Books, music, paintings and objets d'art surrounded him as he grew more aware of the wider world. As soon as he could ride he was able to visit the various farms, and roam further and further along the dale. Everywhere he went he met friends – tenants and their families who knew him. There was always an oatcake or a drink of milk ready, and a word and a smile for the boy on his sturdy pony.

His first boarding school was Dr Sharpe's preparatory school in Doncaster, and from there he followed his brother to Eton. During his Eton days he read the latest novels by Dickens, Thackeray and Trollope, and studied the ideas of Ruskin and later, Darwin. He was taken to see the Great Exhibition and the amazing Crystal Palace in Hyde Park. By the time he went up to Cambridge, over one third of the total mileage of the railways had been completed. He took a first class degree at St John's, then, having a keen interest in agriculture, he went up to the Scottish Borders to study farming for two years.

On his return he made his home at Halton, which he grew to love greatly. On his brother's marriage, his mother and two sisters came to live with him, and it was from there that Caroline was married, in January 1861, to The Rev. St John Tyrwhitt, Vicar of St Mary Magdalene, Oxford.

The following year Edward and his sisters and brother-in-law made a trip out to Cairo, visiting the Holy Land and Jerusalem, Damascus and Syria. Edward and the other men made the ascent of one of the highest peaks in the Desert of Sinai, the first Europeans, as they believed, to do so. He left an excellent account of the expedition, with some family details like the following,

Jerusalem, March 16th, 1862,
'So far my sisters like their new tent life and Fanny gets on better than I expected on. . . the little Arab horses which are very sure footed. . . . We are encamped not far from the Damascus Gate. . . and it is very much pleasanter than being in an hotel, tho' we have had a good deal of rain on our beds. . . .

While his mother was living at Halton she kept careful records of her household expenditure and a keen interest in the estate. There were six or seven servants to feed every day as well as four or more of the family. The number of meals provided was totalled up each month. In April 40lbs of butter were made, (of which 32lbs were sold), 188lbs of meat consumed, 136 eggs produced and eaten during 221 breakfasts, 217 lunches and 213 dinners. Whilst Edward was in the East and the servants left alone in the house, five of them ate 139lbs of meat, 110 eggs, 8lbs of butter and 240lbs of flour in a month.

Mary saw that the four old cottages near the Old Hall, which had been thatched and built in 1668, were in a bad state, so she had plans drawn up to rebuild them. This was done for a cost of £496, and a room in one of them was fitted up for Sunday evening services.

It was in 1862 that Edward met his future wife Augusta. She was the daughter of Canon the Hon. John Baillie, Rector of Elsdon, Northumberland, and brother of the Earl of Haddington. They were married in February 1863 at Elsdon with Edward's mother and sisters present, and spent a month travelling around Cheltenham, Oxford and Torquay.

On their return home, their carriage was met at the top of Bridge Banks up from the river, the horses taken out, and the carriage drawn up the drive by the men of the village. Edward's delighted mother and excited sisters joined in the great welcome. Two days later a supper party was held in the village to which seventy people came. Twenty-six children had a delicious tea first, then the grownups came along, (after milking). Augusta's silk crinoline dress must have made a great impression.

It was with heavy hearts that Mary Yorke and her daughter Fanny left Halton in April to live in York, in a house Edward had bought for them in Fishergate. Like Mary's mother-in-law before her, she had twenty long years of widowhood ahead, but like her too, she used her energies in keeping up the family links through correspondence, and by her interest in the history of the Yorke and Wright families.

Edward and Augusta began their married life at Halton just a hundred years after Thomas and Jane. The house was exactly the same, though no doubt differently arranged, nor were the garden, stables or park much altered, excepting that the trees planted by Thomas had matured.

Edward took on the home farm in 1857 from his brother John. It was 160 acres, at a rent of £288.13.0. It was all under grass but Edward ploughed up Little Long Roods and sowed eight acres with oats, (using 4 to 5 bushels to the acre), in the last week in March. The rest of the field was burnt off and sown with turnips and rape. Seventeen acres were left for hay and the rest was pasture.

'The farm generally,' wrote Edward, 'was, as far as the land went, in good order, most of it being dry and the quality generally very good, but the buildings were sadly out of repair, and the fences, from neglect and want of cutting, very indifferent. My brother undertook to put the Buildings in order. Most of the old walls surrounding the Farm Yards were pulled down and rebuilt, and a new Shed erected for wintering stock.

I bought fifteen Irish and six English heifers in Nidderdale, and fourteen Scotch and twenty-three Irish for grazing. My mother made me a present of two milk cows which were bred at Bewerley, and I bought another of my brother for £23. I also bought two horses, a mare and a horse for either cart or carriage work. Also 80 Cheviot ewes and 2 tups. These, with two small pigs, some turkeys and poultry from Bewerley, made up my farm stock. I took in four cows from the villagers for the summer, at £3.10 a piece. I took four men and a boy as labourers, viz. Parker, two Natiers, Thomas Shorrock and R. Edmonson.'

The field names on the home farm then were Sandholes, Mill Field, Great Ing, Sadler Pasture, Back Sadler meadow, Spring Field, Long Roods, Little Bank, Longlands, Faultless (now Blacker Meadow), Marrils and Old Close.

Thanks to Edward's habit of keeping a detailed journal,[1] we can follow his farming year accurately, as well as his work on the rest of the Halton estate.

He noted down the dates for washing the sheep in the river, ewe clipping, hay making, corn cutting and the quality of each crop. He bought in 60 more ewes at 23/- each and forty more at 24/6, and sold 110 lambs at £1 a piece. He grew potatoes, both black and white oats, and some swedes, and reseeded the Marrils with clover. After five years he bought a single horse grass mower for £20, 'an American machine. This we found a most invaluable help in haytime, it being able to cut nearly an acre per hour. I worked it three years then exchanged it for a two horse machine, for only a further £6, which had many improvements.'

Ten years after starting he had eight cows, forty-three heifers, two calves, three horses, 141 sheep, 173 lambs and two pigs. His pasture was 130 acres, meadow 21, crops 35, (oats, potatoes, turnips and clover). His rent had risen to £382.16.9.

The rent roll from the estate in 1870 was £2,082. [A hundred years earlier it had been £500.] The tenants were Johnson, Petty, Parkinson, Dugdale, Cockshutt, Rumney, Bronnan, John Wilson, Derby, Sugden, Parker, Thompson, T.C. Moon, Mason and Shorrock.[2] John Wilson had been the tenant of Cow Hill from 1832, and Moon had been at Old Hall since 1859.

Edward noted when drainage was done on Nappa Flatts, Low and High Scale, and the Thornbers; houses painted, roofs re-slated, new shippon and pigstye built at Panbeck, dairy fitted up at Long Bank, barns re-slated, new Farm House built at Low Scale in 1884 (by Bewerley masons and joiners), wash house made for T.C. Moon, new water cistern installed, and so on. These notes are intermingled with others about planting, clearing and thinning woods, making fences and repairing the river banks.

'1868   Brother John bought Nappa Flatts from Lord Ribblesdale for £11,500, a valuable acquisition.
1869   Sold 2,764ft of timber to S. Widdup for £181.8.7
       Enlarged village service room, £114
1876   New school and school house built by Miss Fanny Yorke, for £585.'

As well as his farming journal there is a household book kept in turn by Edward's mother, himself and his wife. From this we learn that when they first moved in to Halton they kept between five and seven servants. This meant there were ten to twelve people to feed every day, and with visitors, a good many more.

In the month of July 1860, 402 breakfasts, 341 lunches and 404 dinners were cooked and served. Some of the food consumed that month was noted down,

75lbs butter made, 15lbs used, the rest sold.
225lbs of meat, 1 hare, 22 rabbits
6lb coffee, 6lbs tea
32lbs lump sugar, 84lbs brown
95 eggs
240lbs fine flour
120lbs brown flour

This then was the household into which Augusta came as a bride. She was evidently an energetic and lively girl, brought up in a loving and godly home and not at all spoilt. She needed all her energy, for her own and Edward's personal diaries give a vivid picture of their early married life.

As Jane Yorke had done, she supervised the production of much of the food they ate. The dairy, garden and poultry were her special domain, but she also ordered the dressing of the game, and all the complicated uses of a pig after killing. Like Thomas and Jane too, she and Edward lived on very close terms with their servants, and knew their Halton tenants and their children like an extended family. They were perhaps more social than their predecessors, and were of course able to make longer journeys with greater ease by train.

They frequently rode together to call or to lunch at Gisburne Park, (the Ribblesdales), or to Gargrave, (the Marsdens), Flasby, Broughton, Coniston, Gledstone and Bolton. They walked to Hellifield to lunch at the Vicarage, or to the Peel to fish for perch. They rode to Settle, and drove to Malham to fish there in the Tarn.

They entertained at Halton a good deal too. The Tyrwhitt family, Mary and Fanny Yorke (and their servants), and John and Alice often visited. They gave archery and croquet parties, went to theatricals at Gisburne, and never missed the balls at Ripon, Knaresborough or York. They went to stay at Bewerley, and Cambridge, and at Oxford with the Tyrwhitts.

Augusta entered in her diary some of Edward's many and varied public duties as well as such important matters as the garden and farm produce,

'Six turkies hatched. Bought six ducks. Cow died. Edward caught a 16lb salmon. First gooseberries in. The harriers met here. Halton school examinations. Edward to sheep fair. Went to The Residence, (in York where her parents lived). Eight lbs of butter made. Four partridges shot. Edward to a meeting of the Highway Committee.'

Edward attended a constant round of meetings. He was a governor of Giggleswick, Long Preston and Halton West schools, each of which required careful oversight. The yearly examinations were all important. The grant made to elementary schools then depended on the exam results, so a poor teacher could be disastrous to the district.

He was an Income Tax Commissioner, and a J.P. for the West Riding. This also involved serving on the Grand Jury in Leeds and Wakefield four times a each year. (Local government was by then mainly carried out by elected bodies, so the justices had lost much of the administrative power which they had held since Tudor times.) As a riparian owner, he served on the Board of Conservators of the Ribble Fishery, in which he was keenly interested.

As churchwarden he had to attend the Archdeacon's Visitations, and was responsible for the fabric of the church and the welfare of the parish.

The elected wardens and overseers still looked after many parish matters, although like the J.P.s their responsibilities were not as all embracing as in earlier days. The Parish Church was in Long Preston, (where Edward built a coach house and stable in which to put his carriage during the service), but a Sunday evening service was held in the top floor of Library Cottage, in Halton West, and Edward sometimes led this. Family prayers were the custom then, and Edward and Augusta held them with their household each morning.

He also belonged to the Yorkshire Agricultural Society, the Yorkshire Club and the local Conservative party.

His rent days, manor courts, estate repairs, book keeping and charitable works were all carried out with care and thoroughness. He was constantly studying new farming ideas and was beginning to use the oilcake and cattle feed which was coming in, and some chemical fertilisers too.

The first wave of depression in agriculture was caused by the quantity of grain imported from America. This affected all the farming community, but on the whole, beef and milk were still in great demand so the stock farmers fared better than the arable ones.

As well as his local interests, Edward read widely about the many new scientific inventions of the age, and kept up to date on the development of the railways, and the telegraph, and steamships. He was a keen photographer, and amateur archeologist. His library contained books by John Stuart Mill, Darwin, Matthew Arnold, Huxley, and George Eliot, as well as Tennyson, Swinburne, Kipling, Macaulay and Carlyle. (His children read The Water Babies, Grimm's and Hans Anderson's fairy tales, Gulliver's Travels and Robinson Crusoe, and loved Alice in Wonderland.)

His natural kindliness and sense of duty did not prevent him from enjoying all that his life offered. He was a good shot, a skilful fisherman and a knowledgeable naturalist. He enjoyed travel and the company of his friends, neighbours and tenants. One of the latter said of him, "E liked 'is pipe and 'is glass, but 'e liked 'is pipe the better.'

Augusta, who was twenty-two when she married, had three years to enjoy her life with him before her babies came. In March 1866, Mary Augusta was born, after a journey to York and a day out, next day, in Scarborough. (Her mother, in her neatly written and factual journal, permitted herself one exclamation mark for the birth of each baby.) Agnes Rae was installed as the baby's nurse and the household doted on the little auburn haired girl, who was always known as May.

John Cecil, the heir, followed the next year, in November, and nineteen months later the twins, Helen and Louisa arrived. By now Halton was becoming rather crowded, so plans were made to build on. The new nursery wing was added on to the north end of the house, making four new rooms and a game larder. New plumbing for the W.C. and sinks brought in the fresh spring water recently piped down from Long Bank. The total cost of this was £575.11.1 and Mary Yorke contributed towards it.

The new wing was completed in 1872, just in time, for Katharine was born in Settle, where the family were staying while the work was being done. Exactly one year later Ethel was born, and she was only eighteen months old when the second son, Henry Reay, arrived.

Mrs Rae, loved by them all, had her nursery full, so Miss Jackson, a new governess, came for the older children, and Johnnie went off to school in Harrogate. At last poor Augusta had a breathing space, and was able, in 1877, to enjoy a visit to Paris with Edward for ten days.

It was this year that, Halton West having been made a district on its own, they were obliged to provide an elementary school in the village under the Education Act. Edward's sister Fanny offered to build one, with a house for the mistress. The first page of the log book reads,

"This school was built in 1876 by Miss F.M. Yorke. The materials carted by the tenants. It was opened June 27 1877 by the Revd. J. E. Coulson, Vicar of Long Preston. The site and foundation stone were given by John Yorke of Bewerley Hall."

'Miss S. M. Temperton took charge of the school, which was 22ft in length, 14ft in breadth, 10ft in height, and 2,737ft in cubicle (sic) content.'

By 1879 Augusta was carrying another child. She went to her parents' house in York in February and Arthur was born on 23rd March. The excited elder children were taken to York to visit their much loved mother whom they had missed, and the new little brother. One of them must have carried the germ of scarlet fever which their mother then caught. In her weak state she could not fight it, and on Easter Day, April 13th, she died, aged thirty-eight. The only photograph of her shows her looking far older than that, wearing a ribboned cap under which her fair hair is tightly drawn back from her pale worn face.

'My dear wife died; a terrible loss to me. Thy Will be done,' wrote Edward. His mother wrote,

'After a week of *deep* anxiety, dear Augusta was taken from us and her dear husband and 8 children, to our unsurpassible grief.'

Canon and Mrs Baillie, who had helped with each confinement and baptised each child, were stunned. Mary came to try to comfort the stricken Edward, who then had to go home to his eight motherless children, the eldest of whom, May, was only thirteen.

41. Augusta, first wife of Edward Yorke

Augusta was buried at Long Preston, followed by the saddest procession one could wish to see.

With the invaluable help and devotion of Agnes Rae, Edward tried to carry on his normal life. Miss Flowers was engaged as governess, and in September, Johnnie went off to Elstree school. May missed him dreadfully, as well as her mother, although Edward took great trouble to make her his special companion. There are many entries in the diary of trips with her to York Agricultural Show, or to the Leeds Festival, or to stay at Bewerley. Edward's friends clearly did their best to help and console him too and he was invited out and away a good deal.

The next year brought severe frosts and Edward took the children skating on the river at Long Preston, and also skated himself from Mitton Bridge to Preston, returning by train. By the prevailing standards of strict Victorian Papas, Edward seems to have been a gentle and approachable father, but his many duties and occupations meant that he had to be away a good deal. He bought ponies for the children, and took great care of their health and wellbeing. He even took seven of them to the Pantomime in Leeds . . . but only once. They had annual seaside holidays at Morecambe and Lytham, where he would join them for a few days.

In January 1882, John went to Harrow, and in the following August another tragedy struck. Agnes Rae, the lynch pin of the family, overburdened by the work and responsibility of so many young children, fell ill and died. She was buried at Long Preston, near Augusta, and once more the poor children walked behind a coffin.

'A grievous loss to us all,' wrote Edward.

May, still only sixteen, was now mother to them all, and her father's companion too. He was fortunately very strong, and had a remarkable ability to withstand pain, both physical and mental. Riding home from Settle one day, 'my horse Donald came suddenly down without warning and put my shoulder out. I immediately returned to Settle where it was put in again.' He then rode the seven miles home.

One of their mutual interests and delights was collecting and reciting local dialect poems and stories. They both spoke Yorkshire as a second language, and belonged to the Dialect Society. As well as the usual accomplishments of a young lady then, the music, water colour sketching, and dancing, May entertained her father's guests with these Yorkshire stories, and became extremely good at their delivery and timing.

> Ah's waitin' and Ah's watchin' on tha, darlin'
> By t'intak edge o' bonny purple ling.
> But Ah sees ony 'alf a score o' moor birds
> Flit passt me on their strong brown wing.
>
> Ah's plagued tha, and tormented tha, ma poor lad,
> Forgive thi lass, she'll never dae it more,
> Ma heart is oppen noo, sae cum an' fill it,
> 'Stead o' beatin' on a fasst closed door.
>
> Tha'll 'appen 'od me close an' say tha loves me

That's what Ah's fair longin' just ter 'ear,
Ne'er heed if, shaming,
Ah sould turn away like,
Kiss me sweet'eart, kiss, an' ev no fear.

May also went fishing with her father and was thrilled when he caught a fine salmon. There was great excitement when three men were caught and taken into custody by the keeper, Thomas Shorrock, for netting trout at Nappa. (There had been Shorrocks working at Halton since 1819.)

The year 1883 brought more sorrow to the family, for Mary Yorke died in June, aged eighty-seven. She had been ailing for some two years, with failing sight, but still had been an indomitable support to Edward and her grand children since Augusta's death. A pathetic last scrawl in her most private diary says,

'1881, Dec 22 Alas! sight almost gone.'

Her funeral took place at Pateley Church, so I hope that only the elder children had to attend yet another black Victorian funeral.

One is thankful to read that the little ones went for their annual seaside holiday at Lytham in August, and that Edward took May and Johnnie on a most exciting ten day trip to Ireland. They visited Donegal, and Belfast and returned by Stranraer and Carlisle.

Edward took them on this tour, I think, to spend some time closely with them before preparing them for a plan he was forming. He had met, the previous December, Fanny, daughter of Sir John Walsham, of Knill Court, Hereford, who was a distant cousin through Mrs Bell. He needed a wife very badly, and chose with great care someone who was close to him in age, and whom he considered would make a kind and loving step mother.

He met her at Mrs Bell's in August and in York in September with his sister Fanny. In October, brother John finally died after a lingering illness and Edward inherited all the responsibilities of the Bewerley property. By the end of that month, he was in London, and,

'was married the next day to Fanny Walsham, in St Mark's North Audley Street. A very quiet wedding, my sisters present, luncheon in Piccadilly afterwards.'

They spent two weeks in the Isle of Wight and the New Forest and returned home on November 16th. We are not told whether the children had ever met their new stepmother before, nor do we know their feelings as they saw her. The younger ones probably warmed to her kind face quite soon, but poor May, at seventeen, with those years of responsibility and position behind her, felt most dreadfully ousted.

It must have been hard too for Fanny, who was gentle and easily flustered, to have a rather resentful step daughter with a very strong character at such close quarters, and there were some difficult periods from time to time.

42. Fanny, May, Kathie, Harry and Arthur, with their governess and Edward Yorke at Halton 1883

The move to Bewerley the following year improved matters and there were plenty of new activities for both of them. Edward wrote,

'1884 May 7th we all left our dear old home and went to Bewerley. During the winter a great deal had been done to the house. A new W.C. at the end of the nursery passage, a new main drain taken down to the iron gate. Many rooms papered and painted, new grates in morning room and boudoir. Dear Arthur had a bad attack of bronchitis. Miss Flowers left and Fraulein Schloifer came.'

(Edward's sister Caroline Tyrwhitt had died the previous December, to his very great grief, and the children had been particularly fond of and close to her.)

The next year saw much entertainment. There was a servants' ball given in the laundry in January, and a Gala in the park in the summer. The Nidd Valley railway line had attracted tourists to the area, and two or three thousand people came by special trains, and visited the gardens and walked up Ravensgill. What they saw has been described by William Grainge in his inimitable style, in the account written for these very tourists.

'Bewerley Hall is pleasantly situate on a gentle eminence, a park, studded with timber trees, extending down to the River Nidd sheltered by a range of hills and woods, and commanding beautiful views. The grounds are romantic, and . . . leaving the smoothly shaven lawn with its beds of flowers and clumps of evergreen shrubs, the walk winds up the Fishpond Wood, principally of beech trees of a great height. The pond, a fine sheet of clear water . . . is a cool and delightful spot on a summer's day. Crossing Fossbeck, romantic Ravensgill is entered. On one side is a plantation of tall larches on the slope of a steep hill, on the other, deep down below, flow the waters of Raven's Beck. In winter there are a thousand small cataracts. The walk keeps winding up and upward still – near the top, grey crags and cliffs of gritstone rise abruptly. Seats are placed at intervals and from one can be seen a view of Pateley Bridge, and of Brimham Rocks.' (Six more pages describe the ferns, mosses, lichens and heather, and the paths and rocks which may be explored.)

It is no wonder that the Bewerley Gala attracted more and more people each year, running to six or seven thousand before the war. The money collected was usually divided between the Temperance Society and the village school, or some other good cause.

[Young John went off to Christchurch, Oxford, to rooms in Peckwater. Before leaving Harrow he had gained both the first and second prizes for music there.]

The second wave of agricultural depression was coupled in Nidderdale, as elsewhere, with a very severe winter. Edward described the huge snow drifts round Greenhow, and May wrote a poem about the silence of the white world buried there. Much local distress resulted. A relief fund was set up, and free dinners were provided. After several trials in different areas, Edward opened up a quarry of good stone, which gave work, for what lead mining there was had been made impossible by the weather conditions. Good gritstone, slate and flags were all available and easily worked, and the advent of the railway had expanded production. (Rights for quarrying had been granted to the abbeys in the twelfth century.) At Rent Day Edward returned 15% of each man's rent both at Bewerley and Halton, and reduced some considerably. [Gladstone had recently given the farm workers the vote, but many employers found it hard to pay their wages.]

To the sorrow of the Yorke family, little Arthur, who was only seven, had a stoppage of the bowel and died. The only picture of him shows a little sad faced child with long curls, holding a toy bird. Although much loved, his health was poor and the succession of people who looked after him cannot have made his life very happy. His father could not bear to bury him in the family vault so bought a plot in Pateley cemetery.

Queen Victoria's Jubilee was celebrated everywhere with real pride and thankfulness, and Edward and Fanny travelled to London to watch it. They joined in the Bewerley celebrations later too when the Volunteers marched to the park, and athletic sports were organised, followed by a huge tea.

The same year the grouse season proved especially good, due to the dry hot summer. Some of the mining ground was now being thought more valuable for rearing grouse than raising ore. The drought resulted in a poor crop of hay, and Edward made 'an ensilage stack' for the first time for winter feed.

May went off on a memorable visit to Florence and Rome with her uncle Tyrwhitt and his two daughters, and her father had his portrait painted. He was then fifty-five although his full bushy grey beard and moustache make his strong face seem considerably older.

For the second year running Edward felt obliged to return 15% of the rents. The introduction of frozen meat shipped in from Australia, New Zealand and South America had depressed the price of beef and mutton, keeping pace with that of corn. Many farm workers moved away into the towns, but in Nidderdale there was no great exodus. The dalesmen were used to hardship, and knew how to survive on very little. For centuries, oats had formed the main cereal crop in the dale, but higher imports after the Repeal of the Corn Laws had made it safer to rely on the cheaper

43. Thomas Edward Yorke

bought grain. More meat and wheat bread was gradually replacing the old staple diet. Some of the craftsmen went out of business now that goods came in so easily by train. Shops even in as small a place as Pateley could supply a far greater variety of merchandise than ever before.

Nevertheless the old traditional way of life continued in Nidderdale. Many of the solid stone farm houses with their mullioned windows, still had the hay mow and shippon adjoining under one roof. (This warmed the house and gave easy access to the cattle in bad weather.)

The cooking was done on a big black iron range with a hot air oven. The old kail pots still hung over the fires on a hook in some houses, and a bakstone, now made of iron rather than stone, was used for baking the still favourite oatcakes. The stone flagged floors downstairs were cleaned and polished with fine sand after washing. Rugs, made from pieces of clean rag hooked through a sacking base, were only put down on Sundays, or when company came. Beautiful patterns on these rugs were made, as in patchwork, by varying the coloured strips of cloth. A hard backed bench, called a settle, ran from one side of the fire, and a wooden armchair for Father stood opposite. A dresser or cupboard, a well scrubbed table and a few other chairs made up the rest of the kitchen furniture, though there might be a grandfather clock and a bible box in the front room. Overhead hung hams and sides of bacon, pickled beef and herbs. On the airing rack, (or flake), hung the damp oatcakes along with the clean socks, caps and shirts. All was spotlessly clean, with a delicious compound of smells – baking, freshly laundered clothes, wholesome bodies and a fresh tang of cow.

The next most important room was the dairy, with its slate shelves, on the north side of the house. Here were the dairy utensils, the milk bowls, churns, butter bowls and hands, crockery and the baking utensils. The farms within reach of the railway sold their milk, but quantities of butter and cheese were made on the 'outside shops', and each farm had its own mark or print for the finished product. The skim milk was fed to the calves. Great pride was taken in learning the skills needed to make the havercake or oatcake, the butter, the cheese, to pickle the meat and salt the bacon and cure the hams.

These daleswomen were wonderfully thrifty, hard working and hardy, and were truly working partners with their men. They kept the poultry, shared in the haymaking, the rearing of weak lambs, the upbringing of the young dogs (so vital to the sheep farmer), the calving, lambing, foaling, the making of remedies for all ills, animal and human alike. There were a few self taught 'Cow Doctors' in the area, but membership of the Pateley Bridge and Bewerley Cow Club was about the only way to afford the services of a qualified vet. Even then they were seldom called in. Tallow, turpentine, Stockholm tar, tobacco and herbs were all used, and some of the treatment was rough and painful for the animals.

The men followed the seasonal round, walking 'monny a weary mile' up hill and down dale in all weathers, tending their beasts, with faithful Moss, Jip, Nell, Jet or Lassie alongside.

If the farm had an outbarn, it meant two journeys a day in the winter, carrying creels of hay out, and a backcan of milk home. There was washing, shearing, wrapping fleeces, trimming feet, burning horns, marking and checking the sheep on the moors. There was foddering and watering the cattle all winter, and some to milk daily. There were walls to build, ditches to dig, fences to mend, tools to keep in order, and the all important journeys to market with stock and produce.

Peat cutting, bracken scything and haymaking were heavy summer jobs, but spreading muck on the good ground after winter was one of the heaviest. To load the muck forkful by forkful from the midden on to a cart, then cart it, drop it in heaps on the field, and finally spread it by hand was hard work. A skilled man could fling the muck from his fork so that it fell in a wide arc and was evenly distributed over the ground. The right rhythm, a twist of the body and a flick of the wrist to clear the last remains of each forkful, enabled a man to keep going steadily for hours.

The whole family took part in haytime, and in bad weather the work had to be done over and over again. Mowing with a scythe meant rising at two or three o'clock in the morning. After mowing came strewing (by hand or fork), turning (by rake), making footcocks, rowing up, and finally leading, using either a cart or a sledge. On steep slopes the hay was heaped into pikes, about six foot high, and left out until dry. Then the whole pike was pulled by rope on to the sledge. The made hay was tossed up through the forking hole into the barn, and on to the mow, where a sweating man or woman spread it evenly and trod it down. On larger farms an Irishman was hired to help, at £5 a month plus his board and lodging. The youngest children loved to ride back to the barn on the sweet smelling load, but all too soon they grew old enough to join in the work with their parents.

On the Bewerley estate the larger farms were between 120 to 160 acres, but these also had sheep gaits on the moors for extra grazing. An argument arose in the late eighties, and it was settled at the Ramsgill Manor Court that each tenant should have twenty sheep gaits for every £20 of rent paid. The Nidderdale half breds, developed from a cross between Scotch ewes and a Leicester tup, and the Masham, a cross between a Swaledale ewe and a Teeswater tup, fattened earlier and produced more wool than the pure Scotch sheep.

More than twenty families, such as the Hardcastles, Baynes, Thackerays, Clarkes, Bells, Darnboroughs, Suttles, Horners, Inmans, Myers, Newboulds, Parkers, Wards, Calverts, Harrisons, Moors, and Richmonds had lived and farmed in the dale for well over a hundred years, and some of those for five hundred. The skills and customs, beliefs and remedies had been handed down and strictly adhered to, in spite of the advance of new ideas in the rest of the world. The relationship between landlord and tenant had also been a steadily growing bond.

The many smaller holdings were usually farmed along with a second occupation or craft, though the tailors, watchmakers, weavers and knitters produce had been undercut by goods brought in by rail. The specialists were the joiners, masons, slaters, drainers, saddlers and ropemakers. Every man, woman and child on the farms wore wooden soled clogs, iron shod with leather uppers, fastened by a bar, clasp or laces. They were warm and airy, and didn't pick up dirt or slip on grass or wet flagstones. The cloggers were seldom short of work. The blacksmiths too were in constant demand: apart from shoeing horses they were the equivalent of today's agricultural engineer.

Miners tended then to work full time for one of the big companies, such as the Pateley Bridge Mining Company or the Old Merryfield, and just keep an acre or two, a garden, a pig and a cow as a sideline.

They worked in shifts. After doing his shift a man might go on to cart a heavy load all the way down to the railway station at Pateley. Greenhow village was a close community, centred round T'Miner's Arms and the church. Their code and traditions were as strong as those of the farming community. There were no secrets, and they were nearly all related. They stood by each other through thick and thin, but if the unwritten law was broken, the breaker would have to go. There was no way he could remain. They were great tellers of tales in t' Miners, tales of lucky strikes, of undreamed of wealth, of hardship and pain, of humour and wit. Owd Ned, as decent a chap as you could meet, was kept short of beer money by his wife. This was because, when he was in drink, he'd smash everything in sight. One day he sold a bull calf. He spent his threepence of beer money, then he started on the money from the sale. Roaring drunk, he set off for home, and met Squire Yorke on the way. 'Ah've swallered a girt bull corfl' he bellowed, but t'Squire saw he was drunk and went on his way. No one ever knew whether he realised what Ned was on about.

Fred Walker of Burnsall has been down nearly every shaft in Nidderdale in his time. Now eighty, he says, 'I'm still prospecting. I said I'd niver go down t'shaft, but on the morning of my eighteenth birthday the gaffer coom up and gev me a lamp. He said, 'Yer goin' down today. Don't look down, and don't let go of one stepper till you've got hod of another.' The ladder went down eighty feet and I just peddled on down. After a while I could run up and down like a cat. Worst bit was passin' t' balance wheel. I used to try to race t' tub to t'top. I was fixing shafts and stoups, stemples, pins and lugs. A good vein could just blow out, and be full of sand, then it were finished.[19]

The price of lead was low, so were wages, and so were rents. It has never been easy to find a tenant who thought he had a good landlord, and no doubt the age old arguments and bargaining went on in Edward's

44. Miners at Harris Shaft, Greenhow 1890
North Raikes Vein, depth 70 fathoms. Photo, Marsden, Pateley Bridge

manor courts and rent days, just as they do today. A list of some of the major works done in one year of the depression on the Bewerley estate, makes interesting reading however.

In 1892 Edward gave back 10% of the rent to each tenant and did these major works,

New shed and cartshed	enlarged dam, replaced
New shed	windows, made new
New barn roof	flow and repaired
New W.C. at Ramsgill Inn	water wheel
New outbuilding	Re-roofed barn burnt
Rebuilt blacksmith's shop	down by vagrant
New roof to cottages	Enlarged and converted
New roof to shed	Bewerley school and
New barn roof	boarded classroom
Roof re-slated	Boarded classroom in
New shed at Shaw's Mill,	Ramsgill School

These were major works but of course, every day of the week, there were jobs such as fixing a loose slate here, fettling a window latch there, pointing up a barn end, mending an easing trough or 'loisin' a drain' which were not included in this list.

By the time Queen Victoria's long reign came to an end, the Bewerley household was well settled in its ways. Edward and Fanny were nearing seventy, Helen, Isa and Harry had married and gone, John was living at Halton, and 'the girls' were thirty-five, thirty and twenty-nine respectively. The household was run on oiled wheels under the ponderous and inappropriately named old butler, Mr Swift, and tiny brisk little Mrs Ismay, the cook. Two footmen, and Mrs Yorke's jolly Scottish ladysmaid, Miss Dodd, (always dressed in black silk with a choker), attended to all the personal needs of the family, assisted by four housemaids, a stillroom maid, a kitchen maid, a scullery maid and various 'odd men'.

Breakfast was a serious affair preceded by family prayers for the whole household. Edward read the Gospel for the day, a collect and the Lord's Prayer, and everyone knelt against their chairs. Swift found it hard to rise off his knees and wheezed a good deal.

In the dining room afterwards there was a great bowl of porridge, and lashings of thick yellow cream to go on it. Dish after covered dish was set round on heaters – sausages, bacon, eggs, devilled kidneys, fresh mushrooms, kedgeree or trout out of the Nidd. A vast ham, and sometimes a tongue as well, stood on the sideboard, with a dish of cold game in due season. Oatcakes, toast wrapped in a napkin, slabs of Jersey butter, heather honey in the comb, home made preserves and bowls of fruit from the greenhouse covered the snowy damask table cloth.

The sounding of the great gong for lunch, for dressing at 7.15, and finally for dinner, at three minutes to eight, was an art in itself. Taking the gong stick, its round end well padded with wash leather, Swift executed one or two preliminary flourishes, then let the padded end fall on the exact centre of the gong, drawing out a low ringing note. With increasing force the sound filled the whole house, booming through corridors, vibrating in every beam. To the end of their days 'the girls' would fly downstairs like the wind if they were not already assembled by the first strokes. Then Swift majestically opened the double doors to the dining room. If there were guests, each lady was escorted into dinner on the arm of a gentleman. The polished table set with silver, glass and damask napkins, gleamed in the gas light. Trailing greenery and small vases of carnations were used as decorations, or sometimes a huge central épergne filled with fruit.

The footmen, smart in the Bewerley livery of blue tail coats and buff waistcoats, (they wore short black coats in the daytime), handed round the six or seven courses in a deft and unhurried manner. For dessert, everything was cleared from the table and finger bowls set on delicate plates, with pearl handled silver dessert knives and forks, were laid before each guest. Dishes of hot house grapes, nectarines, peaches or cherries were handed round in their season. The old Bewerley Madeira was famous throughout the West Riding, and was often served instead of port.

Edward himself ate and drank sparingly, though he appreciated excellent food and wine. Vast quantities of Mrs Ismay's good cooking was consumed in the servant's hall, and by the upper servants in the housekeeper's room, with much merriment and good companionship. A barrel of beer was kept near the back door, from which callers and workmen were sustained after walking or driving a horse and cart to the Hall. Motor cars were indeed coming in, and the speed limit had been raised from 4 to 12 m.p.h., but the Yorkes did not own one till 1912.

On a shooting morning the gentlemen had a very early breakfast, then carved slices of ham for themselves and put them between bread in their pockets. At 7.30 the open wagonette drawn by two fat horses collected the guns, and another followed with the loaders and cartridges. They drove five miles to Ramsgill at a very slow trot. From there, the guns walked for three quarters of an hour straight uphill to the butts, and the cartridges and guncases went up in the spring cart. After three or four drives on the wet and windswept moor, they walked to a stone hut where they ate their sandwiches and had a nip from their flasks. They walked back down to Ramsgill, to where the open brake was waiting, and so home about 5.30pm. The ladies greeted them in their tea gowns, then everyone changed into full evening dress for dinner. Next day the same was repeated, but on Heathfield moor. Edward particularly enjoyed walking up grouse over setters in the early part of August, when many miles were covered. Each beck had a small stone trough cut in it by a spring, for the dogs to stop and have a drink.

Their comfortable way of life, no more luxurious at the time than that of their neighbouring landowners, the Ingilbys, Mountgarrets, Tempests and so on, was balanced by the strong family sense of duty and responsibility. Edward, as we have seen, interspersed his seasonal round of farm, mine and estate management, with his manifold duties as Deputy Lieutenent, Chairman of the Bench (for thirty or more years), High Sheriff, Churchwarden, Govenor of three or four schools, Income Tax Commissioner, Chairman of the Parish Council, and President of innumerable societies. He was constantly asked to give or help to raise money for the Temperance society, the Boys Brigade, relief funds, the Clothing Club, the Burial Club, the Primrose League, the Mechanics Institute, the Reading Room and several churches and schools in Nidderdale and Halton. Every Sunday morning he walked to Pateley Church together with his daughters and as many of the staff as could be spared, including one footman. (The others attended Evensong, which afforded an opportunity for doing a bit of courting on the way home.) He read the Lessons regularly. Fanny and the delicate Kathie were driven there in the brougham, which waited in the coach house beside the church.

Because of his example and their upbringing, his three unmarried daughters also took a lead in all the local affairs. May deputised for her father in various capacities in the dale, opening sales of work and bazaars, visiting the tenants, taking gifts to the sick, and helping with the Clothing Club. She always said that the nicest welcome she could have when she knocked on a door was, 'Coom on in luv, and set tha down. Put thi umberella in't slopstone to sype, and reach to, an' 'elp thi'sel.'

From their earliest days, the eight Yorke children had made their own home entertainment. John had a wonderful gift for music and rhyme. He wrote humorous plays and songs, while May wrote poems, skits and monologues in dialect. All of them were well used to putting on these happy amateur performances. They sang together at home and in church with great gusto and considerable harmony, and kept the warm family ties strong, right on from their motherless childhood days until they were all grown up. Kathie and Ethel taught in the Sunday School, entertained at the school treats, sang and acted in the parish evenings, and took a lead in the Girls Friendly Society.

Their own social life was bounded by visitors, shooting parties and garden parties at home, the occasional visit to London, York or Leeds to attend a concert, a royal occasion, an agricultural show or a county ball. York races were seldom missed, and music festivals, such as the one at Hovingham, were specially enjoyed. With five daughters there were many prospective suitors including the Watson boys, introduced by their cousins the Walshams. All family occasions naturally included the tenants, the work people and their families. John's coming of age was celebrated by dinners both at Halton and Bewerley, where the tenants presented him with a set of Dicken's works and a handsome gold watch. Helen's wedding to Arthur Bailey from Wramplingham Hall in Norfolk, in April 1896, was a cause of great local excitement. It took place in Pateley church and the Dean of York officiated. Nine bridesmaids, including her four sisters, attended her. Triumphal arches were erected at the Park gates, Pateley was decorated with flags and scrolls, and a special train brought guests from Harrogate. The laundry was draped in pink for the reception. Presents were displayed in the morning room, and a ball was held in the dining room.

Bertie, (the Rev. A.H. Watson), had first proposed to Helen, but had been refused. In 1900 he married gentle Louisa but this was a quieter affair. Harry's marriage to Dora Bateman, in Tralee in 1901, was marked by a workmans' supper and a dinner for seventy tenants at the King's Arms, Pateley Bridge.

An east window in Pateley church, designed by Comere and Capronnier of Brussels, was unveiled by the Dean of Ripon in 1893, and six years later the music loving Yorkes gave a new organ, which had more power and a beautiful tone. Bridgehousegate School became a National School in 1894, and though that meant that Edward was no longer entirely responsible for it, he still supported it both personally and financially.

The news of the old Queen's death reached the Yorkes the day after Harry's wedding. The family had watched the Diamond Jubilee processions in London and now Edward went to meet the three Lords Lieutenant in York Castle to send a message of sympathy to the new king. He also attended a crowded memorial service in the Minster. The proclamation of King Edward VII was read out at Pateley station by Mr Harker, who kept the Yorke Arms at Ramsgill. Later in the year Edward took the girls to London for the Coronation. In Halton and Bewerley the schools celebrated with tea and games, and on July 1st a torchlight procession went up on Pateley Moor, and Edward lit a huge bonfire.

When Colonel Harrison, the tenant at Halton Place, died, John decided to live there. His bailiff was T.C. Moon of Old Hall Farm, whose life had been spent in the Yorkes' service. There was no land in hand for when Edward had gone to Bewerley he had let the Home Farm to John Thompson and built the farm house for him. John enlarged and improved the service room at Halton by taking away the staircase, doing away with the cottage, and building a new vestry and a family pew. A new Reading Room was built by Edward and John, and was opened with a successful dance. A new farm house had recently been built for R. Swinbank, who had married one of the Miss Moons, and old James Parker, for years the tenant at Nappa, died. John also followed his father as one of the school managers.

Between them they bought back Parcevall Hall, in Appletreewick, which had been out of the family for some long time.

Edward's diary tells us in March 1903, 'John and his intended bride, Miss May Stansfeld, paid us a visit, and we were all much pleased at the engagement'. They were also much surprised because John was thirty-five and had shown no sign of courting. Then he made up his mind in a short time.

'In June,' wrote Edward, 'We had the pleasure of seeing John married in St Paul's Knightsbridge by the Bishop of Ripon.' He always referred to John's wife as Mrs May thereafter.

In Nidderdale a new railway line for mineral traffic was opened from Pateley to Lofthouse, a tramway on to Angram having been previously constructed. Edward rode on this line with great enjoyment the following year.

Many improvements and alterations at the Hall took place. 'I converted the old laundry,' wrote Edward, 'into a ball and smoking room. Over the new fireplace I put a fine old piece of oak carving, formerly Reay property from Hunwick Hall. It is said to be early Jacobean, and needed complete restoration.' In this new Oak Room the servants gave the tradesmen a ball in the new year.

A new oven was put into the kitchen. The story is told that Mr Boord, the agent, (known always to the locals as 'Yon Board') asked Mrs Yorke if she would like to see the new stove. She said she would, so he escorted her to the back regions. They reached the first, old, kitchen, no longer used. Mrs Yorke stopped. 'Very nice, Mr Boord,' she said, turned and went back to the morning room. He always said she never actually saw the new stove at all. . . .

Harry and Dollie went back off leave to India. Fearful for their two young boys, Richard and Reggie, (for their eldest had died in India), they left them in the care of their grandparents at Bewerley. This livened up

45. Jacobean Oak Overmantel from Hunwick Hall, purchased by T.E.Yorke

the household and 'the girls' loved them. Bertie and Isa Watson also brought their boys over to play with them, and John and May's sons came as well.

Edward's great physical stamina is evident from the things he did in his seventy eighth year, in 1907. He rode regularly around the estate. He skated on the reservoir, and bicycled from Weetwood to Harewood, then back to Harrogate. He shot, walking miles over the moors, fished, played golf and drove his dogcart. He attended thirty meetings, fortnightly courts, four Quarter Sessions and thirteen fundraising events in the year, as well as going to the races, to six concerts, and four visits away to London and the Continent. (Petty Sessions could now be held at Pateley Bridge, both for the West Riding and the Liberty of Ripon, so many cases which formerly would have gone to Knaresboro' were now tried locally.)

Edward was always ready to try new ideas. He went in a charabanc with May in the Isle of Wight. He motored through the Dukeries, and bought his first car, a Berliet cabriolet, in 1912.

His old keeper Merrington was soon going to retire. When shooting with Lord Mountgarret, Edward heard a beater ask his keeper, Simpson, "'ow did Lordy do at yon drive?' Simpson replied, 'Thirty-seven shots and not a bloody feather'. Unfortunately his Lordship heard this too. Stepping out from behind a tree he said, 'You can take a month's notice, Simpson'. Edward went up to the keeper a few minutes later. 'I'd be very glad to have you at Bewerley' he said. Simpson became head keeper there soon after, and stayed many years.

The outbreak of World War One was an unbelievable shock to the whole country. Life had been so calm and secure for so long, safe behind the shield of the Navy, and the Victorians and Edwardians knew more about life in the Colonies than the politics and aspirations on the Continent.

Edward Yorke was called upon to preside at two great meetings in

Pateley to attract recruits. Intercessions for the troops in church, on that first Sunday of the war, brought home to everyone some of the impending tragedy. A Colonel Dickinson came to ask for land on which he could encamp and train 17,000 men, and he too held an open air recruiting meeting. The next year the Yorkshire Hussars and infantry marched a battalion of 632 men and officers over to the Park and recruited more local men. Many enlisted and many never returned. The carnage of that war is known by the lists of names on the war memorials in even tiny villages.

Young Antony Bailey, Helen's only son, joined up in 1917 and was killed within a month at Delville Wood. John Stansfeld, Mrs May's brother, had both legs shot off and died of wounds after the battle of Loos, along with 94,787 other British soldiers.

John Yorke was unable to go to the front line on account of the accident which had left him with a stiff arm. He toured the country to find remounts, horses to replace the huge numbers which were slaughtered by the guns every week. Chargers, troop horses, and draft horses to draw the gun carriages and provision wagons all had to be found, vetted, bought and transported. Out in all weathers, John was drenched to the skin one wintry March day in 1915. By the time he got home he was running a high fever. Pneumonia set in and there was no medication. Within three days he was dead.

To Edward, in his eighty-third year, this was an end to all his hopes and plans. His constant and unremitting care for the property, his planting, building, and improvements had all been done with dear John in mind. John's elder son Jock was only eleven years old, and fond as Edward was of the boy, he was too young to be taken about and shown the things he would need to know. The whole family was stricken, and felt deeply for forlorn Mrs May with her three little boys.

Miss May, heart broken too, determined to do her part in the war work, so she went over to Harewood Hospital, and enrolled as a V.A.D. She was forty-eight, and used to an orderly life, but her strength of character and knowledge of all types of people made her an invaluable, [if sometimes dictatorial] nurse.

Bombs were dropped by Zeppelins in the autumn of 1916, and the winter was very severe. Sheep were buried in the snow, and the thorn fences were damaged by starving rabbits. The boiler burst when the pipes froze at the Hall, and it was three long months before they could be repaired. The lists of casualties in the papers each day grew longer and longer. It seemed indeed that the flower of English manhood was lost. At long last an Armistice was declared.

Edward's diary was kept just as before, but although his activities remained unabated, and the same duties were carried out, his hand writing grew progressively more shaky and more crabbed. A revival in lead mining occurred with a demand for fluospar and calcite and a rise in price. Edward granted a lease to the Greenhaugh Mining Co. in 1915, and they reopened several old shafts, including Appletreewick Mine.

With his wife and daughters he enjoyed the visits of his ten grandsons and three grand daughters. John's sons, Jock and Peter, used to come over, bringing their ponies by train, and spend a month or more at Bewerley in the summer. They loved their grandfather, who taught them how to fish, and shoot, and showed them birds and butterflies in the garden, chatting away as they walked. His sturdy figure, dressed almost invariably in plus fours, with rather wrinkled stockings, and surmounted by a shapeless old hat, could be seen out in all weathers talking to the men, visiting the Estate Office, inspecting a drain, calling at a mine, discussing timber sales, looking at a new bull, visiting the school or tying a fly, his dogs always beside him. His knowledge of the branches of the local families was encyclopaedic and every day brought a new story to be enjoyed about some local happening.

When he finally weakened and died, in his ninety-first year, a whole way of life went with him. His funeral was held in a packed church, and people came from all over the county as well as all down from the dales to pay their respects to a well loved man.

He was buried beside his youngest son and his sister Fanny, and his butler and his keeper lay close by. A recumbent cross in Nidderdale marble marks his grave, and the family put a memorial tablet in the chapel beside his father's window, 'Sacred to the memory of Thomas Edward Yorke, the last Squire of Bewerley'.

CHAPTER XVII

JOHN CECIL YORKE   1868 – 1915
OF
BEWERLEY AND HALTON PLACE

JOHN WAS BORN IN 1868 AT HALTON, the eldest son and prospective heir. His first curls, which were preserved by his mother, were of a definite auburn hue. His other brother and sisters followed soon after him so his earliest memories were of a large and united family. He went to school at Dr Blackwell's in Harrogate, from where he wrote,

'A master comes and teaches us Latin. He talks very Yorkshire and shakes the boys. I like Miss Blackwell very much, she is not at all what I expected. We have music and drawing from a master. He is German and cannot speak properly.'

His mother knew her boy's interests and wrote back,

'Papa went ferreting and got twenty rabbits in Worthy Hill.'

He went on to Dr Sanderson's school at Elstree, where he was reported to be excellent in every way. It was while he was there that his mother had her last baby. Together with the others, he visited her in York, where she was staying with her parents, the Baillies. It seems possible that the scarlet fever which caused his mother's death may have been brought by him from school, but I hope he was never told that. He was just twelve when she died.

His grandmother did her best to comfort him. She wrote to him at school, 'My dearest Johnnie, my A 1 boy. . . with cartloads of love and blessings, your fond old Grannie'.

Dr Sanderson evidently was kind and understanding. He wrote to John's father, 'He is a very dear boy, and he has taken an excellent place at Harrow'.

When John left Harrow he took the two music prizes for the school. Since his earliest days he had a superb ear for music, and being well taught, soon began to compose songs, hymn tunes, psalm chants and other pieces. It was one of his chief delights, and he was the instigator of many happy family evenings around the piano. He wrote skits, plays, pantomimes and rhymes too and thoroughly enjoyed amateur dramatics, using his willing sisters and brothers in the various parts. Several of his written and musical pieces have been preserved, and they show the flavour of the humour of that time. One of his choruses ran,

"They sang God bless the weasel

And, pop goes the Prince of Wales."

He went to Christchurch, Oxford, where he had rooms in Peckwater Quad. There his sisters visited him and went to some of the balls. His father had remarried, and Fanny proved a loving step mother to them all, even though May and John found it harder to accept her at first than did the younger children.

He lived at home for some time, joining in the local social round, shooting, riding around the estate with his father, and learning much as he went. His father tried to make up the loss of their mother and, especially to the two elder children, made himself as much of a companion as was possible with his busy life.[1]

John joined the Royal Artillery Garrison and travelled the country with them. He also became a J.P. for the West Riding, and joined in many local functions. He was a delightful person, gentle, entertaining, kind and amusing, and much liked by all. His sisters were devoted to him, and he found friends wherever he went.

At the age of thirty-one he moved back to Halton Place to live, and there he kept a bachelor establishment, ran the estate, and entered into all the life of Craven. On a visit to London, he met the graceful and pretty May, daughter of Evelyn Stansfeld, and they were immediately drawn to each other. After a few meetings he fell wildly in love with her, and courted her with such success that they became engaged within a very short time.

His family were astonished, but delighted, as snippets from their letters show.

His father: 'My dear John, We certainly were astonished when I opened your letter and heard such wonderful news. . . . I hope that the lady you have chosen will make you a good wife and add much too your happiness. I remember her certainly, and thought her most pretty.'

His sister May: 'How happy I feel that you have secured such a charming girl. She seems to have won all hearts.'

His sister Helen: 'My dear Johnnie, How you took my breath away! I am just delighted. You sound so happy. Is she dark or fair or tall or small?

His youngest sister Ethel: 'My dearest Johnnie, Well you HAVE given us a surprise. We had nearly given you up as a bad job, and now you've gone and got engaged! I hope May realises she is a VERY lucky girl, and if not I shall tell her. We made May guess the news when she came down last, and she guessed quantities of people before you, then nearly fell down with surprise. I hope the Halton people will approve of your choice or else I suppose you'll have to call it off.'

46. John Cecil Yorke

Barbara Lister, an old friend, 'Dear Mr Yorke, How exciting isn't it. . . what is she like to talk to? like me? or much cleverer and more fascinating – no, she's sure to be that. I remember seeing her play croquet one day at Downham, oh so pretty and graceful.'

With great delight the whole family attended John's wedding at St Paul's Knightsbridge. The ceremony was performed by the Bishop of Richmond.

47. Marion Elizabeth, wife of John Yorke, taken on the day of their engagement

They made a handsome pair. The newspaper account said,

'The bride wore a gown of lace, chiffon and satin, embroidered with silver sequins, a Court train of satin, trimmed with Carrickmacross lace, a wreath of green leaves fastening her veil, a diamond aigrette in her dark hair. Master Arthur Bailey was the page, together with six bridesmaids in white muslin dresses and fichus, wreaths of pink roses and long white veils.'

Kathie and Ethel were two of the bridesmaids.

At Halton, over fifty of the school children had a tea party at the house, with games and presents on the lawn afterwards.

So John and May began their married life at Halton, forty years after his mother and father. As his father had done, he had been running the estate with T.C. Moon, who farmed Old Hall, as his bailiff. Moon, who was related to eight out of the fifteen tenant families, was paid £40 a year and took his duties seriously. It was said of him, 'When owd Moon were alive, if a wall fell down, 'e'd 'ave th'estate men out afore t'stones 'ad stopped rollin''. Mr Boord, the Bewerley agent, also gave John the benefit of his advice. Boord was a thorough man and did his best to teach John sound management. He drew up valuations of the farms in some detail. His comments in 1904 on Low Field were,

'This farm is not cultivated to the best advantage. Two of the meadows are very poor indeed and have been badly laid down. Most of the gates require repair, two are missing and all are badly hung. A larger number of milking cows should be considered, in which case, cheese should be made in the summer and butter in the winter.'

In 1915 the Halton farms, tenants, acreages and rents were,[2]

Farm	Tenant	Acres/Rent
Pye Cross,	Ezra Jackson,	193 acres at £80 a year
West Thornber,	Ripley Ashton,	158 acres at £95 a year
North Thornber,	Bailey & Marsden,	162 acres at £136 a year
Low Thornber,	Rbt Capstick,	168 acres at £95 a year
Long Bank,	Thos. Denby,	185 acres at £115 a year
High Scale,	Thos. Johnson,	195 acres at £140 a year
Low Scale,	William Wilson,	124 acres at £160 a year
Cow Hill,	John Wilson,	200 acres at £200 a year
Town End,	Rbt Swinbank,	189 acres at £135 a year
Low Field,	Rbt Whitehead,	172 acres at £224 a year
Old Hall,	T.C. Moon,	112 acres at £167 a year
Home Farm,	J. Thompson,	128 acres at £208 a year
Panbeck,	J. Brown,	133 acres at £125 a year
Nappa Flatts,	G. Moorhouse,	261 acres at £153 a year
The Shop,	J. Chumley,	6 acres at £20 a year
		2,149 acres at £2,053 rent

The nine cottage tenants were Mrs Moon, T. Redmayne, H. Lund, J. Redmayne, T. Nixon, J. Sheldon, R. Bland, Sallie Wincap and J. Wilson senr. The rents were 1/3d a week.

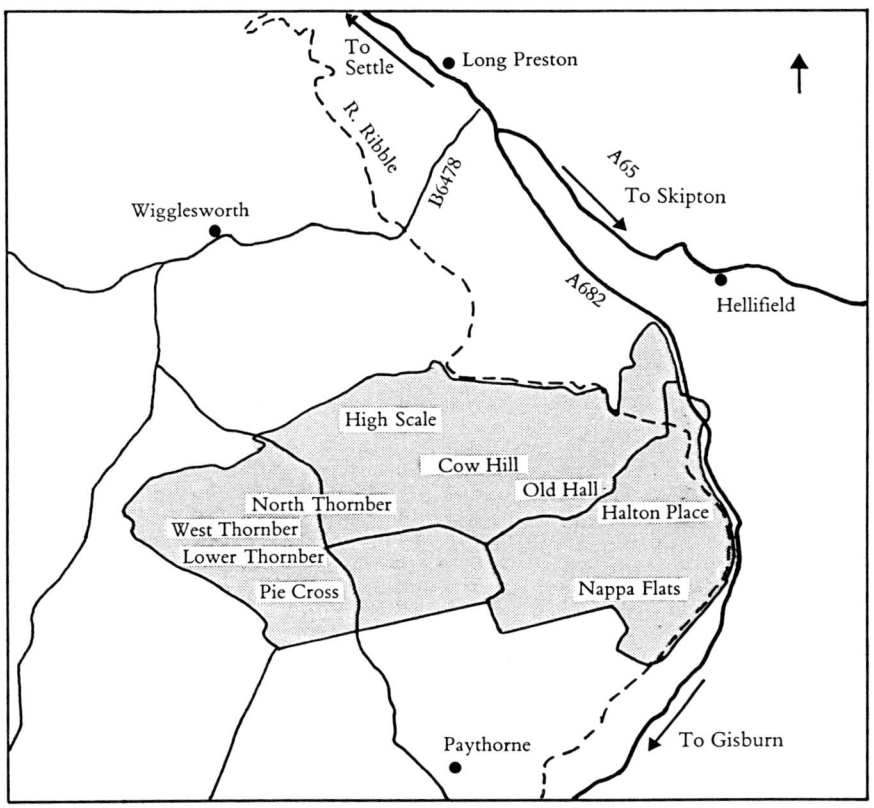

48. Map showing Halton estate

Jim Doyle, the groom, and his wife Nellie, lived in one cottage in the stable yard, and David Jones, the gardener, with his family in the other. Wages for the estate men, Tom Redmayne and Henry Lund, were 3/4d a day, and Sheldon and Bland, the odd men, got 3/-. Thomas Throup, John Carr and William Jackman were doing estate work as plumber, mason and slater then, as their sons still were in the 1950s.

In addition to the farms, there were 120 acres of plantations, plus the grounds of Halton Place. The Church room, the Reading room, the School and the Joiner's shop made up the rest of the village. The total population of the estate was about 120.

In the first log book of the school in 1877 it was stated by H.M. Inspector that "the premises are only meant and only adapted for children under 8 years. At present more than half those on the books are above that age. They have had little or no instruction before attending this school."

The teaching and discipline deteriorated in the period 1885-95, and although Miss Temperton struggled on with poor attendance, (due to necessary farm work, severe weather and epidemics), she felt the last H.M.I. report was harsh. She had had to "bear on her shoulders all the rebuffs and hard words of a bad tempered Inspector." She only received a grant of £34.19.0 for books and equipment for the year, for 20-30 children.

By 1903 Miss Campbell was in charge and things had improved all round but it was still a daunting task to teach children of an age range of four to thirteen, crammed into one small room.

The names of Rumney, Moon and Yorke appear often in the logbook under 'visits of school managers.'

John Yorke was clearly a delightful person and well liked by all who knew him. His extremely capable father and very thorough agent may have made it hard for him to act independently, or develop new ideas, but it does seem that he had a tendency to procrastinate. In one of his letters to May he wrote, 'I took out a mountain of bills to pay, but couldn't decide which. . . so put them back'.

The Stansfeld girls had had a more worldly upbringing, influenced by their mother who herself was both pretty and social. When May married her devoted suitor, she anticipated a considerable inheritance before too long, and saw no reason to stint on entertainment and amusement. She simply had no experience or understanding that in land management or farming there is very little ready cash available.

John wanted to please her in every possible way. After so many solitary years he was enchanted with his beautiful, lively bride, and they lived happily, but in a rather more extravagant style than before. They were not short of friends to visit or entertain. The Edwardian fashions were so splendid – the walking gowns, tea gowns and evening gowns, and above all the fabulous hats, piled with fruit or flowers, were really creations. The art of pleasing the gentlemen was at its height, and was held to be of prime importance in May's world. Every photograph shows how well turned out she always was, whether driving out in the Victoria, fetchingly dressed for tennis, or taking tea on the lawn attended by white flannelled gentlemen in boaters.

A few weeks before the arrival of their first child, John had met with a serious accident in a train. His arm was badly cut when a sudden lurch threw him nearly through the window. Blood poisoning set in and amputation was threatened. He was left with a permanently stiff wrist.

When their eldest son was born there was great rejoicing in the family. John's father wrote to May, 'How pleased I am that you have given me another grandson. I hear he is a fine boy, may God bless him and may he grow up to be a good man, and a credit to the Yorke family.' The boy was named John Edward Evelyn after his two grandfathers, but to distinguish him from his father, he was known as Jock. He shared in the happy, light hearted atmosphere, and was always dressed, (in photographs at least), in the frilliest and prettiest of clothes, standing beside his mother, in a sailor hat and beads.

The blood poisoning which followed his father's accident in the train had prevented him seeing the baby until he was three weeks old, but he and May wrote tenderly to each other while apart. The letters were baked to prevent cross infection.

A party had been arranged at Bewerley to celebrate John's marriage, but it was postponed until he had recovered. Then he took May and the baby over. The tenants had given them a handsome silver mirror and salver as wedding presents, and over a hundred and sixty people came to the Garden Party. Speeches were made, and as well as good wishes to the couple, Mr Hannam said they would give Master Yorke a hearty welcome when he came riding up the dale, and Mr Brown, the old coachman, said he hoped he would prove as good as his father, and live as long as his grandfather, to which there was loud applause.

John was an affectionate father, and close to his sons, as some of Jock's early letters show,

'Darling Dad, How much money for spotting the winner? Love from Jock.'

(From Bewerley) 'Darling Dad, We walked nearly to the moors – oh it was hard work. Mummy has not bought any new hats thank goodness. I love riding the big horse – we rode for an hour.'

49. Edwardian tea party at Halton with May and John Yorke

Jock's love of riding started as soon as he was able to sit up, and his father walked miles beside his pony, with the dogs.

John and the boys loved visiting Bewerley, but May did not always feel at ease there, in spite of a warm welcome and a great desire to draw her into the family. She found the elderly household rather dull and too regular and dutiful in their habits. She would sit sketching on the lawn – she had a great talent for watercolours – but when the gong rang and all were assembled, she'd say, 'Oh the light is just right, I *must* go on for another half an hour'. This would throw everyone out.

When first married and staying for a shoot, she insisted on going up to the moor with John in the dogcart with Temptress, their thoroughbred mare, instead of in the wagonette with the others. They arrived late, an unheard of occurrence, and old Merrington had waited for them. His uncompromising methods with poachers were well known in the dale. 'Fell 'em first, an' agree wi' em after, was mah system,' he always said. His rugged face and keen blue eyes showed his disapproval.

'So sorry we are late, Merrington,' said John.

'Well Maister John,' replied the old man, 'It meks a difference when there's two liggin' a' bed i'stead o' yan'. John, who'd known him all his life, roared with laughter. May was not so amused.

Another factor was Miss May, John's intelligent but reserved sister who, imbued with Bewerley tradition and training, found it hard to appreciate pretty, younger Mrs May. She had not only captivated Miss May's beloved brother, but also seemed not to care about the things his sister believed in.

John, on the other hand, found everything his wife did perfect, but deeply as she genuinely loved him, she did strengthen his natural disinclination to attend to the more tedious of his duties. It is true that they put on concerts to raise money for good causes, playing piano and violin, and singing together, but some of the proper estate maintenance began to be neglected, and debts gradually began to accumulate.

The ten years of gaiety which they enjoyed up until the war were only in keeping with the fashionable spirit of the day – racing, gambling, shooting, tennis and croquet parties, musical evenings, plays and concerts – the world then seemed so safe and secure. Together they built new bedrooms over the billiard room, laid stone steps down to the tennis court, and travelled about. They did however take a leading part in raising the money and planning the building of St Aidan's church in Hellifield, consecrated in 1906. The new parish of Hellifield included Halton West so the Vicar of Hellifield became their incumbent, instead of the Vicar of Long Preston.

Their household resounded with music. With John at the piano, the cook, Violet Lumsden, was called in to sing soprano, the nursery maid Hilda, alto, big Annie, the housemaid, boomed away and the gardener, David Jones, had a fine tenor. John's son always said his parents only engaged servants with good voices, and he remembered practising anthems and getting the giggles when they were singing 'The fool hath said in his heart, there is no God', and his father sang 'The fool! the fool!' then Jones sang 'The fool! the fool!' after him.

John composed songs, waltzes, marches and hymn tunes, and some of them were published and sold for charity. His three boys certainly grew up in a cheerful home, and were devoted to all the staff.

The outbreak of war was a terrible, unbelievable shock. All the interest in social gossip and news suddenly changed to intense patriotism and war news. Miss Delves, the governess, left to become a V.A.D. Troops trained in the Park at Bewerley. John Stansfeld, May's brother went to the front with his regiment. John, whose stiff arm prevented him joining the fighting forces, was made the local Remount Officer, and was sent around the country by train, to buy up for remounts for the army. Travelling through the winter, standing in farm yards, on stations, in stables, he was frequently soaked with rain and chilled through. Hundreds of horses were needed every day, such was the slaughter.

In the March of the second year of the war, John was out in particularly severe weather, and completely drenched. When he got home he was running a high fever, and went straight up to bed. The next day he was worse and May became worried, but still thought it no more than a bad cold. By the second night he was delirious, and the doctor could do little for him. His fever rose still higher, pneumonia set in and by the third day he was dead.

For May the speed of events was unbelievable. Suddenly she, so unused to responsibility, so unversed in business matters, was faced with the loss of her main stay, her husband, adviser and companion. Her father too was dead. Although surrounded by the deepest sympathy and offers of support, she felt totally bereft and desolate, unable to face this disaster.

Her father-in-law, in many ways the ideal person to understand her plight after his own harrowing experience with his first wife, was already eighty-three years old. Grieved beyond measure himself at the loss of all his hopes, he found it very hard to get close to Mrs May. He knew little of their financial affairs. When it was revealed that John had mortgaged the whole estate to raise cash, and had debts as well, the atmosphere in the family grew very cool. However, he wrote kindly of 'poor May in her forlorn position'.

May drew on the support of two friends of John's, Arthur Wauchope, (Jock's godfather), and Wilfred Thompson, a Director of Martin's Bank in Harrogate. Her brother John was at the front. For days before the funeral, a procession of friends and neighbours came to pay their respects. The coffin was laid in the Bow Room, and the queue wound through the hall and up the stairs, along the passage. Jock and Peter, in black armbands, watched solemnly. Each person paused to say a prayer and farewell.

Together they arranged the sad funeral at Long Preston, one of the largest gatherings ever seen there. Most of the farmers and tradesmen from miles around were present. The account in 'The Craven Herald' reads,

'The cortege was headed by a posse of West Riding Constabulary, under Sgt. Arundel. The brass mounted oak coffin was borne on an estate wagon draped with the Union Jack, drawn by two horses, and immediately following was another four wheeled wagon heavily laden with wreaths and flowers.'

Next came the brougham, driven by Jim Doyle, with poor May and two of the three little boys, Jock aged eleven, and Peter, ten. Michael, who was only three, stayed with Nanny Day.

One of the hymns and the Nunc Dimittis were sung to the tunes John had composed, and all the farm tenants acted as bearers. A lump came into every throat as May and the boys walked to the graveside.

So May was left, forlorn indeed, in deep shock and grief, and also in constant anxiety about her brother. The war news alone was enough to cloud everybody's life. The household did all they could to help. Miss Sanderson, the governess, kept the two older boys as busy as possible. Jim Doyle, old Sheldon, and Nixon the keeper took them out whenever they could to occupy them. The crowning blow for May came that summer when her brother, commanding the second battalion of The Gordon Highlanders, had both his legs shot off and died of wounds in the battle of Loos.

As well as her grief, her anxiety about financial affairs was a great burden. She made a will and asked John's two friends to act as guardians for the boys. Wilfred (later Sir Wilfred) Thompson became her most trusted adviser, because, most unfortunately, she simply could not discuss matters easily with any of the Yorkes. Instead of being able to share their mutual grief, and draw comfort, it seems that every meeting ended in misunderstandings. She did make infrequent visits to Bewerley, and

50. St Mary's, Long Preston

Jock and Peter spent a month there in the summer, but in business matters there was a terrible block.

At Halton, the blinds were half drawn, the gardener was given notice, Jim Doyle was called up, and the horses were sold. May kept Corona, Jock's pony, which she drove in a trap, and which pulled the lawn mower wearing leather overshoes. If she needed to go to the station, Joe Coates from Hellifield drove her. The boys' school fees had to be paid, for they went off to Eton. The war dragged on, the lists of the dead growing longer each day. Very many of May's friends suffered and mourned with her. Gradually she took up life again, and rolled bandages, raised money for comforts for the troops, and began to take an interest in local matters, in John's school and the people. In 1917 she was appointed temporary teacher at the school, when there was a severe shortage of trained staff. She played the organ regularly in Halton church, opposite John's memorial tablet, and drew comfort from her youngest son still at home.

Eight years passed, Jock and Peter went on to Oxford, and Michael to Radley. Then came the news that their grandfather, aged ninety, had died at Bewerley. Jock was his heir.

CHAPTER XVIII

JOHN EDWARD EVELYN YORKE 1904
OF
HALTON PLACE

JOHN OR JOCK, AS HE WAS ALWAYS CALLED, was born on June 10th, 1904, at Halton. A fine child, he quickly grew into a lively and attractive boy, full of spirit and fun. He was closer to his parents than most children of his kind and era, and has clear memories of sharing walks and rides with his father. Together they went ferretting for rabbits, shooting pigeons and visiting the farmers. With his mother he sang around the piano, and learnt, from an early age, to entertain the visitors with songs, recitations and stories.

The first public speech he remembers making was, 'Thank God for Mr Moon's good tea', after the old Moons' Golden Wedding in 1909, when he was five.

The tragic loss of his father, when he was only eleven, of course made a great impression on him. He clearly remembers the sorrow, and recalls how he was taken out riding on the fatal morning by kind Jim Doyle. Jim knew Jock's father was dead, but the boy had not yet been told. They trotted up to Three Lane Ends, and on the way various farmers stepped out of gateways and approached them. Each time Jim called out 'Trot her on, Master Jock, keep her going'. He muttered the news to the inquirer, then urged on his horse to catch up the pony.

Somehow his mother managed to tell him herself and they all wept together. The boys had lived a free life, in and out of doors all day, and they enjoyed helping with all the jobs in the stables and about the place. The men encouraged and occupied them. For Jock particularly, Jim Doyle was his mentor and friend. An early photograph shows Jock, still in petticoats, perched up on Mick, a big bay horse. 'Jim used to put me up on him,' he said, 'when I was being a nuisance and getting under his feet. It kept me out of the way.' It also began his lifelong love of horses. Peter was never such a keen horseman, but preferred shooting, so Jock rode his fat pony, Corona, and took out his first 'pack' which consisted of Pauline, a big poodle, and Jummy, the bulldog.

When Jim went on errands in the dogcart, Jock went too, and was taught to drive the lively Temptress, bowling along at a brisk pace. When the meet was near enough, they hunted together, and their companionship was an important part of Jock's life. He always said that he looked on

51. Mr. and Mrs. T. C. Moon's Golden Wedding 1909 L. to R.
Back row: Robert and Mrs. Swinbank, Tom and Mrs. Moon, Rob Swinbank junr. Mr. Moon, Miss S. J. Swinbank, Mrs. Moon, Lizzie Swinbank, Barbara Whitehead, Charlie Whitehead, Mr. & Mrs. Whitehead
Front row: Rob Whitehead, Willy Moon, Maud Ethel & Carrie Swinbank, Arthur Swinbank

all their servants as trusted friends and advisers, and learnt the true values of life from them.

Miss Maud Sanderson came as governess, and later Jock used to ride over to Rathmell to have Latin lessons with her father. Just before he was thirteen he went to Winton House preparatory school. Being war time, the school was cold and that winter was bitterly cold too. It was the first and only time he had chilblains. Due to weak eyesight, he was only allowed to study for short periods. He spent some of his time driving an old buckboard taking Red Cross supplies from Winchester around the various surrounding camps.

He was not unhappy, and enjoyed all the games. His cousin, young John Stansfeld, was with him there too. From there Jock went on to Mr Byrne's house at Eton. Peter joined him the following year, and they shared a room. They also shared in all the games and sports, both being good athletes. High jump, long jump, cross country races, and sprints, as well as the Field Game, and rowing on the river in the summer, were their especial interests. He was keenly interested in the Eton College Beagles, and only missed three half holidays with them in the whole of his school career.

The war came to an end during Jock's school days, and he joined in the peace celebrations in Windsor, when the boys ran up to the Castle and shouted for the King. At Halton later, they celebrated with bonfires, sports and a fancy dress parade. Jock's mother dressed up as a fearsome Druid, complete with flowing beard and draperies, and led a white cow up the village. (In the photograph, Richard Kenyon can be seen following discreetly behind, in case the cow 'struck gad', and got away.)

By now Jock and Peter were invited to the big shoots at Bewerley, where their indomitable grandfather still walked up to the butts, at eighty seven. The keepers and beaters were all old friends whom they looked forward to seeing as the season came round. The moors and the various drives became familiar ground to him, and the second great interest of Jock's life developed.

Staying at Bewerley was an experience never to be forgotten. From his earliest days, when he and Peter hid on the staircase and peeped over the banisters to watch the house party go in to dinner, then sneaked to the back to wheedle some delicious pudding out of Mrs Ismay, the sounds and smells of the old house remained with him. Swift's heavy footfall as he wheezed across the hall, the squeak of a certain door, the boom of the gong, the specially memorable smells of the cedar wood room, the beeswax polish in the hall, and the great bowls of fresh flowers in the sitting rooms, stayed with him all his life, as did the feel of the nursery bath encased in brown wood. With their Watson cousins, Ted, Oliver

52. The stableyard, Halton Place, 1980

and Martin, they played with Miss Dodd and Miss Card, the two ladysmaids, in the sewing room. They rode over to Westcliffe to pick mushrooms with Miss Delves, climbed and fell out of the huge trees, and explored for miles. They joked with the bonneted weeding women wielding their broken-off table knives on the paths, and were friends with everyone. As they grew older, the orderly and substantial meals made a great impression, and they did justice to every mouthful.

Jock went on to Christchurch, Oxford, like his father, and read agriculture. He became first whipper in to the Christchurch beagles, hunted by his great friend Dodie Browne. Once, in the vacation, they took the pack down to the Portman kennels at Blandford. There they had three days beagling, three days fox hunting, and went to four Hunt Balls.

It was while he was at Oxford that his grandfather died, and he inherited the Nidderdale estate. He attended one manor court at Ramsgill, and sat just once at the head of the table for the family lunch after the funeral.

As he was a minor, it fell to Jock's mother to make the decisions. The Trustees of the estate were his grandfather's two sons in law, Arthur Bailey, and Bertie Watson. Over the years unfortunately, Jock's mother had drifted further away from the Bewerley family. Arthur had never recovered from his depression after the death of his only son. Bertie was a busy Canon with five children of his own, and no business experience, though entirely devoted to the family interests. Granny Yorke, nearly ninety herself, and her three daughters nearing their sixties, had no knowledge of finance or land management. Boord, the agent for thirty eight years, was the only key man who knew any of the problems.

Jock's mother was again faced with an extremely complex situation quite outside her understanding. Death duties, leases and tenancies, mining operations, timber sales, regular estate maintenance, even the system used for paying a large work force were foreign to her. All she knew or believed was that her own finances were far from satisfactory, and that this long awaited moment of inheritance had only brought new and larger problems. Jock was of no age to counsel her.

Looking back now it does seem that she was very badly advised. Anything the Trustees on the Yorke side suggested, was immediately suspect to her. Even capable, trusted Boord was felt to be on their side, so his excellent advice was not followed. In the panic over the large sums needed to pay off annuities, death duties and legacies, she and her advisers decided to sell the whole place. In vain the Yorkes tried to persuade her to sell Halton and save Bewerley. This she flatly refused. Relations became even more strained. Letters flew back and forth. The details of how the final decision was reached are lost, but she did take counsel's opinion.

Then, instead of selling part of the whole, say two moors and some of the high ground, or ensuring that it was kept as a whole, the miserable business was carried out in as unsatisfactory way as possible.

At the bottom of the post war slump, the beautiful estate came under the hammer. Some of the tenants bought their own farms, which was the best thing that happened. The rest were bought up by different people. The house, its contents scattered, was sold door by door, fireplace by fireplace, slate by slate and stone by stone. Speculators bought the site.

Only the mineral rights were kept, and about three hundred and seventy acres of rough ground on the Sunside Allotments.

The net result of this potentially huge asset was only one hundred and fifty thousand pounds. After paying off annuities for the two widows, three daughters, the younger son, Harry, and Jock's two younger brothers, the Halton mortgage, death duties and the solicitors' fees, there was only £15,000 left. The speculators, on the other hand, resold the land within a very short time at a huge profit.

The break up of an estate like Bewerley entails so much pain, quite apart from the mishandling. Many men had to go, whose fathers and grandfathers had worked there. Many records, customs, memories and friendships were lost for ever. For Grannie, May, Kathie and Ethel, at their time of life, the move to Sleningford Grange, even with their two faithful old maids, was a terrible upheaval. Had they been able to see Jock move into Bewerley, then they would have felt it all right and proper, however hard, but to have to say goodbye to so many must have cost them much heartache.

All through that summer of 1924 these sad events went on, but to Jock, in the full enjoyment of his Oxford days, they were accepted as his mother's careful decision for the best for them all. Life was for living, and he had been brought up to follow that maxim.

Only a short time after the sale, his mother decided they could not afford to keep him at Oxford, so he was sent to work in Hathorn Davy's engineering works in Leeds. This was certainly a contrast. The first morning he walked in, and said 'Good morning!' to the foreman. The big man glared at him. 'Bugger good mornin',' he said, 'Gerr on wi' thi wark'.

However Jock had a very great talent for getting on with people, and in a very short time, uncongenial as the work was he had made friends, and was swapping stories with all the men.

While he was working in Leeds, he began to court Eleanor, daughter of his neighbour Ralph Assheton of Downham. They were very young, only eighteen and twenty-one, and not at all perturbed by the doubts of their elders as to their wisdom. When they went to Sleningford to meet old Grannie and the three aunts, it was quite an ordeal for Eleanor. Grannie looked her up and down. 'There's not much of her, Jock,' she said.

As Jock had come of age, they got engaged and were married on September 30th, 1926 at Downham. They bought a flat in London, where Jock worked as a wine merchants in the City. His mother moved to Meerbeck, Long Preston, (where she bravely learnt to drive a car), and Halton was let.

Their son, David John, was born in 1927 in London, and their daughter Anne in 1931. By this time they had decided to move back to Halton. The house, which had been lit by gas, was redecorated, and central heating and electric light were installed. In August 1931, the family returned. John Kidd, a land agent from Skipton, had been running the estate and now, with the help of Tom Redmayne, Jock took it on.

Little had changed since 1915. The tenants were nearly all the same. Although most of them hand milked a few cows, mainly young dairy cattle and sheep were kept. Horses were used for all the farm work, as well as for galloping the full milk kits to the station. Farmyard manure and some lime was the only fertiliser. Lambing and haytime were the

53. The Hall at Halton Place

peak periods, but as on any stock rearing farm, the whole family worked from morning till night as the seasons came round. Holidays were virtually unknown. A half day off to attend a local show was a great event.

Although rents were low, it was sometimes necessary to sell a cow to pay the half year's due. Every Thursday, men driving one or two cows, or five fat lambs, could be seen on the roads leading to Hellifield Auction Mart, an important stock centre. The intense concentration on the faces around the auction ring revealed the still narrow margin upon which they lived. (One farmer's wife was heard to say, 'I believe Joe would sell me if he could get a good price!')

Halton West school was flourishing with Miss Haworth teaching thirty-six children, aged from five to fourteen, in the one small school room. The little children were separated from the older ones by a moveable wooden partition, and were helped by one of the older girls as a monitress. Each child brought something with him to eat at midday. The Thornber, Highscale and Swindon children often had a long wet walk of it, both ways, being hustled along by their elder brothers and sisters, but in good weather they played and dawdled along the way.

Regular whist drives, dances and billiards competitions were held in the Reading Room, and Sunday services in the church. The estate men were still the faithful Tom Redmayne and Henry Lund. Charlie Wilson and Sidney Turner were in the gardens, and Alf Smallwood was the groom. In the house, Mrs Appleby was cook, assisted by a parlour maid, housemaid and kitchen maid. Nanny Townsend ruled the nursery wing, with her nursery maid.

Over the next years Jock sat as a magistrate on the Settle Bench, became a manager of Long Preston and Halton West schools, and a district councillor for the Settle R.D.C. He served on the Hellifield Parochial Church Council, and played the organ at Halton West. He also took a great interest in all the local agricultural societies and shows, and was on the Ribble Fishery Board. He played an active part as Fieldmaster, Joint Master and Chairman of the Craven Harriers for the next fifty six years, over the time of amalgamation with the Pendle Forest pack after the war. This gave him an encyclopaedic knowledge both of the surrounding country and of the families who farmed it.

His wife, Eleanor, started a much needed branch of the District Nursing Association in Hellifield and Long Preston, was chairman of the Hellifield Conservative Association, and a member of the Advisory committee for the Skipton Division.

In 1939 she was in a serious car accident, which broke her jaw in two places, broke and crushed her leg and injured her dreadfully. It was over a

54. L. to r. David, Eleanor and Anne Yorke, with Wendy 1936

year before she was able to walk again, and she has endured constant pain ever since.

When the second world war came, Jock was thirty five. Because of poor eyesight he was rejected by the Army three times, so joined the local Home Guard. Eventually he managed to get into a Gunner Training Regiment, near Harrogate. His fellow recruits were a mixed and very tough crop of miners, Welsh, Irish and Geordie. They were, in his words, a splendid collection, and could not think what he had been in Civvy Street. The guesses were either a bus driver or a gamekeeper. This again was as interesting an experience as the engineering works, but again his natural ability to get on with people stood him in good stead.

After some months of training he was granted a General Service Commission and stationed at Darlington, in the Claims Commission. He became Command Compensation Officer and dealt with farmers and landowners who had claims against the Army for all training grounds between North Berwick and Leicester.

While he was away, Eleanor taught herself not only to cook, and do everything in the house that had previously been done by five women, but also to run the estate. She oversaw the two men who were too old to join up, kept a milk cow, grew oats, made the hay, held Rent Days, kept the books, accounts, wages and repairs, measured and sold timber, engaged joiners, masons and builders to see to repairs, dealt with water problems, sewerage and drainage, acted as A.R.P. warden, held first aid classes and unarmed combat classes, and a million other daily matters, and brought up her children, almost single handed. She also had close links with the work of the Land Army, the W.V.S. and the Soldiers and Sailors Family Association, and raised large amounts of money for the war effort.

This was a very hard assignment, with much anxiety about the war news, and many shortages to contend with. The house was commandeered by the Air Force, for use as as an office, but Eleanor said that as the wife of a serving soldier, she would not be turned out of her home. They therefore only took over the ground floor, and we moved upstairs for the remainder of the war. With little or no petrol available our childhood travels were on ponies or bicycles, and our formative years were happily spent in the company of our close neighbours. When we children went away to school, Eleanor lived on her own, keeping everything running and in order, and saving up her meagre rations to use for us in the holidays. She picked the fruit and made jam with her own sugar ration. She wrote to us all each week, and kept the whole family in touch. She visited the old Yorke Aunts at Sleningford, who loved her, and healed the family breach in every way she could. Her mother in law lived nearby, and grew to admire and love the girl whom she had at first felt had driven her from her home.

As in the two previous generations, music and singing were an important part of our lives. Jock inherited his father's talent and can play any tune by ear on the piano, flute or bugle. His repertoire extends from music hall songs from the 1880s, learnt from his father, through negro plantation songs, dance music, songs from shows between, during, and after the two wars, and a huge variety of hymns and psalm chants. His son played with him from a very early age and together they can sit down at the piano for hours on end and never repeat a tune, changing effortlessly from key to key, in any tempo. Eleanor enjoyed playing the violin in an orchestra, and in the family band she joined in, with Anne on the drums, but the singing was the chief enjoyment.

Jock's brother, Peter, went from Oxford to train in Dibb Lupton's, Solicitors, in Leeds. He played squash for his county and won several cups. He married Nora, daughter of the Hon. Alfred Maitland of Kirriemuir, and they had one daughter, Cherry, born in 1943. During the war Peter served in the R.A.F., attaining the rank of Squadron Leader. In 1970 Cherry married Karma Topden and lived in Sikkim.

His younger brother, Michael worked in London, and married Agnes, daughter of George Wilson, of Bolton by Bowland. Their daughter Susan was born in 1937. He joined his uncle's regiment, The Gordon Highlanders, and was Adjutant in Aberdeen for a time. Their son, St John, was born there in 1940, and Michael's mother moved up there to live, remaining until her death in 1955.

Michael served in Orkney, then volunteered for duties in the Provost branch in Kent. In 1944 he commanded 108 Provost Company, (12th Corps) and went over to Normandy. He was posted to Antwerp, and commanded 204 Provost Company, then moved to Brussels to join 21 Army Group as A.P.M. Planning, and promoted to the rank of Major. He was mentioned in despatches. His son married Philippa Barbour, and they live in New Zealand on their farm which they named Bewerley. His daughter married Jeremy Grimshaw.

When the war ended, Jock returned home and we children left school and grew up. It was some years before the war time shortages ended, but the gradual introduction of tractors and farm machinery brought about the replacement of the farm horses. Very few of the farmers owned a car. However, dairying steadily became more profitable and, by the fifties, many were milking twenty or more cattle in shippons. Electricity was laid on and Jock, as landlord, had all the houses and buildings wired to receive it.

He became a member of the West Riding War Agricultural Committee for sixteen years, and a member of the Country Landowners' Association Yorkshire branch. (He received the Queen's Silver Jubilee medal for his services.) He was Chairman of the Settle Bench for over twenty years, and attended Quarter Sessions and Crown Courts. He was on the West Riding County Council Standing Joint Committee for the police, and on the District Council for over thirty years.

Jock was fortunate that the purchasers of the Bewerley moors were kind enough to continue to invite him to shoot grouse regularly, which, with the salmon and trout in the Ribble, and his horses and hounds were his three great joys.

Eleanor took an active part in local politics, like her brother and many of her forbears. She was chairman of both local associations, and later became vice chairman of the Yorkshire Provincial Area Conservative Association, and chairman of the Womens Advisory Committee of the Yorkshire Provincial Area. She drove herself hundreds of miles, and chaired, and spoke at large meetings, despite the great affliction of having been deaf since her early married days.

She was chairman of Governors of Bowland Secondary School, and Governor of Settle High School for many years. In 1956 she was awarded a C.B.E., which she received from the Queen.

55. Halton West Tenants 1955 L. to r.
Back row: Capstick, J. Moon, A. Newhouse, J. E. E. Yorke, Jos. Moorhouse, Alec Parrington
Middle row: W. Kenyon, A. Whitehead, A. Swinbank, F. Moorhouse, E. Cooper, J. Wilson, J. Kenyon
Front row: Tom Redmayne, Henry Lund, W. Wilson, W. Kenyon senr., R. Whitehead

56. John Edward Evelyn Yorke

After we children left school, David went into The Life Guards at eighteen and served in Palestine for a year. There were many terrorist attacks and several of his friends were killed. He went on to Trinity, Cambridge, to read Rural Estate Management, and later trained at Chatsworth under Peter Clive. Then he joined Russell Ingham, and together they started Ingham and Yorke, Chartered Surveyors and Land Agents, in Clitheroe. He married Susan, daughter of Lt Col. Scrope

Egerton, of Pertwood Manor, Wiltshire in 1957, and they live in Worston in Lancashire, (on part of the property owned by Katharine Yorke in 1680).

Their son John Alexander was born in 1958, their daughter Sophia in 1961, and their second son Charles in 1965.

I married James, son of Sir Patrick Ashley Cooper, of Hexton in Hertfordshire, where, with our eldest son, Patrick, we farm 1,250 acres of arable land. We have three other children, Katharine, Felicity and Edward.

After the Agricultural Act of 1958 and government encouragement by grants and subsidies, an explosion took place in dairy farming throughout the sixties and seventies. Some of the Halton tenants increased their herds until they were milking a hundred cows or more. Large modern buildings incorporating cubicle houses, silos, milking parlours and collecting yards, slurry stores, concrete yards and feed hoppers were for the first time built by the tenants, who by then had been given much greater security of tenure, both for themselves and their descendants.

Two crops of silage replaced one of hay, slurry replaced farmyard manure, more 'bag till', (artificial fertiliser) was applied, and more concentrate feeding stuffs fed to the cattle. Larger faster tractors and farm machinery enabled fields to be mown and gathered almost overnight. Some of these factors caused problems, such as overstocking pastures, poaching of the land and gateways, and pollution of becks and rivers.

The dairying explosion coincided with rampant inflation and the combined result made a great improvement in the farmers' standard of living. Halton West had been connected to the main sewerage in 1964 and W.C.s had been added to all the houses. A main water pipe was laid to augment the estate supply in 1978. Cars, television, refrigerators, washing machines, and modern Rayburn and Aga cookers replacing the old black coke ranges, were followed in most houses by central heating.

These comparative figures give the picture: a milk cow in the fifties cost £50 against £600 today, and a half bred ewe £5, against £50 today. Farm wages then were £5 a week against £125 now. A good pointer is the ratio of income to 'proven', (or concentrate feed) to rent.

The natural boundary of the estate formed by the river Ribble has left it relatively undisturbed by major roads, pipelines, reservoirs or other intrusions. Although the closure of the school and the shop are both great losses to the village, many of the tenants are sons and grandsons farming the same land under the same landlord.

No mining operation is being carried on at present in Nidderdale, although various prospectors have made tentative attempts over the

57. Halton Tenants 1964
L. to r.
Back row: P. Dakin, R. Beresford, John Moon, K. Standrill, F. Moorhouse, G. Asquith
Middle row: P. Nelson, L. Kayley, H. Waddington, A. Beresford, D. J. Yorke
Front row: Bronek Kwolek, W. Kenyon, J. E. E. Yorke, H. Walker, M. Thompson

years, but the Stump Cross Caverns have been opened up by Mr and Mrs George Gill and her son Gordon Hanley. The staggering rock formations and the weird shapes of the stalactites and stalagmites attract thousands of visitors each year. They are a unique sight and can now be seen in safety and comfort, with an excellent cafeteria at hand to warm and refresh the explorers afterwards.

David Yorke now helps to run the Halton estate. He also sits on the Clitheroe Bench, of which he was chairman for five years, and is a Deputy Lieutenant for Lancashire. He has managed the Downham estates for his uncle, Ralph Assheton, (later Lord Clitheroe), for over twenty-five years, amongst many others, and, like his father, enjoys all field sports.

His wife Susan took an Arts degree in the Open University, and is Sotheby's representative for Lancashire. She is the founder chairman of the National Association of Decorative and Fine Arts Society for Ribble and Craven, and started the National Arts Collection fund for the area. She served as a school governor of Clitheroe Grammar School and Downham school for some years, and did much work for St Denis's Church of England Children's Home.

58. Stalactite and stalagnite formations in the Stump Cross Caverns.
Photo C. H. Wood, 78 Emm Lane, Bradford

Their son John went to Eton, and is now working for a London estate agent. Sophia took a degree in History at Oxford, and married Nicholas, son of Sir Antony Acland, at Downham Church in 1986. She now works in a publishing house.

Charles went from Eton into The Life Guards on a short service commission. Then he took a degree in Rural Estate Management at Cirencester, and is currently working for a firm of land agents in London.

So they are the seventh generation of Yorkes to know and love Halton, with all the beauty of its surroundings, and the laughter and music which fill the house. 'The atmosphere of Halton,' wrote a frequent visitor, 'always seems to exemplify goodness, and all that is best in our country, the old fashioned virtues of courtesy and neighbourliness, helpfulness and kindness.'

When discussing this book with my brother, I told him he was in it. 'Damn it!' he said, '*I'm* not history *yet*.' But we all are, whether we like it or not.

59. L. to R. Charles, Sophia, Susan, David and John Yorke

THE RIVER RIBBLE

From Deepdale Head to the stepping stones of Nappa, the winding banks of the river Ribble formed the boundary of my childhood days. The quick, flecked brown water sparkles as it ripples and rushes along the edge of the old Mill Field, overlooked by our house on the top of the slope, only five hundred yards away.

At every season of the year the height and condition of the water was a daily topic. My father, with a fisherman's eye, would say happily, "Good water today", or less cheerfully, "Far too big," "Too brown," or "Too low." My mother was also a keen fisherman, but her special joy was to watch the dippers, kingfishers, oyster catchers, mallard, curlews and the occasional sandpiper. For us children the river was a living, always changing friend.

In winter we walked fearfully beside the swirling, swollen, bank-high flood, keeping back the dogs in case they were swept away, and imagining how helpless we would feel if carried along on that surge.

In summer we played during timeless afternoons beside one or other of the bathing pools, paddling, splashing, breathlessly learning to swim, digging in the sandy banks, then sitting on the grass among cowpats, all rumpled and rubbed dry, to eat bread and butter and strawberry jam by the slice, and to drink lovely cold milk.

In between seasons we played ducks and drakes with flat stones to see who could skim them across to the opposite bank, paddled in gumboots, and crossed over the shallows to explore the little island. We knew every rock and bend, every rapid and shallow for nearly two miles of its length.

We hung over the great stone bridge with its massive pillars, to stare into the depths to see a salmon, or, when the water was low, stood under the arches and shouted to make an echo. We swam with the salmon in the big deep pool below the bridge when we were older, and in 1940, (like Thomas Edward), we even skated on the same pool, holding on to my father's coat tails to keep upright.

We crossed the slippery steppingstones, stretching from one to the next, and picnicked on the big island at Nappa in mid stream, but it seemed a long walk home afterwards.

We rode our ponies beside it and across it, walked beside it with our friends, our lovers and our spouses, and, in the course of time, took our own children to play and paddle and enjoy it too. They were the seventh generation of the family to do so.

THE RECORDS OF THE YORKE FAMILY

THIS COLLECTION OF RECORDS SPANS EIGHT CENTURIES, from twelfth century charters granting land to Byland Abbey, through ancient title deeds, manor court rolls, wills and letters.

In 1923 after the Bewerley sale, all the records, which had been so carefully preserved for centuries, were dispersed. In 1939 my mother, Eleanor Yorke, read in the newspapers that solicitors were being advised to burn any papers they had on their upper floors because of the risk of firebombs. She realised the possible danger of loss, and drove at once to Leeds to Dibb Lupton, Solicitors. There she collected several battered tin trunks and boxes containing dusty deeds and documents. She then went to Harrogate, to the family solicitors there, Powell, Son, and Edison, and collected more. In Settle, the local solicitor had died, and his successor had allowed the papers there to become damp, and damaged. She collected a few more unimportant papers from John Simpson, who had been a clerk in the Bewerley Estate office. He said that he had no others. My mother placed them all in a safe place but due to the war and extra responsibilities, she was not then able to sort them.

About 1951 she got in touch with the National Register of Archives in the City Library in Leeds, and slowly together they sorted and transcribed the papers.

Some fifteen years later, my uncle Peter Yorke, who had worked as a solicitor in Dibb Lupton's, received a letter from the nephew of an old friend. The nephew had found a hoard of Yorke documents and medieval charters with their seals in his deceased uncle's attic. These he returned to the family.

During her researches my mother noticed references to some manor court rolls which she had never seen. By now she was like a fell hound on the trail but the line went cold. Ten years later the missing deeds were unearthed in an old house, and returned to the collection.

The seventy-two medieval charters were put on microfilm, which is stored in the Sheepscar Library in Leeds. Mr Collinson of the N.R.A. (with Miss Murdoch, whom he later married), compiled the Yorke Calendar, in which all the papers are annotated and listed. My mother had a special archive made at Halton, with fitted boxes and shelves. Some of the deeds have been transcribed but not all. So it was that this invaluable collection was rescued, restored and preserved by the sole efforts of Eleanor Yorke, one of the many remarkable wives of the Yorke family.

CHAPTER NOTES

PROLOGUE

1. The Friends of York Minster 17th Annual Report 1945
   The stained and painted glass of York Minster, Peter Gibson F.S.A. 1979
   The ancient glass in the Yorke memorial window, MSS by Professor Gwyther Moore of York, 1947. Yorke records 1169

CHAPTER I
EARLY HISTORY

1. Yorkshire from A.D. 1000, David Hey, Longmans
2. A History of Lead mining in the Pennines, A. Raistrick, B. Jennings, Longman's
3. In search of the Dark Ages, Michael Wood, BBC Publications
   William of Malmesbury, Gesta Pontif 216
4. Social History of England, G.M. Trevelyan, Longmans
5. The Ecclesiastical History of Orderic Vitalis, II Oxford, M. Chibnall 1969 : 231–233
6. Yorkshire from A.D. 1000, David Hey
7. Yorke Records 62–68
8. A History of Lead mining in the Pennines, Raistrick and Jennings, Longman's, p. 27
   [E101/598/9]

   The cost of one ox wagon with ten oxen was 3s a day, portage and carriage by water 54s, and transport to London, £26.13.4, a total of £36.11.4

   Descriptions of hushing and firesetting pp. 12, 13
9. Yorkshire from A.D. 2000, David Hey p. 87
10. 'Some of the faithful of Christ, of either sex, have begun to inhabit the places of Dacre and Bewerley, formerly waste, a moor and lacking human dwellings,' Mems. Ripon, 2, 210 No 21. A History of Leadmining in the Pennines p. 34

CHAPTER II
SIR RICHARD YORKE OF YORK 1430? – 1498

1. Test. Ebor.II p. 57
2. Will of Sir Richard York April 8th 1498 (Reg. Horne at Doctor's Commons no LXX)

3. The York Cycle of Mystery Plays, Rev. J.S. Purvis, S.P.C.K.
4. The Paston Letters
5. A History of Hellifield, Tom Merrall, J. Lambert, Settle
6. Eboracum p. 279, Drake
7. Surtees Soc. Trans. 1896 (Vol. I) Vol. 96
8. York Civic Records Vol. I, Angelo Raine
9. Mercers Guild Records, Dr. Maud Sellers
10. Particulars of the Accounts of John Dey
11. Eboracum p. 229. York Civic Records XV, Robert Davies.
12. Eboracum p. 229.
    Medieval English Wool Trade, Eileen Power.
    Studies in English Trade in XV century – Postan and Power, George Routledge & Sons
13. English Country Houses, Mark Girouard, Yale University Press.
    Leland, King's Antiquary.
    'With the help of God I can scale any wall.' Psalm 18. It has been said that the monkey's head was chosen for the crest because a Yorke brought the first monkeys to England.
14. Eboracum p. 363, Drake.
15. Extracts from York Council Minutes, Robert Davies, pp. 120–140.
16. Christian Calendar, Cowie and Gummer, Weidenfeld and Nicholson.
    From 1264 the Corpus Christi festival was the day set apart to teach Christ's last commandment. It was held sixty days after Easter, on a Thursday, like Maundy Thursday.
17. York Mystery Plays, Tony Harrison, Faber and Faber
18. York Civic Records. History of Parliament 1439–1509 edited J.C. Wedgewood and A. Holt.
    Surtees Soc. Transactions 1917 vol. 129
19. York Civic Records, Angelo Raine
20. Medieval Merchant Venturers, E.M. Carus Wilson, Methuen & Co. Ltd.
21. Surtees Soc. Transactions 1871 Vol. I Vol. 57, Skaife.
    York Civic Records
22. Surtees Soc. Trans. Vol. 120 p. 170.
    York Civic Records 29 Aug 1482
23. York Records of XV century, Davies, (Nichols 1843)
24. York Civic Records Vol. I.
    Sir Raufe held the manor of Middleton and had large estates in Ryedale. He was Vice Constable of England in 1483 for Richard III. He was known locally as the Black Lad, and much feared by his tenants. They wrote
     'Sweet Jesu, in this hour,
     By Thy bitter passion,
     Save us from th'axe and t'Tower
     And from Sir Ralph Assheton.'
25. In 1495 every Member of Parliament had to bring from Westminster 'one of every weight and measure as they be in the Exchequer of our Sovereign Lord' to show to the electors, in order that 'one weight and one measure be used throughout this noble realm'.
26. York Civic Records
27. Ibid 13 Febuary 1483
28. Ibid 1 November 1485
29. Ibid July 1486
30. Ibid. Mayne breid, or the Lord's bread was made of very fine white flour mixed with spice and sugar, and only served on important occasions.

31. Ibid
32. 'Appointment of Richard York, Dean of Wells, treasurer of Calais, Lieutenant of Calais et alia to be ambassadors and commissioners for treating with the ambassadors of Maximilian, King of Romans, Duke of Austria etc., with authority to arrange. . . the terms of, and conclude a perpetual treaty and league between the King of England and the King of the Romans.' 15 December 1486
Materials Illustrative of the Reign of Henry VII, Campbell.
33. The Medieval English Economy 1150–1500, J.L. Bolton, J.M. Dent.
34. York Records of XV century – Davies

CHAPTER III

JOHN YORKE OF GOUTHWAITE 1460?–?
(styled thus in Dugdale's Visitation)

1. The District of Nidderdale, William Grainge, Lemare, London
2. History of Nidderdale, edited by Bernard Jennings, The Advertiser Press, Huddersfield, pp. 42–43
   A History of Lead mining in the Pennines, p. 32
3. The District of Nidderdale, William Grainge

CHAPTER IV

SIR JOHN YORKE OF LONDON 1490?–1568

1. The Man with the Rose, A new attribution to the Master of Frankfurt, Dr Stephen Goddard, 1982. Yearbook of the Koninklijk Museum, Antwerp 1983
2. A Survey of London 1589, John Stow
3. Letters and Papers of Henry VIII lx 263
4. The Lisle Letters, ed. Muriel St Clair Byrne, University of Chicago Press
5. Leland, King's Antiquary
6. Abbot Paslew and the Pilgrimage of Grace, William Weeks F.S.A. Wriothesley Chronicle I 65
   Man on a Donkey, H.F.M. Prescott, Eyre and Spottiswoode.
7. Annals of the Coinage 3rd edit. 1840 pp. 34, 40, R. Ruding
8. Ibid
10. Yorke Records 812
11. Yorke Records 475 25 August 1547
12. Ibid 144, 145, (13 June 1549)
    In 1536 Henry VIII sold Appletreewick Manor for £14.10.0
    3 months later the Master of the Rolls sold it for £666.13.4
    2 weeks later Proctor sold it for £1,000 to Sir A. Darcy
    Ten years later Darcy sold it for £2,000 to Yorke.
13. Ibid, 30, [given at York, 23 February Edward III 1328].
14. Dictionary of National Biography 1885 Vol. LXIII, p. 334
15. Acts of Privy Council ii 384
16. Ibid 19 July 1550
17. House of Commons 1588–1603 ed. P.W. Hasler, H.M.S.O. 1981
18. Acts of Privy Council 3 July 1551

19. Annals of the Coinage i 34, R. Ruding
20. House of Commons 1588–1603 ed. P.W. Hasler, H.M.S.O. 1981
    (Christopher Blunt said it was quite exceptional for Yorke to have been allowed to use his own mark.)
    The 1/- coin has a charming portrait of the boy king, crowned. On the obverse side is written Y: EDWARD. VI. D.G. A6L. FRA. Z. RIB. REX. On the reverse, POSUI.DEU? AD. IUTORG? MEUM: Y
    (Psalm 54 v. 4 'Behold, God is my helper')
21. A History of Hellifield, Tom Merrall, (source unknown)
22. Acts of Privy Council 10 May 1552
23. Acts of Privy Council 21 June 1552 and Yorke Records 1078.
24. Calendar of Patent Rolls 1553–1554 pp. 316, 411
    Ibid 1554–1555 pp. 56–57
    Calendar of State Papers Dom. 1547–1580
25. D.L.I Vol. 7 D3; D.L.I Vol. 30 p. 12:
    Yorke Records 1027 et al.
26. Ibid 1030–1033
    Select Cases in the Court of Requests, Seldon Soc. 12 (1898) 201–204.
27. Wriothesley Chronicle ii 92
28. Acts of Privy Council 9 August 1553
29. Yorke Records 1079
    Hippocrass was an aromatic wine, much used in cordials
30. Diary of Henry Mackyn, Camden Soc. 1848 (p. 82)
31. House of Commons 1588–1603
32. Cal. State papers Dom. Eliz. xiv 10.
    House of Commons 1588–1603
    At this time Richard Assheton, grandson of Sir Raufe, was also in Parliament, as member for Aldborough. He had bought estates in Lancashire, Yorkshire and Durham, which included Downham by 1558.
33. A History of Hellifield, Tom Merrall
34. Cal. State Papers 1560 p. 119

CHAPTER V

PETER YORKE OF GOUTHWAITE 1525?–1589

1. A Survey of London 1589, John Stow
2. Peter was Master of the Revels for the Temple in 1561.
   Darkness and Devils, John L. Murphy, Ohio University Press
3. Yorke Records 475
3a. Crisis of the Aristocracy, Lawrence Stone, O.U.P.
    By demanding large entry fines on re-leasing land, the landlord could raise immediate cash even if losing potential future income. The tenant received almost absolute security of tenure at less cost in the long run.
4. History of Nidderdale, ed. B. Jennings
5. The Smelting Mills of the Yorkshire Dales, Robert T. Clough, Jowett and Sowry Ltd, Leeds 1962
6. Yorkshire from A.D. 1000, David Hey
7. Yan, tan, eddero, peddero, pitts,
   Tayter, layter, overro, coverro, dix,
   Yan-dix, tan-dix, eddero-dix, peddero-dix, bumfit,

Yan o'bumfit, tan o'bumfit, eddero bumfit, peddero bumfit, jiggit.
This a phonetic version of the Anglo-Cymric score which I was taught by a shepherd, John Brunskill from Semerwater, and which had been in use since the days of the early Britons. As the counter reached jiggit, he marked, or scored it on a post, so keeping his score. Modern Welsh counting is very similar. I also came across almost the same version in Canada, where it had been taught by an Englishman to a Cherokee Indian. The Indian had passed it on to a Canadian, who thought it was Cherokee. This same link was found by Professor Ellis and a detailed account of some of the variations is given in his paper in the Philological Society Transactions in 1877–1879.
Yorkshire Sheep counting Numerals, Michael Barry M.A. Sheep and sheep scoring in Transactions of the Yorks. Dialect Soc. part xxviii, Vol. IV, J.R. Witty

8. Cliffe 1969: 2–16, 39–48
9. Ingilby MSS 739,
    Vyner MSS 5458,
    Mems. Fount. 1 p. 363
10. Yorke Records 153–160 and 209
    History of Nidderdale, ed. B. Jennings
11. Yorke records 991, 992
    (Meare in Anglo Saxon means boundary mark)
12. The Smelting Mills of the Yorkshire Dales, Robert T. Clough
13. Yorke Records 30
14. Or 'many an umpteen bloody mile' as a local would put it.
15. Diary of Arthur Throckmorton, Raleigh and the Throckmortons, Dr A.L. Rowse, MacMillan. Journal of Nicholas Assheton, (great nephew of Richard of Downham)
16. Yorke Records 1138
    This letter is as clear as the day it was written. It was fortunately preserved by the Danby family and was presented to John Yorke of Bewerley in 1825 by William Danby of Swinton. Sir Thomas was High Sheriff of Yorkshire in 1576, and built Farnley Hall, Otley, in 1586. (Days of Yore, S. Cunliffe Lister)
17. Yorke Records 175
18. Laurence Hamerton was granted a licence by Henry VI in 1440 to fortify and embattle Hellifield Peel. It was one of the southernmost peel towers built for defence against the Border raiders. These lawless men made their living by raiding cattle from each side of the Scottish border, and were feared for generations.
19. The Catholic Recusants of the West Riding of Yorkshire 1558–1790, Dom Hugh Aveling O.S.B. 1963
20. When the news came of the execution of Mary, Queen of Scots, bells were rung and bonfires lit in London, but in Nidderdale it was a cause for grief.
21. Yorke Records 73, 74 and Merrall p. 128
22. Sandys, having been born in Hawkeshead, Cumbria, (where he was also buried), founded his Grammar School there for 100 boys. The Master was 'to teach Grammar and the principles of the Greek tongue, with other sciences necessary'. From March to September work was from 6 a.m.–5 p.m., break 11–1. In winter, 7 a.m.–11 a.m. and 12.30–4 p.m. No weapons were allowed in school, or gambling or frequenting taverns.
23. Dictionary of National Biography Vol. ix III
24. Ralegh and the Throckmortons, Dr A.L. Rowse, MacMillan
    Markham's Fighting Veres p. 46

25. Cal. State Papers Dom. 1547–1684
26. Grimeston History of the Netherlands p. 827
27. Leicester Corresp. Camden Soc. 1844
28. Tozen i 351
29. Cal. State Papers Dom. 1581–1590 p. 466
30. Yorke MSS (T.E.Y.)
31. Annals of Great Britain in the Reign of Queen Elizabeth, 1615, William Camden.
32. The three voyages of Martin Frobisher, Vilhjalmur Steffanson, Argonaut Press 1938.
    What glistened in the ore like gold turned out to be flecks of biotite mica. The worthless crushed ore was used to pave the streets of London.
    Company of Adventurers, Vol. I, Peter Newman, Viking Press
33. 'The moustre or showing and view of all men of arms, men able to bear them, as well archers as other men on horse and on foot, together with the names and surnames and diversity of their harness, viewed and seen in the Wapentake. . . 1538'
34. Yorks. Arch. Jnl. xxxiii
35. C.S.P. Dom. Add 1566–1579 p. 156.
    D'Ewes 431
36. Yorks. Arch. Soc. rec. ser. xxii 145
    Yorke Records 73

CHAPTER VI
SIR JOHN YORKE OF GOUTHWAITE 1566?–1634

1. Harrington's Nuga Antiqua by T. Park 1804
   (Advice to Sir John Harrington 1611)
2. Assheton's wife, Christiana, was sister to Frances, second wife of Thomas Yorke. Thomas was John's younger brother.
   Yorke Records, 1170
3. Ibid 425, lease 21 February 1597
4. There are eight documents in the Yorke Records, 138–146, concerning Appletreewick licences and sales between Thomas Proctor, Christopher Hales and Sir Arthur Darcy in 1539
5. Sir John Yorke of Nidderdale, Christopher Howard, Sheed and Ward 1939. State Papers Dom. 14/ccxvi
6. History of Nidderdale, ed. B. Jennings
7. Ibid
8. State Papers Dom. 14 lxxxi f. 59
9. Star Chamber Stac. 8/19/10 f.9
10. Sir John Yorke of Nidderdale, Christopher Howard, Sheed and Ward
11. Darkness and Devils, John L. Murphy, Ohio University Press
    P.R.O.Stac. 8/19/10
12. Yorke Records 1065
13. Ibid 147–159
14. Hilar. 1 Car. Comer. Cumbria v. Yorke Esq
    Whitaker's Craven
15. Yorke Records 528
16. Anatomie of Melancolie, Burton, 1624
17. Company of Adventurers, Vol. 1, Peter Newman, Viking Press

18. Assheton Journal, Assheton Records, Downham Hall
19. Yorke Records 1094

CHAPTER VII

JOHN YORKE OF GOUTHWAITE 1592?–1638

1. Yorke Records 73, 74, 75
2. P.R.O. DL 4/85/54
3. History of Hellifield, Tom Merrall p. 156
4. Harrison and Hutton 1984 8–9

CHAPTER VIII

JOHN YORKE OF GOUTHWAITE AND RICHMOND 1633–1663

1. Yorke Records 1097, 1067, 1139
2. Notes by Thomas Edward Yorke (T.E.Y.)
3. Raleigh and the Throckmortons, Dr A.L. Rowse, Macmillan
4. Yorkshire from A.D. 1000, David Hey p. 179
5. David Leslie fought under Alexander Leslie, 1st Earl of Leven, who later entrusted command to him. Webster's Biographical Dictionary
6. History of the English Speaking Peoples, Vol. II, W.S.C.
7. Yorke Records 80
8. History of Richmond, Clarkson.
9. Dugdale's Visitation of Yorkshire, ii 281, Clay
   'Col. Thomas Danby received the sum of £63.10.0 for fees due to the King's servants for the honour of knighthood conferred upon Sir John Yorke. Geo. Owen, York Herald.'
   History of Richmond, Clarkson.
   H.M.C. 8th rep. pt. 1 (1881) 275
   North Riding Records vi, 25 63.
   History of Richmond, Clarkson, 330, 332
10. A History of Richmond and Swaledale, Fieldhouse and Jennings, Phillimore & Co
11. The Whitcliffe Common pasture was enclosed in 1696.
12. These courts of summary justice were called pie-powder courts, derived from the French 'pied poudreux', meaning vagabond or wanderer
13. North Riding Records vi 25 63
14. House of Commons 1660–1690 ed. B.D. Henning
15. Ibid
16. Yorke Records 1096

CHAPTER IX

THOMAS YORKE OF RICHMOND, GOUTHWAITE AND BEWERLEY, 1658–1716

1. Yorke Records 836
1a. Ingilby Papers
2. Yorke Records 1139
3. Ibid 992
4. Ibid 1041
5. Upper Nidderdale, Harry Speight, Elliot Stock, 1906
6. Yorke Records 1085
7. Ibid 498
8. Ibid 1139 (i)
9. Ibid 1139 (ii)
10. Ibid 85, 86
11. Ibid 87–94
12. History of Parliament 1660–1690 ed. B.D. Henning
13. Yorke Records 991
14. Leadmining in the Yorkshire Dales, R. Clough
15. Yorke records 1021
16. Ibid 1012 and 96
17. Ibid 967
18. Ibid 1038–1044
19. Ibid 924–933
20. Ibid 488, 684–767
21. Ibid 1098
22. Ibid 426
23. Ibid 850
    Dacre Hall farm comprised 13 named closes, 11 beast gates on Dacre Pasture, (an area of 1,180 acres), and two parcels of land called Calfe Garth and North Field Pasture.
24. P.R.O./DL/44/1022
25. Yorke Records 1044
26. Ibid 1083
27. Ibid 1087
28. Her step grandfather, Sir John Assheton, died that same year so may have left her a legacy with which to buy the set.
29. Yorke Records 1100
30. Ibid 95
31. History of Parliament 1660–1690, ed. B. Henning
32. Travels throughout Great Britain, Daniel Defoe
33. Yorke Records 491
34. Ibid 1102, 1103

CHAPTER X

JOHN YORKE OF RICHMOND, GOUTHWAITE AND BEWERLEY 1685–1757

1. History of Parliament 1754–1790 ed. L. Namier & J.B. Brooke
2. History of Richmond and Swaledale, Fieldhouse and Jennings, Phillimore and co.
3. Ibid, and Yorke Records 1139 and 802
4. Ibid
5. Ibid. see Whitcliffe pasture explanation by Fieldhouse and Jennings, in History of Richmond and Swaledale.
6. Yorke Records 102, 103, 104.
7. Yorke Records 802
8. Ibid 1139
9. Ibid 1139
10. Ibid 939, 940
11. Ibid 313
12. Ibid 850
13. Ibid 1176
14. Ibid 851
15. Thomas Edward Yorke [T.E.Y]
16. History of Nidderdale, ed. B. Jennings
17. Ibid
    A workhouse was built at Bishopside near Bewerley in 1746
18. Walpole, Coxe iii 583
19. T.E.Y.
20. Up until the Maxwell Fyffe reform in 1952, a man with private means could still 'buy' his candidature by offering to pay the agent or fund the local party machine. Few selection committees could resist that lure.
21. Yorke Records 1104
22. T.E.Y.

CHAPTER XI

THOMAS YORKE OF HALTON WEST AND GOUTHWAITE 1688–1768

1. Yorke Records 96
2. T.E.Y.
3. Ibid
4. Yorke Records 852
5. T.E.Y.
6. T.E.Y.
7. Yorke Records 1139
8. History of Parliament 1754–1790 ed. L. Namier and J.B. Brooke
9. Yorke Records 1139
10. Ibid
11. Ibid

12. Life of Mrs Gladstone, Georgina Battiscombe, Constable
13. Yorke records 1139
14. T.E.Y.
15. Yorke records 1108

CHAPTER XII
JOHN YORKE OF RICHMOND AND BEWERLEY 1733–1813

1. Yorke Records 1157
2. Journal kept by John Yorke 1776–1857
3. T.E.Y.
4. Yorke Records 1139
5. Ibid 1109
6. T.E.Y.
7. History of Nidderdale, ed. B. Jennings
8. Ibid
9. The Expenses Extraordinary on a/c of ye Sheriffwick, Pulter Forester of Broadfield Hall, 1717
10. In 18th century, 50,000 negro slaves had been transported each year by British ships to the colonies.
11. Alumnis Cantabrigensis
12. Yorke Records 1139 (26)
13. Ibid 1139 (25)
14. Ibid 1112, 1114
15. Ibid 1109

CHAPTER XIII
THOMAS YORKE OF HALTON PLACE 1738–1811

1. English Country Life, 1780–1830, E.W. Bovill, O.U.P.
2. John Crunden, 1740–1828, was born in Sussex and said to have been a pupil or assistant to Henry Holland the elder.
3. Yorke Records 1139
4. On December 29th 1987 the course of the old mill stream, or Goat Stream, filled with an exceptional run of flood water, making it possible to see exactly how it used to be.
   The Halton West Poll Tax payers in 1379 were, Halton, Lawkland, Thornber, Youlrig, Thwaites, Stringer, Sherburn, Grenfell, King, Harris, Cooper Denison, Thomson, Nelson, Fairey, Stevenson, Wheelwright.
   History of Hellifield, Tom Merrall
5. The licence was granted under the Toleration Act. History of Dales Congregational Churches
6. The Drovers, K.J. Bonsor, Macmillan
7. Thomas Grey's Journal 1759
8. Yorke Records 1139
9. Ibid 1139
10. Hunting in Craven, Wm. Gomersall
11. Richmond Parish Registers

CHAPTER NOTES

12. Yorke Records 1111

CHAPTER XIV

JOHN YORKE OF BEWERLEY AND HALTON PLACE 1776–1857

1. Yorke Records 1127
2. Ibid 1132, 1134, John and Mary's Journal
3. Ibid 866
4. In the Act for enclosing Lands in the Township of Appletreewick in the Parish of Burnsall... Royal Assent 12 May 1815, it says,
   'And that the said John Yorke... and all the future Owners of the said Manor... shall and may at all times have, hold, work and enjoy all Mines, Minerals and Quarries, of what nature or kind soever, within or under the said Stinted Pastures, Open Field Lands, Moor or Common intended to be divided and inclosed as aforesaid... and be vested with all convenient and necessary Ways, Wayleaves, and liberty of laying Waggon Ways... along the same... and of searching for, draining, winning and working the Mines and Quarries and dressing, smelting and... carrying away the Coals, Lead, Tin, Copper, Stones, Limes, Slate, Metals and Minerals to be gotten thereout... and of making Pits, Shafts, Drifts, Levels, Heights, Dams and reservoirs and Watercourses, and taking, diverting and using Springs, or brooks or other Waters etc. etc. without paying any Damage or making any Compensation, in the same manner as if this Act had not been passed.
5. Yorke Records 1132, 1134, John and Mary's Journal
6. Ibid 1142
7. Ibid 1141
8. Edmund became a Fellow of St Katharine's, Cambridge and died unmarried in 1871
9. Rev. Moseley Atkinson, Vicar of Catterick, had died in 1824, as had his wife also. John bought back the painting of his uncle, which had been left to her, for £30.
10. Ibid 974
11. Ibid 1014, 1020
12. Ibid 1063
13. Ibid 1142
14. Ibid 1141
15. Bewerley Bridgehousegate School, 1678–1978, Muriel Swires
16. John and Mary's Journal
    Education enquiry 1833
17. Middlesmoor Church was consecrated 1484, altered 1775.
18. Character Sketches of Old Yorkshire Lead Miners, H. Bruff, Waddington's, York, p. 58
19. Yorke Records 1142
20. The District of Nidderdale, W. Grainge
21. Yorke Records 1120

CHAPTER XV

JOHN YORKE OF BEWERLEY AND HALTON 1827–1883

1. John and Mary's Journal
2. T.E.Y. notes
3. Alice became Madame de Veysey, and received an annuity of £800
4. History of Nidderdale, ed. B. Jennings

CHAPTER XVI

THOMAS EDWARD YORKE 1832–1923

1. All the information in this chapter is taken from the two journals kept by Edward and his mother, (1132 to 1137), with the addition of the two notes below
2. Life in the Yorkshire Dales by Joan Ingilby and Marie Hartley, J.M. Dent
3. Character Sketches of Old Yorkshire Lead Miners, Harold Bruff.
4. In 1893 the Bradford Corporation decided to obtain water from Nidderdale, by constructing a reservoir between Wath and Ramsgill. They purchased the land and the work continued for many years. The site of Gouthwaite Hall was submerged and, as Edward Yorke wrote, the face of the valley was changed. Some of the old stone from the Hall was used to build the houses now standing near the old site.

CHAPTER XVII

JOHN CECIL YORKE OF BEWERLEY AND HALTON PLACE 1868–1915

1. T.E.Y. notes
2. Yorke Records 881
3. Formerly Stubbe Cross.

CHAPTER XVIII

JOHN EDWARD EVELYN YORKE OF HALTON PLACE 1904

Sources for this chapter were letters, photographs, records and much invaluable information told me by my parents, and by my brother.

1. Moorside Farm, Worston, has the Yorke arms over its door. The mill mentioned in Katharine Yorke's will could have been worked by the beck nearby.

BIBLIOGRAPHY

For further reading I recommend this selected list of books which have contributed both material and illumination to my own.

A History of Hellifield, Tom Merrall, Lambert's Settle
Domesday Book, Yorkshire, Part I & II, ed. John Morris, Phillimore
MSS Dr Gwyther Moore for Miss M.A. Yorke
History of the English Speaking Peoples, Sir W.S. Churchill, Cassells
Merchant of Prato, Iris Origo, Jonathan Cape
Medieval Merchant Venturers, E. Carus Wilson, Methuen & Co.
Medieval English Wool Trade, Eileen Power
The Paston Letters
Life in the English Country House, Mark Girouard, Yale University Press
The Medieval English Economy 1150–1500, J.L. Bolton, J.M. Dent
English Trade in the Middle Ages, Salzman, Oxford Clarendon Press
Yorkshire from A.D. 1000, David Hey, Longmans
The Atlas of Medieval Man, Colin Platt, Crescent Books, New York
Civilisation, Kenneth Clark, B.B.C. and John Murray
Renaissance Essays, Hugh Trevor Roper, Fontana Press
Medieval English Trade in XV century, Power and Postan, George Routledge and Sons
The District of Nidderdale, William Grainge, Lemare, 1863
Upper Nidderdale, Harry Speight, Elliot Stock 1906
The History of Nidderdale, Pateley Bridge Tutorial Class edited by Bernard Jennings, Advertiser Press, Huddersfield
English Social History, G.M. Trevelyan, Longmans
Story of English, Professor Tom Sheppey, McCrum, Cran, Macneil B.B.C.
Raleigh and the Throckmortons, A.L. Rowse, Macmillan.
The Great Lucifer, Margaret Irwin, Chatto and Windus
A Survey of London, John Stow, Vol I and II 1603, Clarendon Press 1908
The Lisle Letters, ed. Murie St Clair Byrne, University of Chicago Press
The Catholic Recusants of the W.R. of Yorks 1558–1790, Dom Hugh Aveling OSB (printed for the Leeds Philosophical and Literary Society by Chorley and Pickersgill 1963)
York Civic Records, Angelo Raine
A History of Lead mining in the Pennines, Raistrick and Jennings, Longmans

The Smelting Mills of the Yorkshire Dales, R. Clough, Jowett and Sowry
The Pennine Dales, A. Raistrick, Eyre and Spottiswoode
England in the 17th Century, M. Ashley, Penguin 1966
Company of Adventurers, Peter Newman, Viking Press
History of England, A. Maurois, Jonathan Cape
Days of Yore, a history of Masham, Susan Cunliffe Lister
English Country Life 1780–1830, E.W. Bovill, O.U.P. 1962
Bewerley Bridgehousegate School 1678–1978, Muriel Swires
The Church of St Cuthbert Pateley Bridge, Muriel Swires
Life and Tradition in the Yorkshire Dales, Hartley and Ingilby, Dent
Travels throughout Great Britain, Daniel Defoe, Penguin Books
A History of Richmond and Swaledale, Fieldhouse and Jennings, Phillimore 1978
A Daughter of Time, Josephine Tey, Penguin Books
Annual Reports and Bulletins of the W.R. Northern Section of the National Register of Archives 1961 onwards
Abbot Paslew and the Pilgrimage of Grace, William Weeks F.S.A.
Man on a Donkey, H.M. Prescott, Eyre and Spottiswoode.
Darkness and Devils, John L. Murphy, Ohio University Press
Sir John Yorke of Nidderdale, Christopher Howard, Sheed and Ward 1939
Life of Mrs Gladstone, Georgina Battiscombe, Constable.
The Age of Plunder, W.G. Hoskins, Longmans

GLOSSARY

To addle = to earn
Agate = busy with
A beck = a brook
A bielding = a shelter
To bray = to hit
Capped = dumbfounded
Clammed = hungry
Champion = excellent
Fast = tight or secure
Fog = new growth of grass after mowing
Fother or fodder (of lead)
To fettle = to mend
To flay or fleer = to frighten
To flit = to move house
Ghinnel = alleyway
To gang = to go
Gate = way or street
(Beast gate or pasture gate = stint)
Grand = fine
Galloway = pony
Gimmer = female sheep
Gyste stock = agisted stock grazing for rent
Happen = perhaps
Hog = male sheep
Hoofed or hefted = sheep kept on one area until they remained for good
I just bethowt mesel' = I just thought
Jyste = agisted
To laik = to play
A laithe = a barn
Lish = supple, fit
To lug = to pull or drag
Lad = boy
Lass = girl
Look sharp = be quick
Mind thi wark = pay attention
To mar = to spoil
Mug = a Teeswater/Blackface cross sheep
Nesh = soft, not hardy
Neb = nose
Owt be = however, anyway
Out barn = a barn away from the farm
Settle = a bench
Shippon = cow shed (from sheep pen)
Slopstone = a stone sink
Snig = piglet
Sneck = a latch
Sitha = do you see?
Stirks = young cattle
Stag = a young horse
Starved = cold
A stot = a young ox
A stint = permitted number to graze an area
To shape = to prepare
A syle = a sieve
To sype = to drain
Tek hod = take hold
Tup = ram
Think on = remember
To teem = to pour
Throng = busy
Wick = lively
Whye = a heifer
Yow = a ewe

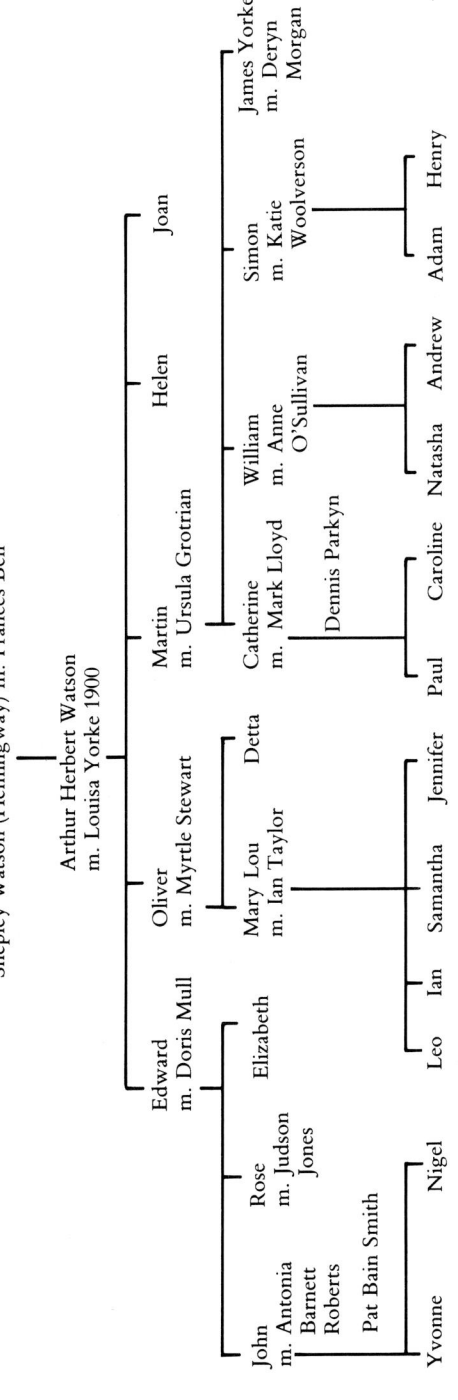

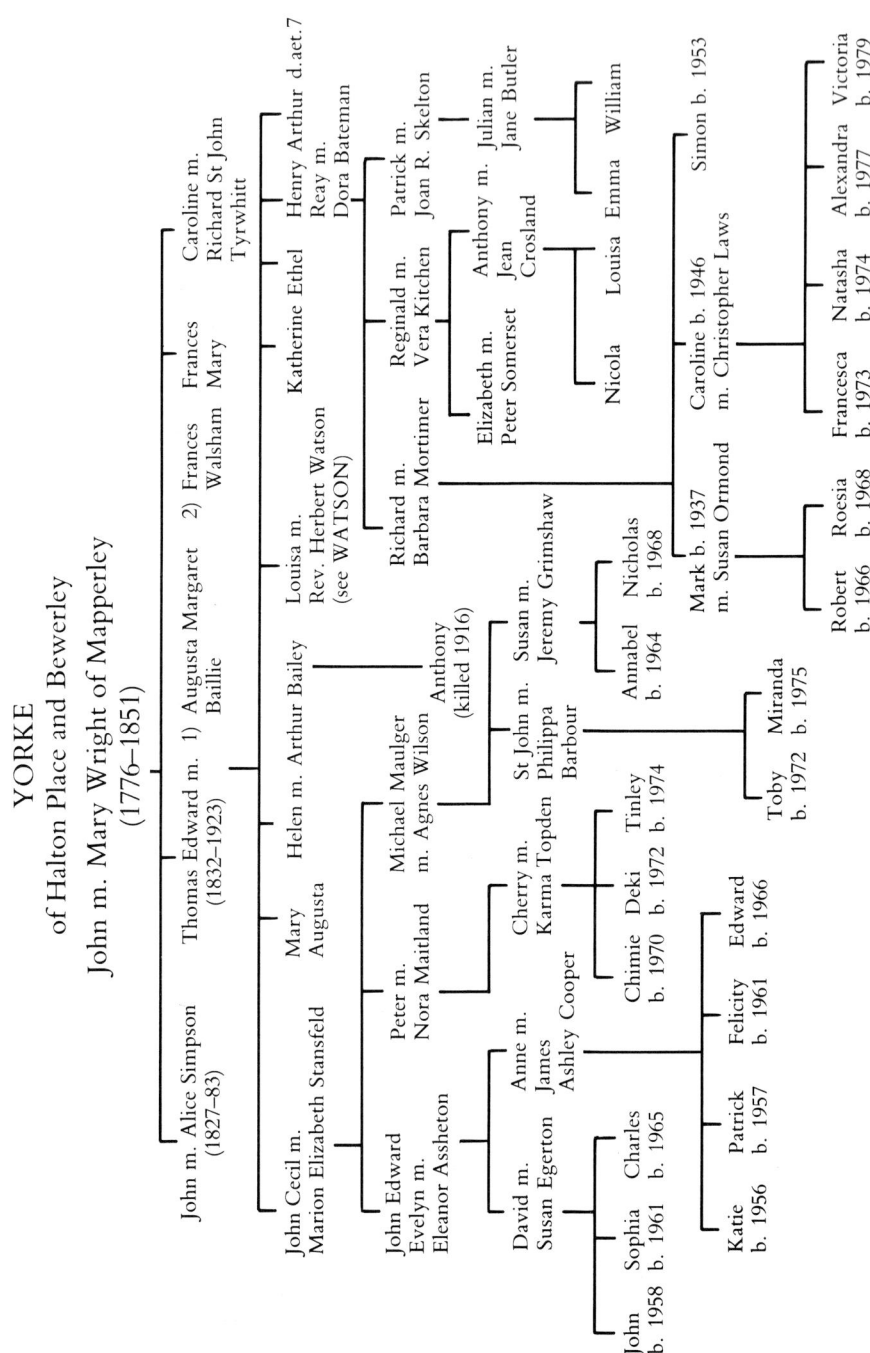

INDEX

Abbey, Byland, 6, 40, 48, 52
   Fountains, 6, 39, 40, 46, 83, 112
   Rievaulx, 6
   Salley, 46
   St Mary's, York, 34, 35
   Westminster, 129
   Whalley, 46
Abbeys, Benedictine, 6
   Cistercian, 6, 40
Abbot Huby's chapel, 112, 170
Acland, Sir Antony, 277
   Nicholas, 277
   Sophia, 274, 277
Act, Agricultural, 1958, 274
   Catholic Emancipation, 1830, 205
   Poor Law Amendment, 1833, 211
Act of Settlement 1701, 129
   Succession 1534, 45
   Supremacy 1534, 45
   Treason 1534, 45
   Union with Scotland 1707, 132
Acts of Enclosure, Nidderdale 143, Halton West 179
Airton, 151
Allerton cum Wilsden, 150
Andrews, William, of Barneshall, Worcs. 150
   Abigail, 150, 153, 156
Anglo–Saxon Chronicle, The, 3, 4
Anglo–Cymric score, 61, (see Sheep counting)
Angram, 74, 244
Antwerp, 14, 18, 41, 45, 55, 271
Appletreewick Fair, 48, 64, 125
   Enclosure Act, 1804
   Lord of the Manor of the Underworld of, 145
   Lead Mining Company, 215, 220, 247
   Manor of, 48, 52, 55, 64, 74, 78, 83, 88, 89, 91, 111, 112, 123, 145, 171
Apprentices, 12, 14, 44, 96

Armada, Spanish, 76, 80
Armathwaite, 98, 123
Arncliffe, 71
Arthingtons of Spofforth, 73
Aske, 98, 108
Aske, Robert, 46
Ashley Cooper, Sir Patrick, 274
   James, 274
   Anne, 267, 269, 273, 274
Ashton, Ripley
Assheton, Sir Raufe, 1484, 28
   Nicholas, 1611, 81, 88, 91
   Sir Ralph, 1661, 108
   Sir John, 1680, 117
   William, 1813, 190, 197
   Ralph, 1860–1955, 266
   Ralph, (later Lord Clitheroe), 1902–1984, 276
   Eleanor, 266, 268, 269, 270
Atkinson, The Rev. Richard Moseley, 173–176, 191, 193
   Mary, 173, 174, 175, 176, 191
Austwick, 50, 74, 78

Babthorpe, Sir William, of Babthorpe, 91
   Frances, 91, 94
Bailey, Arthur, of Wramplingham Hall, 243, 265
Baillie, Canon the Hon. John, of Elsdon, Northumberland, 223, 228, 248
   Augusta, 223 et seq., 228
Bank of England, The, 121
Barbour, Philippa, 271
Bardon, Forest of, 51, 111
Barrmaster, see Lead mining
Barmoot Courts, see Leadmining
Bargate Green, Richmond, 103, 105
Barnby, 35
Barton, Yorks., 98, 123, 145
Basford Church, Notts., 203
Bateman, Dora, 243

Bathurst of Arkengarthdale, 135, 136
Bayne, Dorothy, 85
  family, 62, 237
Beckwith family, 52, 72, 91, 113
Belfield House, Weymouth, 179
Bell family, 237
Berwick on Tweed, 11, 34, 36
Bewerley Hall, 40, 61, 83, 112, 134,
  145, 151, 166, 170, 173, 188, 200,
  201, 203 205, 208, 212, 218, 219, 220,
  221, 228, 232, 247, 255, 257, 263
Bewerley Chapel, 113, 211
  Clothing Club, 212, 220, 242
  Estate, 112, 139, 145, 172, 175,
    197, 205, 214, 224, 231, 234, 240
    260, 265, 271, (271 N.Z.)
  gardens, 170, 233
  School, 113, 170, 213
Birtwistle, John, 184
Bishopthorpe, 35
Black ink, recipe for, 189
Blackett, Sir Edward, of Newby Hall,
  114, 115, 118, 126
Bland family, 252, 254
Bloomsbury Square, 128
Bolton by Bowland, 271
Bolton Priory, 79, 88, 183
Bonaventure, The, 76
Boord, Bertram, 244, 252, 265
Boroughbridge, 7, 55, 83, 150
Bosworth Field, 30
Bouverie, Captain, 193, 194
Boundaries, disputes over, 52, 70, 89,
  162, 207
Bowes family
Bowland Secondary School, 271
Brabant, 24
Bradforddale, 123
Bridgehousegate school, 170, 211, 243
Bristol, 18
Brown family, 255
Bruges, 14, 18
Burgage properties, 105, 108, 121, 127,
  135, 136, 156
Burgesses, 23, 105, 108, 127, 136
Burneston, 98, 123
Burnsall
Byland Abbey, 6, 39, 40, 46, 83, 112

Cabot, Sebastian, 51

Calais, The Staple at, 7, 18, 19, 27, 49
  Lord Deputy of, 45, 51
Calvert family, 237
Campbell, Peter Woodstock, of
  Kilmory, Argyllshire, 166
  Elizabeth, 166, 173, 174, 175, 176,
    192, 197
Campbell, Miss, 254
Capstick family, 252, 272
Card, Miss Emily, 265
Carr, John, 254
Cathay Company, 76
Catholic persecution, Chapters V and
  VI
Cattle droving, 184
Cavalier Parliament, 107
Cavaliers, 100
Cave, Sir Ambrose, 55
Cawood Palace, 19
Caxton, William, 11, 19
Cecil, Robert, Earl of Salisbury, 55, 84
Chancery suits, 112, 144
Charles I, King, 90, 95, 100, 102
  II, 102, 103, 105, 110, 119
Chaytor, William, 175, 176
Christchurch, Oxford, 249, 265
Civil War, 100, 101
Clare Hall, Cambridge, 154, 155, 164,
  173, 178
  college bills 1728, 155
Clarendon Code 1662, 107
Claro, wapentake of, 72, 105
Clarke family, 144, 184, 237
Clavering, Sir James, of Axwell Park,
  Co. Durham, 127, 133
  Sir John, 167, 168, 186
  Sir Thomas, M.P. 187
Cleasby, 98, 123, 150
Clitheroe, borough of, 108
Clitheroe of Downham, Lord, 276
Clitheroe Grammar School, 276
Close, Ralph, 136
Coats of arms, 10, 20, 37, 126, 139,
  145, 149
Coates, Joe, 260
Coffee houses, 129
Coinage, 50, 55
Company of Merchants and Mercers,
  The, 24
Company of Mines Royal, 64

INDEX

Coniston, 82
Convention Parliament, 121
Coppergate, York, 12
Corpus Christi festival, 21
    Guild, 21, 39
Coulthursts of Gargrave, 190
Country Landowners' Association, 271
Cow Bridge, Long Preston, 183
Cow Hill, Halton West, 183, 225, 252
Cranmer, Archbisop Thomas, 45
Craven, 59, 72
    Archdeaconry of, 72
Craven Arms, Appletreewick, 64
Craven Cross, 171
Craven Harriers, 268
Craven Herald, The, 259
Craven Longhorns, 143, 184
Craven Moor Mines, 172, 176
Craven, wapentake of, 72
Crest, Yorke family, 20
Cromwell, Oliver, The Lord Protector, 90, 101, 102, 108
Cromwell, Thomas, Lord Great Chamberlain, 43, 45
Crundon, John, 1740–1828, 179
Culloden, Battle of, 148
Culloden Tower, Richmond, 148
Cumberland, Earl of, 61, 88, 122, 148
Cuthbert, Joseph, of Witton Castle, Co. Durham, 187, 191

Dacre, 39, 64, 88, 112, 212
Dalton, John, 31
Danes, 3, 4, 5
Danish language, 61
Danby, Sir Thomas, of Swinton and Farnley, 70, 73
    Earl of, 121
Daniel, Sir Ingilby, of Beswick, near Beverley, 94
    Katherine, 94 et seq.
Darcy, (de Arci), Lord, 37, 39, 46, 72, 111
Darcy, James, M.P., 1st Baron Darcy of Navan, 121, 127, 136, 156
    Hon. Anne, 136, 139, 141, 142, 149
d'Arcy, Sir Conyers, 135, 136, 156
Darnborough family, 237

Davile, Mayor of Richmond, Yorks., 135, 136
de Halton family, 183
de Moubrai, (Mowbray), Roger, 6, 39
de Poitou, Roger, 83
Defoe, Daniel, observations of, 122, 128, 134, 142
Delves, Miss, 258, 265
Denholme, 123, 150
Dialect Society, Yorkshire, 230
Dibb Luptons, Solicitors, 270
Dissenters, 212
Dodd, Miss, 240, 265
Domesday Book, extracts from, 5, 183
Donnington, 34
Downham, Lancs., 81, 94, 152, 267, 276, 277
    school, 276
Downing College, Cambridge, 214
Doyle, Jim and Nellie, 254, 259, 260, 261
Drake, Sir Francis, 76

East India Company, 90, 129, 163, 168
East Marton, 190
Edward III, King, 18, 30
    IV, 16, 19, 20, 23, 24, 27, 29
    VI, 47, 49, 51, 53
    VII, 243
Egerton, Lt. Col. Scrope, of Pertwood Manor, Wilts., 273
    Susan, 273, 276
Election of Sir Richard Yorke as Lord Mayor of York, 23, 28
    as M.P. for York, (1472), 23, (1483), 30
    Thomas Yorke as M.P. for Richmond, (1689), 121, 127
    John Yorke, as M.P. for Richmond, (1727), 135, 136
    Thomas Yorke, as M.P. for Richmond, (1759), 156
Elslack, 190
Emperor Maximilian, 33
Emperor of Russia, 194
English Revolution, The, 121
Erdigg, Co. Denbigh, 149
Essex, Earl of, 75, 100
Eton College, 134, 218, 222, 260, 277

Fairfax, Lord, 123
Falmouth, 164
Fawkes, Guy, 84, 85
Ferrybridge, 202
Fishergate, York, 12, 32, 223
Flanders, 14, 24
Flaxby, 35
Fleet, Prison, 87, 89
  River, 43
Fountains Abbey, 6, 39, 40, 46, 83, 112
  Earth, 207
Frankland family, 183
Frobisher, Sir Martin, 40, 52, 74, 75, 76, 80
Fugger family, 49

Gallyon's Farm, Woolwich, 48
Garforths of Coniston, 190, 204
Gargrave, 190
George I, King, 132, 135
  II, 154, 156
  III, 156, 172
  IV, 203
Giggleswick School, 226
Gill, Mrs Barbara, 276
Girls' Friendly Society, The, 242
Gisburn, 117, 152
Gledstone, see Roundells
Gloucester, Duke of, (see Richard III)
Glynne, Sir John, of Hawarden, 158, 160, et seq., 164
  Sophia, 158, 160, 164
Goosemere Heights, 180
Gordon Highlanders, The, 259, 271
Gouthwaite Hall, 39.48, 52, 60, 65, 66, 69, 80, 81, 86, 91, 97, 112, 150, 151, 207
Grand Jury, The, 226
Granges, monastic, 6, 40
Grassington, 60, 62, 64, 122, 151, 238
Greenhow Hill, 2, 60, 83, 108, 112, 145, 207, 220, 234, 247
Greenhow church, 212
  school, 175, 212
Gresham, Sir Thomas, 55
Grey, Lady Jane, 50, 53
Grimshaw, Jeremy, 271
  Susan, 271

Grindal, Edmund, Archbishop of York, 71
Guilds, 8, 13, 14, 17, 106
Guisecliffe, Bewerley, 170
Gunpowder Plot, 85, 86

Halifax, 150
Halton Place, 179, 181, 187, 188, 196, 199, 200, 201, 204, 218, 222, 223, 224, 225, 244, 249, 260, 277
  architect, 179
  household 1780, 188
  household 1860, 223, 225
Halton West bridge, 96, 186
  church, 227, 254, 260, 268
  Enclosure Act, 1759
  estate, 152.153, 163, 170, 181, 182, 197, 225, 265, 267, 274
  farms, 183, 224, 252
  school, 225, 226, 228, 254, 268
  shop, 252, 274,
  tenants, 225, 226, 252, 272, 274
Hamertons of Hellifield Peel, 72, 73, 184, 190, 204
Hampton Court, 129, 130
Hannam family, 255
Hanley, Gordon, 276
Hanover Square, St George's, 162
Hanse, 33
Hansby, Sir Ralph, of Beverley and Tickhill, 81
  Juliana, 81 et seq., 91, 94, 95
Hardcastle family, 92, 237
Hardwicke, Earl of, 149
Harrison family, 83, 237
Harrogate, 228, 245, 248
Harrow School, 230, 248
Hatchment, 110
Hathorn Davy, Leeds, 266
Hatton Gardens, 132, 150
Hawkins, Sir John, 76
Hawkshead school, 74
Haworth, Miss, 268
Haynes, Mary, 175
Healaugh, 108
Heathfield, 83, 146, 207, 242
Hebden, 111
Hellifield, 152, 184, 226, 260
  Auction Mart, 268

INDEX

Church, 257
Peel, 226
Hellifield District Nursing Association, 268
Helmsley, 6
Helperby, 149, 150, 153, 154, 164, 178
  household expenses, 151, 152
Henry VI, King, 11, 12, 16, 24
  VII, 30, 31, 33, 41, 58
  VIII, 41, 44, 47, 51, 53
Hertlington, 111
Heyshaw Bank, 2
High Scale, Halton West, 225, 252
High Sheriff of Yorkshire, 172, 199, 242
Hipperholme cum Brighouse, 150
Holland, 24
Holderness, Lord, 121, 135, 136, 139, 156
Holtby, 35
Home Farm, Halton West, 225, 244, 252
Horner family, 62, 237
Horton, 184
House of Commons, 100, 103, 108, 109, 129, 135, 148, 187
Hovingham Hall, York, 214, 243
Hudson's Bay Company, 90, 129
Hudswell church, 176
  Peel, 103, 106
Hull, Kingston upon, 7, 13, 17, 24, 27, 31, 32, 34
Humber, River, 3, 5
Hunting, 51, 70, 88, 89, 101, 123, 126, 148, 170, 174, 185, 190, 218
Hunwick Hall, Northumberland, 244

Ice hills, 194
India in 1777, 178
Ingham, Russell, 273
Ingham and Yorke, Chartered Surveyors and Land Agents, 273
Ingilby, Sir William, of Ripley Castle, 55, 60, 62, 83, 85, 86, 88, 190, 242
  Elizabeth, 60, et seq.
Ingleborough, 179
Inman family, 113, 237
Ismay, Mrs, 240, 241, 263

Jackman, Arthur, 254

Jackson, Ezra, 252
Jacobites, 121
James I, King, 78, 84, 90
  II, 119, 121, 129
James V, King of Scotland, 47
Jones, David, 254, 258
Justices of the Peace, 45, 62, 72, 77, 88, 96, 105, 107, 218, 226, 249
  Petty Sessions 245
  Settle Bench 271
  Clitheroe Bench 276
Justices' room, 109

Kensington, 154, 178
Kenyon family, 263, 272
Kidd, John, 267
Kilnsey, 48, 64, 71, 78
Kirkby Malham, 118
Kirkby Malzeard, 83, 85, 125
Knaresborough, 7, 226, 245
  Castle, 5
  Forest of, 52, 60, 111, 112, 162
  Honour of, 60
Knitting of stockings, 106, 171
Kwolek, Bronek, 275

Lancashire, 3, 91, 117, 118, 184
Lancastrians, 12, 16, 23, 29
Lawkland Hall, 50, 190
Leeds, 226, 230
Lead mining, Roman, 1, 2
  medieval, 7, 66
  18th century, 145, 171, 207
  19th century, 215, 234
  20th century, 247, 274
  Barrmaster, 62
  Barmoot courts, 63, 69, 107, 122
Lead miners' lives and customs, 122, 145
Leicester, Earl of, 75
Leigh, 56
Leland, John, King's Antiquary, 32, 65
Leslie, General David, Lord Newark, 100, 101
Liberty of Ripon, 39, 79, 218, 245
Life Guards, The, 273
Lisle, Lord, Deputy of Calais, 45
Lister, Thomas, of Arnoldsbiggin, 117
  Katherine, 117 et seq.

301

Listers of Gisburn, 73, 118, 152, 190, 204
Littledales of Bolton Hall, 190
Lodge, Francis, 139, 141, 144
Lloyd's, Edward, Coffee House, 129
Lofthouse, 212, 244
London, Pool of, 129
   16th century, 41
   18th century, 129, 148
   Sheriff of, 48
   Streets of, 43
   Tower of, 49, 51, 53, 86, 90
Long Bank, Halton West, 183, 225, 228, 252
Long Preston, 183, 184, 189, 230, 267
   Church, 196, 216, 227, 228, 229, 257, 259
   School, 226, 268
Low Field, Halton West, 183, 252
Lowson family, 113
Low Scale, Halton West, 225, 252
Low Thornber, Halton West, 184, 225, 252
Lund, Henry, 252, 268
Lupton, Marmaduke, 95

Maitland, Hon. Alfred, of Kirriemuir, Angus, 270
   Nora, 270
Mallory, Sir William, 72, 78, 79
Malham, 59, 64, 151, 184, 226
Manfield, 98, 123
Manor courts, 69, 97, 107
Marriage settlements, 60, 103, 115, 117, 118, 150, 162
Mary, Queen of Scots, 47, 56, 71, 74
Mason family, 225
Mauleverer, Nicholas, of Allerton Mauleverer, 15
   Jane, 15 et seq., 31, 37
Maximilian, Emperor, 33
Mercers and Merchants, Company of, 24
Merchant Adventurers Company, 24
   Hall, York, 25
Merchant Taylors Company, 48, 56, 58, 80
Merrington, Robert, 245, 257
Merryfield Mines, 173, 176, 207, 238

Metcalfe family, 184
Micklegate, York, 16, 22, 25, 203, 204
Middleham Castle, 20, 30, 125
Middlesmoor, 64, 73, 85, 88, 91, 93, 110, 112, 207
Middlesmoor Church, 93, 110, 125, 171, 212
Midsummer Watch, 44
Militia, The Yorkshire, 193, 195
Miners' Arms, Greenhow, 238
Mint, The Royal, 47, 51
   Master of the, 50
Mitton Bridge, 230
Montagu, Charles, 1st Earl of Halifax, 121
Moon T.C., 225, 244, 252, 254, 261
Moon family, 262
Moorhouse family, 252, 272
Moors family, 237
Morecombe, 230
Morton, (Malton?) 35
Mountgarret, The Viscount, 242, 245
Muker, 108
Muscovy, Adventurers to, 51
Music, 67, 242, 248, 258, 270
Muster Master, 77, 78
Myers family, 237
Mystery Plays, York, 13, 14

Nanny Townsend, 268
Napier, The 8th Lord, 169
Nappa Flatts, Halton West, 152, 184, 225, 244, 252
National Association of Decorative and Fine Arts, 276
Netherlands, The, 31, 33, 49, 75, 80
Neville, George, Archbishop of York, 16, 19, 20, 27
Newark, Lord, see Leslie
Newbould family, 220, 237
Newby Hall, 114, 126
Newcastle, 27, 34
New House, Halton West, 183
Newsholme, 152
Newton Morrell, 98, 123, 145
Nice, 169
Nidd, River, 2, 46, 52, 94, 95, 143, 233, 240
Nidderdale Agricultural Society, 218

INDEX

Nidderdale Enclosure Act, 1804, 148
   farming in 17th century, 59 et seq.
   farming in the 18th century, 143
   farming in 19th century, 207, 235, 236, 237
Norman castles, 5, 6
Norse tradition, 13, 61
Northern Earls, The Rising of the, 74, 80
Northowram, 150
North Thornber, Halton West, 183, 225, 252
Northumberland, Earl of, 19, 27, 30, 71
   Duke of, 51–54
Northumbria, 23
Norton, Maulger, of Richmond, Yorks., 73, 91, 98, 102, 110, 118
   Mary, 102, 105, 107, 110, 211
   Welbury, 91, 98, 111, 113
Nussey Knot, 2

Oatcake, 236
Oath of Allegiance, 1606, 78, 85, 94
Old Hall, Halton West, 183, 184, 223, 225, 252
Ouse, river, 7
Ousebridge End, York, 34, 36
Ousegate, York, 25, 39
Ovenden, 123, 150
Oxford, 222, 223, 226, 260, 265, 266, 270

Pageant, The, York, 21, 22
Panbeck, Halton West, 225, 252
Pancake Lane, London, 57
Parcevall Hall, Appletreewick, 55, 65, 69, 79, 80, 91, 244
Parker family, 225, 237
Parkers of Browsholme, 190
Parliament, Member of
   in 15th century, 24, 42
   in 17th century, 100, 108, 127
   in 18th century, 129, 148
   Cavalier, 1661, 107
   Convention, 1759, 121
Parrington, Alec, 272
Pateley Bridge, 64, 66, 73, 83, 112, 212, 233, 244, 245
   Church, 212, 216, 221, 231, 234, 242, 243
Pateley Bridge and Bewerley Burial Club and Cow Club, 236, 242
Pateley Bridge Mining Company, 238
Patterdale, Katherine, 39
Pavement, The, York, 22
Paythorne, 152
Peasegate, York, 12
Pechell, Sir Thomas Brooke, 169
Pedderthorpe, 56
Peel Hill, Hellifield, 179
Peels of Knowlmere, 73, 190
Pendle Forest Harriers, 268
Pendle Hill, 180
Pen y ghent, 179
Pepper family, 108
Peterhof, 195
Peterhouse, Cambridge, 58, 134
Pilgrimage of Grace, 46
Pitt, William, 148, 156
Pitt the Younger, 172
Pontefract Castle, 5
Pope, The, 45, 84
Pope, Sir Thomas, 43
Poultry, The, London, 43
Preston, 230
Proctor, Thomas, 83
   Sir Stephen, 83, 85, 86, 87
Prosperous Mine, 207
Pye Cross, Halton West, 184, 252
Pym, John, 100

Queen Anne, 131
   Elizabeth I, 55, 70, 74
   Mary, 53, 54, 58, 70
   Victoria, 211
Queen Victoria's Diamond Jubilee, 234
Queen's College, Cambridge, 102
Quarrying, 234

Rae, Agnes, 227, 228, 229, 230
Radley School, 260.
Radcliffe, William, 93, 95
Railway Company, North Eastern, 220, 234
Raleigh, Sir Walter, 75, 90, 100
Ramsgill, 48, 64, 95, 97, 115, 207, 214, 241, 242

303

Church, 212
Manor court, 97, 237, 265
School, 212
"The Yorke Arms," 212, 243
Ravensgill, Bewerley, 203, 233
Reay, Joseph, of Killingworth, Northumberland, 180
  Jane, 171, 180, 181, 187, 192, 203, 204, 212, 226
Recusants, Chapters V and VI
Redmayne, Tom, 225, 267, 268
Reformation, The, 11
Restoration, The, 105
Ribble, River, 3, 96, 151, 179
  Board of Conservators, 226, 268
Ribblesdale, Lord, 208, 225, 226
Richard III, (see Gloucester), 24, 30, 31
Richmond, Yorks., 64, 97, 98, 103, 105, 106, 111, 112, 123, 145
Richmond, Bargate Green, 103
  Bishop of, 250
  borough of, 110, 121, 135
  fairs, 107
  Friary, 170
  parish church, 133, 145, 173
  races, 139
  The Green, 103, 109, 115, 118, 132, 136, 149, 162, 166, 175, 188, 197
    household expenses, (1729), 144, 145
Richmond family, 237
Ringhouse, 35
Ripley Castle, see Ingilby
Ripon, 72, 77, 78, 91, 207, 226
  Bishop of, 212, 244
  Fair, 65
  Grammar School, 105, 113
  Liberty of, 39, 79, 218, 245
  M.P. for, 78, 115
  Minster, 116
Roundells of Gledstone, 190
Roundheads, 100, 101
Rudston, 56
Rumney family, 225, 254
Rupell, Richard, 11

St Aidan's, Hellifield, 257
St Blaise, feast of, 20, 29

St John's College, Cambridge, 191, 193, 214, 218, 222
St John the Evangelist, York, 34, 36, 39
St Paul's Cathedral, 129
St Petersburgh, 191, 193, 194, 195
St Stephen's, Wallbrook, 43, 54, 55, 78
St Stephen's Hall, Westminster, 129
Sanderson, Miss Maud, 263
Sandys, Archbishop, 72, 74
Scale Farm, Halton West, 183, 184
Scarborough, 36, 215, 227
Scarlett, Sir James, later Lord Abinger, 176, 197
School, Bewerley Bridgehousegate, 170, 211, 243
  Bowland Secondary, 271
  Clitheroe Grammar, 276
  Downham, 276
  Giggleswick, 226
  Greenhow, 175, 212
  Halton West, 225, 226, 228, 254, 268
  Hawkeshead, (see Sandys), 74
  Lofthouse, 212
  Long Preston, 268
  Ramsgill, 212
  Richmond Grammar, 105, 113
  Skipton Grammar, 71
  Settle High, 271
Scotland, 47, 106
Scots, 27, 28, 45, 100, 102, 106, 132, 183
Settle, 184, 226, 230
  Bench, 271
  High School, 271
  Rural District Council, 271
  "Spread Eagle Inn", 178
Sharpe, Florence, 94
Sheep counting, (see Anglo Cymric score), 61
Sheldon, John, 252, 254
Ships, merchant, 17, 18, 24, 51, 76, 90
Shorrock family, 199, 224, 231
Simpson, James, of Westcliffe Farm, 218
  Alice, 218, 219, 220, 221
  gamekeeper, 245
Sinclair, Jack and Elijah, poachers, 207
Skeeby, 123, 145
Skipton, 64, 95, 189, 190, 221, 268

INDEX

Bow Bearer of the Forester of, 88
Castle, 5, 15, 61, 88, 89
Forest of, 88,
Grammar School, 71
Sledmere, 34, 56
Sleningford, 91, 94, 266, 270
Smallwood, Alf, 268
Smyth, Robert, of London, 41
Anne, 41, 49, 53, 56
Soper Lane, London, 56
Somerset, Duke of, 47, 48, 49, 51
Southwark Place, 47
mint, 47
inns, 47
ward, 129
South Sea Company, 129, 163
Stansfeld, Evelyn, 249
John, 245, 258, (son, 263)
May, 244, 249, 252, 255, 256, 257, 258, 259, 261, 265, 267, 271
Staple at Calais, The, 7, 18, 19, 27, 49
Star Chamber, Court of the, 62, 83, 85, 87, 89
Starkies of Huntroyde, 190
Stean, 74, 114, 207
Stinting, 59
Stocks Market, London, 43, 129
Stonebeck Up and Down, 39, 48, 62, 83, 89, 97, 114
Stow, John, 44, 58
Stubbs family, 87
Stump Cross Caverns, 220, 276
Suffolk, Duke of, 50, 53
Suffolk House, 47, (see Southwark Place)
Suttle family, 237
Sunside Allotment, 146, 266
Swaledale, 64, 106
Swale, River, 103, 105
Swift, Mr, 240, 241, 263
Swinbank, Robert, 244
family, 262, 272
Swindon, 184
Swinegate, York, 12
Swire family, 207
Swires, William, 211
Miss Muriel, 217

Talbots of Halton, 73

Long Preston, 183
Taylor family, 113, 189, Taxes, 152, 157, 199
Tax Commissioner, 226, 242
Tees, River, 3
Temperance Society, The, 233, 242
Temperton, Miss, 228, 254
Tempests of Broughton, 46, 62, 73, 190, 204, 242
Tenure, systems of, 67, 88, 123, 125
Thackeray family, 237
Thames, River, 43, 47, 129
Theakeston, 98, 123, 145
Thompson, John, 225, 244
Thompson, Matt, 275
Thompson, Sir Wilfred, 259
Thornton, 72, 97, 150
Throckmorton, Sir Nicholas, 50
Throup, Thomas, 254
Titulus Regius, 29
Tolls, 29, 125, 207
Topden Karma, 270
Cherry, 270
Tories, 120, 121
Town End, Halton West, 183, 252
Trinity College, Cambridge, 273
Triumph, H.M.S., 76, 80
Turner, Sydney, 268
Turnpike Trusts, 171
Tyrwhitt, The Rev. St John, 222, 226, 234
Caroline

Vavasour family, 32, 73, 91
Vikings, 3, 4, 5
Volkonski, Prince, 194

Wakefield, 16, 226
Walker family, 238
Wallbrook, London, 43, 44, 48, 49, 56, 80, 128
Walpole, Sir Robert, 132, 135, 148
Walsham, Sir John, of Knill Court, 231
Fanny, 231, 242
Wandesford family, 91, 98, 108, 115
Waltz, 194
War Agricultural Committee, 271
Warley, 150
Warren, Sir John Borlase, 169, 191, 193, 194, 195

305

Lady, 169, 195
Wars of the Roses, 16
Warwick, Earl of, 19, 20, 30, 47, 48, 51
Watson family, (see also Family Tree) 242, 263, 265
Wauchope, Arthur, 259
Wensleydale, 64, 106
Wesley, John, 212
Westcliffe, Bewerley, 218, 266
Westminster, 15, 23, 30, 42, 84, 128, 156
Westmoreland, Earl of, 71
West Riding of Yorkshire, 54, 71, 72, 84, 94, 96, 101, 218, 226, 241, 245, 249
West Thornber, Halton West, 184, 225, 252
Wharton, Lord, 108, 121, 127, 132
Wheeler, Rev. John, 169, 172
Whigs, 108, 120, 121, 132, 148, 156
Whitby, 54, 86
Whitcliffe Common, 105
    Pasture, 136
White, Sir Thomas, 171, 173, 175, 191, 207, 220
Whitehead family, 252, 272
Whitfield, John, 31
    Joan, 31, 32, 34
William I, King, 5
William of Orange, 119, 121
William III, 128
    IV, 205
Wilmot, Henry, 159, 160
Wilson, Charlie, 268
Wilson John, 225, 252
Wilson, George, of Bolton by Bowland, 271
    Agnes, 271
Wincap, Sallie, 252
Winter, Robert, 84
Wood, William, 171
Worsley family, 214
Worston, Lancs., 117, 123, 150, 152, 163, 197, 274
Wrangwyshe, Richard, 23
    Thomas, 27, 29
Wright, Ichabod, of Mapperley Park, Notts. 199, 223
    Mary, 199
Wyvills of Constable Burton, 108, 127

Matt, 135, 136
The Rev. Christopher, 164

York, 3, 7, 18, 21, 27, 30, 202, 203, 205, 209, 226, 228
    Archbishop of, 5, 32, 71, 123
    Aldermen of, 20, 23, 26, 28, 32, 33, 34
    Assizes, 172, 208, 209, Castle, 46, 73, 101, 243, Chamberlains of, 16, 28, 32, 39
    City of, 3, 5, 11, 16, 21, 31, 34, 37, 39
    City Council of, 7, 16, 20, 24, 26, 27
    Council Minutes of, 26, 28
    Dean of, xi, 243
    Lord Mayor of, 20, 23, 27, 29
    Member of Parliament for, 23, 30
    Minster, 2, 13, 34
    Recorder of, 32
    Races, 243
    Sheriff of, 20, 32
York, Duke of, 12, 16, 118, 154
Yorke, Arthur, 1879–86, 228, 234
    Charles, 1965, 274, 277
    Edmund, 1575–16?, 75, 80
    Sir Edward, 15?–1621, 75, 76, 77, 78, 80
    Ethel, 1873, 228, 242, 249, 252, 266
    Henry, 1875–1940?, 228, 243
    John Alexander, 1958, 274, 277
    Katherine, 1872, 228, 242, 252, 266
    Mary Augusta, 1866–1959, 227, 231, 232, 234, 242, 245, 249, 257, 266 271
    Michael, 1912, 259, 271
    Peter, 1906–1984?, 259, 261, 263, 270
    Roland, 1550?–1588, 74, 75, 80
    Richard, 1570–?, 75, 77, 80
    Richard, 1902–19..., 244
    Reginald, 1904, 244
    St John, 1942, 271
Yorke coat of arms, 10
Yorke crest, 20
Yorke Folly, The, 170
Yorke motto, 20

INDEX

Yorkists, 12, 16, 29
Yorkshire, 1, 2, 91, 118
Yorkshire Agricultural Society, 221, 227, 230
Yorkshire Archaeological Society, 221
Yorkshire Dialect Society, 230
Yorkshire horses, 134
Yorkshire people, 1

Yorkshire Post, 221
Yorkshire Provincial Area Conservative Association, 271
Yorkshire Ridings, 3
Yorkshire, High Sheriff of, 172, 199, 242
Zeeland, 24
Zutphen, 75